the MOTOR CAR

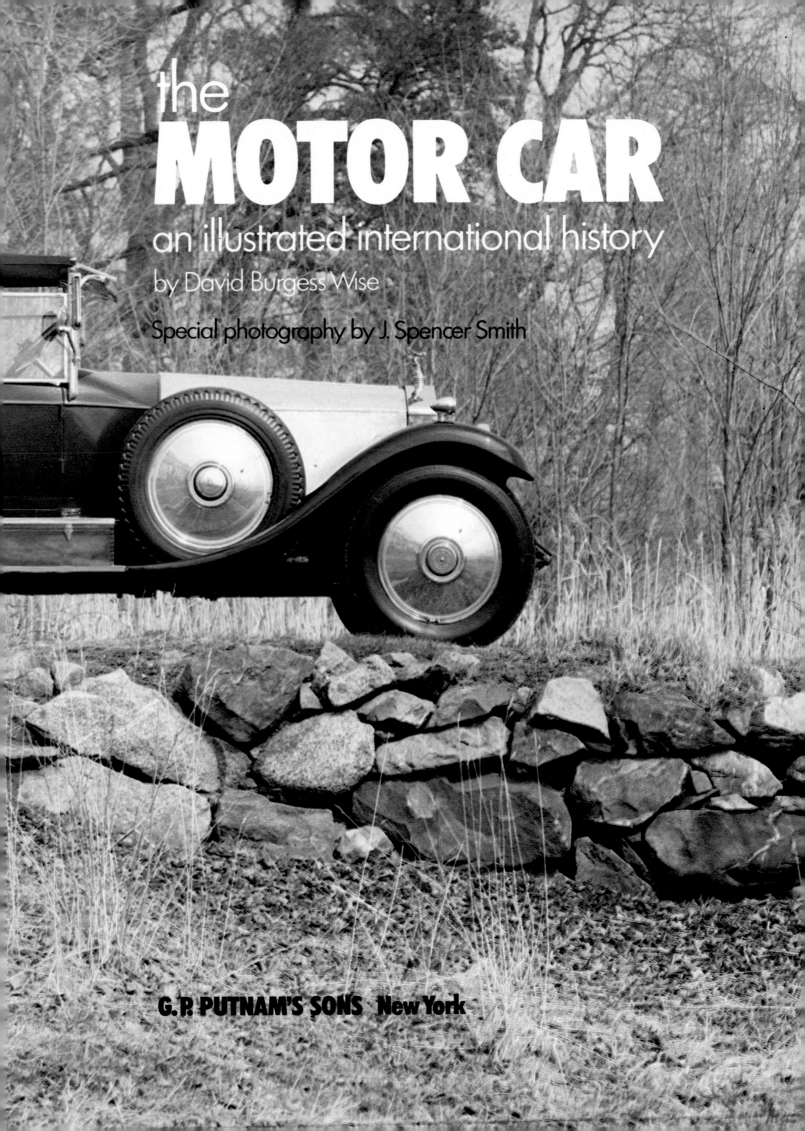

the MOTOR CAR
an illustrated international history

by David Burgess Wise

Special photography by J. Spencer Smith

G. P. PUTNAM'S SONS   New York

Orbis Publishing is indebted to the following for allowing their cars to be photographed:
Château de Grandson, Switzerland; Cheddar Motor Museum, England; Coventry Motor
Museum, England; Fiat Centro Storico, Italy; Peter Hampton, England; Dr John Mills,
England; National Motor Museum, England; Peugeot, France; Saab-Scania, Sweden; Franco
Sbarro, Switzerland; E. Schmidt, Switzerland; Hank Schumaker, England; Science Museum,
England; Skokloster Museum, Sweden; Stratford Motor Museum, England; Ben Wright,
England.
The Turner on page 153 and the Austro Daimler on pages 184-5 belong to the Cheddar Motor
Museum; the Porsche on the front jacket belongs to Porsche Cars.

Picture acknowledgments
Autocar: 156, 162, 164b – Automobile Museum, Turin: 44a–b, 46–7, 54b–d, 55 – Bayer Armée
Museum: 166a – Belli: 60 – British Leyland: 281 – Bundesarchiv: 166b, 167 – C. Burgess Wise: 2b,
193, 241a – L. J. Caddell/Orbis: viii, 22–3, 295, 299a, 300 – D. Copsey/Orbis: 81, 93a–c – Daimler-
Benz: 48a–b, 49b, 50–1, 53b, 62, 63, 66a, 110 – Deutsches Bunde Library: 158–9 – Fiat: 44c, 47a – Ford:
160, 161, 241b, 249, 250–1, 252–3 – Robert Hunt: 157a, 254a – IGDA: 3a–b, 49a, 54a, 65, 66–7, 68,
72a, 75b – Imperial War Museum: 164a, 166c – Mansell Collection: 16, 18–19, 20, 21a, 24–5, 26–7,
30–1, 36a, 58a & c, 59c, 72b–c, 74a, 79a, 80, 86a – Mary Evans Picture Library: 1a–b, 2a, 4a–b, 6a, 8c,
9, 15b, 22, 29, 30a, 32–3, 34, 35b, 37, 42a–b, 48c, 52a–b, 69a–b, 75a, 87, 88, 95, 96a, 97, 100 – Musée
de la Guerre: 165 – Musée National des Techniques: 5, 6–7, 40, 53a, 56–7 – National Motor Museum:
v, 8b & d, 10–11, 15a, 47b–c, 73, 88–9, 92, 94–5, 102, 105, 107, 109, 116, 119, 120, 121, 123, 144, 202a,
213, 228, 233, 234, 242, 243a, 261, 264, 266, 269, 273, 275, 276, 278, 280 – Orbis: 8, 12, 13, 14, 21b, 35,
39a–b, 41, 74b – Quattroruote: 36b–d, 43, 59a–b – Sport & General: 217c – Volkswagen: 243b –
I. Ward/Orbis: 18b, 26a – N. Wright: vi, viii – all other photographs were taken specially for Orbis by
J. Spencer Smith
Front cover photograph by W. Forman and L. J. Caddell
Back cover photograph by J. Spencer Smith

This edition published by G. P. Putnam's Sons
200 Madison Avenue, New York, NY 10016

Printed in Great Britain by Jarrold & Sons Limited, Norwich
Library of Congress Catalog Card Number: 77-2500
SBN: 399-12025-4

Contents

Foreword
by Lord Montagu of Beaulieu

Top: motoring in the early days was very much an open-air hobby, as represented by this 1898 Daimler (Coventry Museum, England)

Above: cars like this elegant Cord 81.2 of 1936 made America the centre of grandiose styling of the motor car

Right: Lord Montagu of Beaulieu with a magnificent 4½-litre Bentley

Foreword

by Lord Montagu of Beaulieu

Motoring history is now entirely respectable, and a recognised branch of scholarship. The literature of the automobile has become an essential concomitant of the museum, the rally and the motor race.

It has been my good fortune to be associated with the furtherance of this branch of the art. From earliest days we at Beaulieu recognised that people like to know more about the cars they drive or even observe upon the museum floor. They are fascinated by the pioneers whose faith enabled the motor car to overcome the prejudices of the early vehicles, by the designers who strove to conquer their imperfections, and by the engineers who made roads worthy of the new locomotion. Automobile competitions have attracted a following surpassed perhaps only by football. Restorers of barn-weathered wrecks need to know the correct equipment with which to refurbish their discoveries, be this a carburettor or merely a colour scheme. To this end we have sought to create one of the finest centres of specialist documentation in the world, and also to produce or sponsor serious historical works. By so doing we also contribute to such books as the present one. Perhaps the greatest attraction of motoring history is that it is still being made. Everyone knows Henry Ford's damnatory dictum 'History is bunk' – perhaps excusable in the case of one who was himself too busy making history – but even the great American industrialist has given us the magnificent Greenfield Village museum complex in the United States. In any case it is now recognised that history does not stop at 1914, or even 1939. The story is gaining in scope as the automobile's protagonists face new hurdles – congestion, emission, safety and now the energy crisis, allied to a worldwide inflation that once again highlights the need for a new people's car to follow in the wheeltracks of the Model T, the Volkswagen and the Mini.

It is, of course, impossible to break entirely new ground in any written history, be it of motoring or of any other subject. *The Motor Car* has, however, avoided every pitfall that attends the unwary historian. There is often a tendency for authors to skip smartly through the periods that interest them least. This David Burgess Wise has not done, giving a fair share of the text both to the primordial (on which nothing new remains to say) and to the modern.

Better still, he has used illustrations and captions to add a third dimension that will appeal to the more selective and knowledgeable reader, and here, the book scores an unqualified 'alpha'. Immense pains have been taken, not only to eliminate hackneyed shots but to seek out illustrations of less obvious cars from less obvious places. Where lesser works have contented themselves with easily available, if not very original, photographic material, the publishers of *The Motor Car* have gone out to look for vehicles rather than for prints and transparencies.

Above left: a car which ably illustrated how far motoring had progressed in a technical sense by the 1970s was the Citroën SM with its hydro-pneumatic steering and suspension

Below: on performance, this Barker-bodied Model J Duesenberg of 1929 is not far behind the space-age Citroën although its speed was achieved more with brute force than finesse

Montagu of Beaulieu

CHAPTER 1

The Horseless Carriage

Top: an early 'technological dead end' is portrayed here with Simon Stevin's two-masted carriage of 1600. Looking like a latter-day sand yacht, this huge vehicle was not a resounding success

Above: this vehicle bears more resemblance to a soap-box cart than anything else. However, motive power for this vehicle is provided by a man on a treadmill, which must have presented real problems on anything other than the slightest of gradients

'There is in this city', wrote the Parisian Gui Patin in January 1645, 'a certain Englishman, son of a Frenchman, who proposes to construct coaches which will go from Paris to Fontainebleau and return within the same day, without horses, by means of wonderful springs . . . If this plan succeeds, it will save both hay and oats . . .'

So it was, over three hundred years ago, that the first horseless carriages crept onto the scene, not with the hiss of steam or the bark of internal combustion, but with the whir of clockwork and the rumbling of crude wooden gearing like that of a mill; not that such machines were anything but elaborate and costly toys. The invention of the anonymous Franglais ran strongly, it is recorded, on trial within the confines of the Temple in Paris, but the wages of the two strong-arm men who turned the handles to wind up those 'wonderful springs' were found to exceed the cost of horses, hay and oats by an unacceptably excessive degree.

The ingenious inventors persisted, however. In 1649, Hans Hautsch of Nuremberg built an elaborate triumphal carriage with the forward end in the shape of a sea monster. This was, it seems, the fifth carriage built by Hautsch, who was born in 1595 and died in 1670, and was the most celebrated mechanic in that city of clockmakers; his inventions were powered by springs and could travel at two thousand paces an hour. He even established an export trade, selling one carriage to Prince Charles-Gustav of Sweden, for 500 rixdollars, and another to the King of Denmark. The latter machine, built in 1663, 'could go forward, backwards and turn without the aid of horses, and cover 3000 measured paces in an hour, solely by the action of cranks turned by two children concealed in the body of the carriage, which make the rear wheels revolve, and he who is within a rod which turns the front of the carriage, where are attached two little wheels to point at the desired place'.

Another technological dead-end which was being avidly pursued at that period was the sail-powered carriage, pioneered by Dutchman Simon Stevin, who in 1600 constructed a vast two-masted 'flying chariot' for the Prince Maurice of Orange-Nassau, which was mentioned in Laurence Sterne's rambling novel *Tristram Shandy* and was thus, if only peripherally, the first horseless vehicle to be featured in literature.

In 1648, one Bishop Wilkins proposed a windmill-driven carriage, while in 1714 a French inventor named Du Quet patented two extremely curious wind-powered carriages, one using a two-bladed sail to work little legs which pushed the vehicle along, while the other had a twelve-bladed fan operating racks geared to the wheel hubs. Du Quet's patent drawings also included the first-ever suggestion for wheels pivoting on stub-axles instead of the centrally pivoted cart-axle, fine when a vehicle was being drawn by horses, but liable to cause it to tip over when it was driving itself along.

Even in the nineteenth century, experimenters were still building sail-driven vehicles, and seemed to have virtually overcome the problem of running against an opposing wind, so that the carriage could be used on roads rather than on beaches (like their lineal descendants, the sand-yachts of today).

In 1826 and 1827, the *Charvolant* of the Englishman George Pocock ran successfully at speeds of 15–20mph, drawn by a train of steerable kites. One useful side-effect of this method of propulsion was that the lift of the kites lessened the effective unsprung weight of the carriage, and made it extremely smooth-running. One evening, Pocock had halted in front of an inn on the Bath Road. 'Just as we were preparing to depart, the London stage came by; it was almost fifteen minutes ahead when the *Charvolant* set out, but after a run of four miles, the *Charvolant* was alongside it; its efforts were fruitless, and after a run of ten miles, we entered Marlborough twenty-five minutes ahead of the stage-coach.'

A Frenchman named Hacquet was seen in the streets of Paris in 1834 with a three-masted carriage named *l'Eolienne*, which had a mainmast forty feet high. On 18 September it gave a public demonstration: 'Leaving the Ecole Militaire with a south-westerly wind, it crossed the Pont d'Iena, followed the Quais with the same wind, finally halting in the Place Louis-XV. The most curious features of this experience were having weathered a violent squall and having taken the rise of the Pont Louis-XV against what was virtually a head-wind.'

However, by that time the wind wagon had become an obsolete curiosity; for many years, inventors had been turning their attention to less fickle forms of propulsion. As far back as the 1680s, the Jesuit priest Ferdinand Verbiest had built a little steam-powered model carriage while he was on missionary duty in China. In 1685, he wrote a treatise in Latin, *Astronomia Europaea*, which was published two years later. In it he wrote: 'About three years ago, while I was making some researches into the power of the aeolipyle (a small boiler), I constructed a little chariot about two feet in length, in the middle of which I placed a container full of glowing embers, and then above this an aeolipyle. On the axle of the front wheels, there was a ring of bronze with teeth engaging in wheels linked to a shaft carrying four blades, on which the jet of the aeolipyle impinged. By means of a tiller linked to the rear axle, which could pivot, the machine could be made to describe a circle.'

In 1690, Denis Papin, the Frenchman who invented the pressure cooker, proposed an 'atmospheric machine' driven by a piston acting on a ratchet wheel, then in 1698 he built a little model steam carriage: 'As I believe that this innovation can be used with advantage for other ends than raising water, I made a model of a little chariot which moved itself by means of this force, and it achieved all that I had anticipated . . . I believe that the inequalities and twistings of the main roads will make it very difficult to develop this invention for use in land carriages.'

At the beginning of the 18th century, Father Grimaldi, another Jesuit on the China Mission, is said to have followed in the wheeltracks of Father Verbiest, building a little model steam carriage propelled by an aeolipyle in an attempt to convert the Chinese Emperor, Kang Hi, to Christianity. The machine ran successfully; whether the proselytisation of Kang Hi was as successful is not recorded.

The first British inventors to move into the as yet ethereal realms of self-propelled vehicle design were two optimists named Ramsey and Wildgoose, who in 1618 took out a gloriously vague patent for 'newe, apte, or compendious formes or kinds of engines or instruments to plough grounds without horse or oxen; and to make boates for the carriage of burthens and passengers runn upon the water as swifte as in calmes, and more safe in stormes, than boates full sayled in great winnes'.

All this, mark you, without specifying any precise form of motive power. Nor was Ramsay any more specific when he subsequently patented: 'a farre more easie and better waye for soweing of corne and grayne, and alsoe for the carrying of coaches, carts, drayes, and other things goeing on wheels, than ever yet was used and discovered'.

In 1680, Sir Isaac Newton, who had been laughed to scorn when he prophesied that one day men would be able to travel at fifty miles an hour, described

Abriß vom Triumphwage

den von einem Meister deß Circkelschmidt Handwercks/ist so gro geht/wie er da vor Augen sicht/vnd bedarff keiner Verspannung der lincken Hand ein Flammkopff inhanden/damit kan er den W Thal/wie er dann vnterschiedlich mal/ist die Vestung zu Nürnb umb/vnd geht solcher Wagen in einer Stund 2 tausent Schritt/ alles von vhrwerck gemacht/wird alles mit der lincken Hand reg het/die Augen verwenden/der Meerdrach kan Wasser / Bier /

Dargegen kan er allerley wolriechende Wasser geben/als Zu Posaunen auffheben vnd blasen/vnd ist solcher Wagen alle S

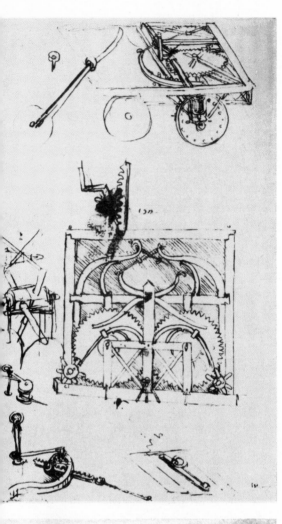

Far left: the inventor of the pressure cooker, Denis Papin, produced in 1698 a model steam car, although he believed at the time that the idea would not work on full-size 'land carriages'

Left: long before it was generally thought to be needed, Leonardo da Vinci had already produced a differential drive system. In fact, even when motor vehicles had reached quite an advanced stage, the use of a device to distribute dissimilar amounts of torque to each wheel was still thought to be unnecessary

Below: a different and probably less efficient way of using wind power than that proposed by Stevin is seen on this model of Valturio's carriage of 1472. Even at this early time, it was realised that there was a future in vehicles powered by means other than oxen or horses

Left: the elaborate *Triumphwagen*, built by the famed Nuremberg mechanic Hans Hautsch in 1649. The vehicle, with a front shaped like a sea monster, could cover 2000 paces in an hour, powered by its clockwork mechanism. Perhaps greater mileage could have been attained had there not been so much decoration on the body to weigh the machine down

a 'scientific toy' in the shape of a little boiler mounted on wheels and propelled solely by the force of the jet of steam issuing from a nozzle leading backwards from the boiler, a concept unlikely to succeed in model form and doomed to failure in full-scale.

By the mid eighteenth century, the steam engine had been developed to the extent that it could be built sufficiently small enough and sufficiently powerful enough to propel a road carriage, and such a vehicle was proposed in 1759 by one Doctor Robinson, a student at Glasgow University, who subsequently became Professor of Natural Philosophy at Edinburgh University. Robinson mentioned his scheme to his friend James Watt, but soon afterwards went abroad, and proceeded no further with his invention.

Six years later, three distinguished scientists began a correspondence regarding the use of steam as a motive power. It seems that one of them, Matthew Boulton of Birmingham (who became partner to James Watt), had built a little steam engine, and had sent it to Benjamin Franklin, who was then the London agent for the United Provinces of America. Franklin, his mind already abuzz with political matters, dismissed the invention with the throwaway remark that: 'It was believed to be practicable to employ it as a means of locomotion'.

This caught the imagination of the third member of the group, Doctor Erasmus Darwin, a poet as well as a physician, who wrote to Boulton: 'As I was riding home yesterday, I considered the scheme of the fiery chariot, and the longer I considered this favourite idea, the more practicable it appeared to me. I shall lay my thoughts before you, crude and undigested as they appeared to me ... and as I am quite made of the scheme, I hope you will not shew this paper to anyone. These things are required: (1) a rotary motion, (2) easily altering its direction to any other direction, (3) to be accelerated, retarded, destroyed, revived, instantly and easily, (4) the bulk the weight, the expense of the machine to be as small as possible in regard to its weight'.

Darwin then went on to describe a rather crude device mounted on three or four wheels, driven by a two-cylinder Newcomen engine of the type used for pumping water out of mines. 'And if this answers in practice as it does in theory,' concluded the good doctor, ignoring the fact that the Newcomen engine, in which the pistons were sucked down by the condensation of steam in the cylinders creating a partial vacuum, was a bulky, slothful, inefficient device, quite unsuited to powering a road vehicle, 'the machine could not fail of success'.

It could, though, and it did. Boulton was unwilling to become a partner in Darwin's enterprise, and the scheme was allowed to lapse, although Darwin did turn the experience to some account by composing a poem which started: 'Soon shall they force, gigantic steam, afar haul the slow barge or urge the rapid car ...' It was left to his grandson, Charles, to establish the fame of the family name.

In 1769, came the most fanciful scheme yet proposed. One Francis Moore, a rich linen draper, announced that he had obtained a Royal Patent for 'a new machine made of wood, iron, brass, copper or other metals, and constructed upon peculiar principles, and capable of being wrought or put in motion by fire, water or air, without being drawn by horses, or any other beast or cattle; and which machines, or engines, upon repeated trials, he has discovered would be very useful in agriculture, carriage of persons or goods, either in coaches, chariots, chaises, carts, wagons, or other conveyances, and likewise in navigation, by causing ships, boats, barges, and other vessels to move, sail or proceed, with more swiftness or despatch'. So confident in the omnipotence of this new motive power was the inventor that he had not only disposed of all his horses, but had also persuaded many of his friends to do the same.

James Watt dismissed the news of Moore's invention with scorn: 'If linen draper Moore does not use my engine to drive his chaises, he cannot drive them by steam. If he does I will stop him. I suppose by the rapidity of his progress and puffing, he is too volatile to be dangerous.'

However, the same year that Moore proposed his 'new machine', the first full-sized steam carriage made its appearance in Paris, the work of a French military engineer named Nicolas Joseph Cugnot, born at Void, in Lorraine, in

Left: Erasmus Darwin (the grandfather of Charles, whose biological theories were to provoke such a furore a half-century later), *above*, and Matthew Boulton, *below*, who together with Benjamin Franklin corresponded on the use of steam as a motive power. Boulton had, in fact, built a model steam engine and had shown it to Franklin. Although Franklin was indifferent about the whole idea, Darwin was most impressed. Darwin's idea centred around using a two-cylinder Newcomen engine, as utilised in mining-pump engines. This, however, was not to Boulton's thinking, so it was left up to the poet Erasmus to wax lyrical about the prospects of the steam engine

1729. As a young man, Cugnot lived in Germany, where he entered the service of the Emperor. He was, it seems, posted to Brussels in the early 1760s and, according to tradition, built a model steam carriage there in 1763.

It was in 1769, though, that Cugnot was enabled to realise his brainchild in full scale, as L-N Rolland, Commissaire-General of Artillery, recalled in a report published on the 4th Pluviose in Year VIII of the French Revolution (1801): 'In 1769 (old style), Planta, a Swiss officer, proposed a number of inventions to Minister Choiseul. Among these was a carriage moved by steam.

'General de Gribeauval, having been called in to examine the prospectus of this invention, recalled that a certain Cugnot, who had worked as an engineer in foreign parts, and author of a work entitled *Fortification of the Countryside*, was then engaged in the construction of a similar machine in Paris; the Swiss officer was instructed to make an examination of it. He found it in all ways preferable to his invention, and Minister Choiseul authorised Cugnot to complete at the State's expense that which he had begun on a small scale.

'In the presence of General Gribeauval and many other spectators, and carrying four persons, it ran on the level, and I have confirmed that it could

Above: the mechanism of Nicholas Joseph Cugnot's *fardier*, showing a ratchet from the cylinders (one either side) that turned the front wheel. Interestingly, the latest French Citroëns use a similar layout to that of the Cugnot wagon, with the engine mounted forward of the driven front wheels

have covered 1800 to 2000 *toises* (2.1800–2.4222 miles) an hour if it had been run without interruption.' However, the capacity of the boiler had not been accurately enough proportioned to that of the pumps, and it could only run for twelve to fifteen minutes at a time, and then had to stand for nearly as long so that the steam could build up to its original pressure; besides, the furnace being badly made allowed the heat to escape and the boiler seemed hardly strong enough to contain the full strength of the steam.

This trial having shown that a full-scale carriage would actually work, engineer Cugnot was ordered to build another, this time capable of carrying a load of 8 to 10 *milliers* (about 4 tons) at a steady speed of around 1800 *toises* per

5

hour; it was completed at the end of 1770, at a cost of 22,000 livres.

Cugnot's second carriage had twin cylinders (cast in the arsenal at Strasbourg and brought from there with all possible speed to Mazurier, quartermaster of the Paris Arsenal, where the *fardier* was being built). Steam was admitted to the cylinders through a rocking valve, the pistons going up and down alternately and turning ratchets either side of the single front wheel. Ahead of this wheel was supported the massive boiler, which could only (and then with difficulty) be replenished when the vehicle was at a standstill. This whole clumsy mass turned with the front wheel; steering was through handlebars which operated a geared-down pinion acting on a curved rack. It must have been a near super-human operation, as the entire power pack was supported only by one in-

Below: seen in the Conservatoire des Arts et Métiers in Paris is the Cugnot *fardier*. One can see how unstable the machine would be with all the weight at the front and also how heavy the steering must be. The difficulty involved in steering the Cugnot was proved, *inset*, by the wagon destroying a wall which was in its path. There is still some confusion over which museum possesses the original *fardier*. Although the concensus of opinion suggests that the Paris museum has the original, sources at the museum have volunteered the information that the machine is in fact a replica

substantial-looking kingpin, which gave the driver a lot of work.

As the Cugnot carriage was intended as an artillery tractor, there was no superstructure on the rear part of its wooden chassis. Without a load to keep the back wheels on the ground, the *fardier* must have been terrifyingly unstable. Nevertheless, a letter written on 20 November 1770 recorded '. . . a fire engine, for the transport of carriages and, especially, artillery, has been developed to the point where, last Tuesday, this machine has pulled a load of 5 *milliers* while simultaneously carrying a cannon of around the same weight, covering five quarters of a league in an hour. The same machine can climb the rockiest heights and overcome all irregularities of the terrain.'

The last comments were, it seems, mere embroidery for, although it seems likely that the Cugnot did run under its own power, it was manifestly not a success. Cugnot's obituary, published in *Le Moniteur* of 6 October 1804, stated that the carriage was 'built in the Arsenal and put to the test. The excessive violence of its movements prevented its being steered and, as early as its first trial, a piece of wall which happened to get in its way was knocked down. That's what prevented it being put into service.'

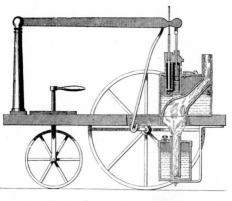

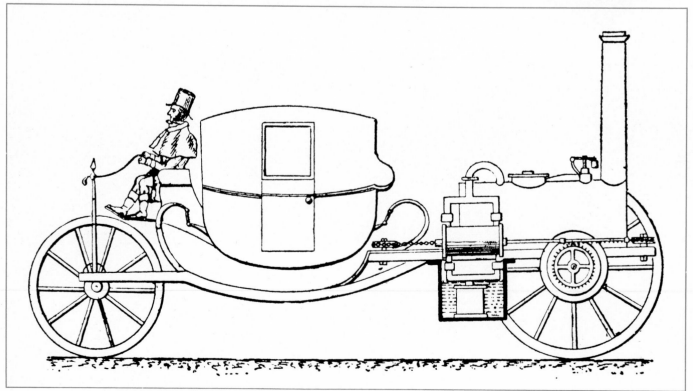

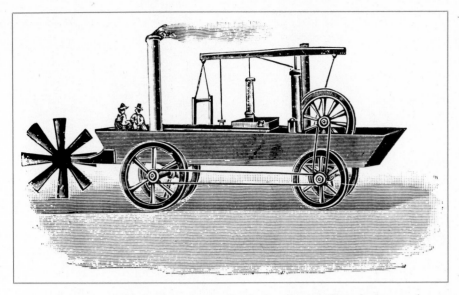

Far left and top: this model steam engine was built *circa* 1784 by William Murdock of Redruth, Cornwall. The little vehicle, standing just over one foot in height, was tested by its designer. 'The night was dark, and he alone sallied out with his engine, lighted the fire, a lamp under the boiler, and off started the locomotive, with the inventor in full chase after it. Shortly after he heard distant despair-like shouting; it was too dark to perceive objects, but he soon found that the cries for assistance proceeded from the worthy pastor, who, going into town on business, was met on this lonely road by the fiery monster, whom he subsequently declared he took for the Evil One *in propria persona*'

Left and below: William Symington and his model steam coach of 1786. The state of the roads in his native Scotland at that time meant that such a vehicle in full size would not be practical. Thereafter, he concentrated on the use of steam to propel boats

Above right: Oliver Evans, in Philadelphia, built this twenty-ton amphibian, *Orukter Amphibolos*, in 1805. It was powered by a twin-cylinder grasshopper beam engine and made what is generally accepted as the first journey by a steam-powered vehicle on the American continent

It was preserved, though. It survived the French Revolution and was acquired for the Conservatoire des Arts et Métiers in 1799. Put on display in 1801, it has remained the star exhibit of this museum of technology ever since. Also surviving is a little model steam carriage built around 1784 by the Englishman William Murdock, who was in charge of the construction of Boulton & Watt beam engines in the Cornish mines around Redruth. It was a far more practicable design than that of Cugnot, but unfortunately lacked the massive Government backing which had enabled the French inventor to realise his project as a full-size machine. Indeed, it seems that James Watt was more than a little jealous of his assistant's model carriages, and sought to divert him from such projects, although on several occasions the models made successful test runs. In September 1786, Boulton wrote to Watt that Murdock had caused his little steam carriage to run for a mile or two (doubtless in a circle!) in the drawing room of a mutual friend, carrying as ballast the fire-tongs, poker and coal-shovel.

Several other inventors were also working on the development of steam carriages around the same time; they, too, got no further than the model stage. For example, in Edinburgh in 1786, William Symington proposed a curious steam berline, but the dreadful state of the Scottish roads at that period caused him to turn his attention to the more immediate problems of applying steam power to the propulsion of boats – in 1788, he built the first British steamboat to the order of Patrick Miller of Dalswinton, Dumfriesshire, which on its initial trial carried the poet Robert Burns among its passengers.

In 1788, Nathan Read, of Massachusetts, built a model steam carriage of curious design, while around the same time one Doctor Apollos Kinsley is reported to have driven a steam carriage through the streets of Hartford, Connecticut . . . although it has been recorded that it is doubtful whether the story has much basis in fact.

The true pioneer of steam propulsion in America – although his activities in other aspects of engineering outshadowed his achievements in vehicle manufacture – was Oliver Evans, born in Newport, Delaware, in 1755. Today, Evans is chiefly remembered as a pioneer of automation in manufacturing processes, but as a young man he devised a high-pressure steam engine and considered its application to land carriages.

He petitioned the Legislation of Delaware in 1786 for an exclusive licence to use his automatic mill machinery and to build and use steam wagons. The Board granted the privileges he prayed for, respecting the improvements in flour-milling machinery, but they quietly ignored his steam carriage schemes altogether . . . they believed him to be somewhat deranged.

A similar request was placed before the Legislature of Maryland, and here Evans's case was pleaded by a friend on the committee, who stated that 'no one in the world had thought of moving carriages by steam, and by granting the request, no one could be injured, and there was a prospect of something useful

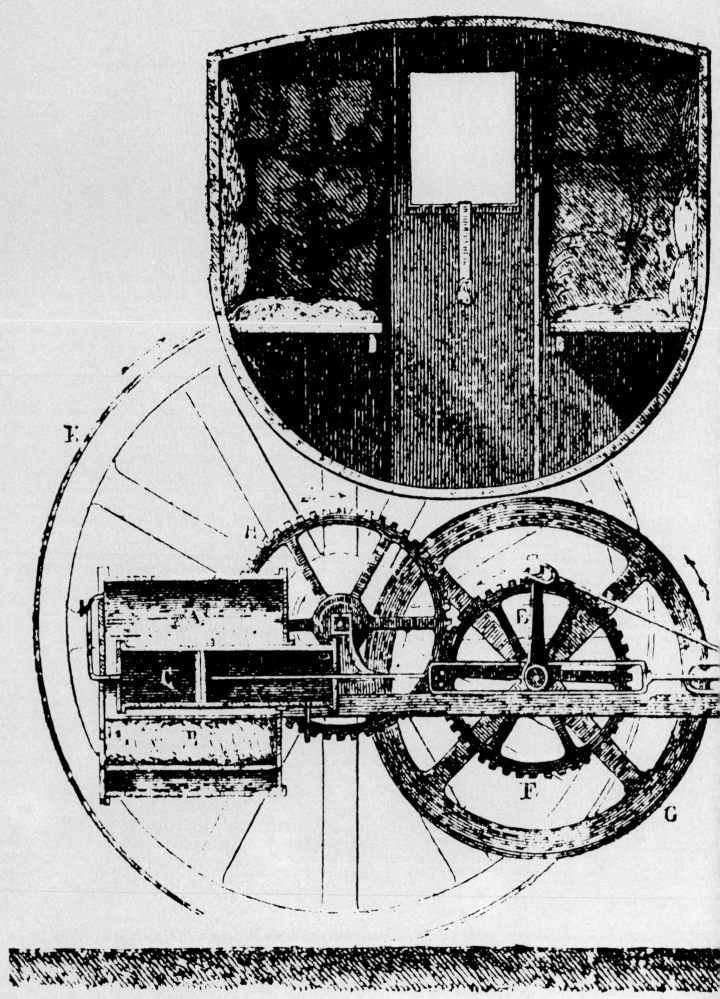

Trevithick and Vivian's second carriage was a massive piece of equipment with the boiler at the rear. Built in 1803, it proved quite successful, making many journeys through London and the provinces. The Felton body, mounted above the engine, could hold eight or nine people. The machine was so reliable that John Vivian, who himself was no great engineer, would take the carriage out on his own without Trevithick, so sure was he that it would not break down. It was while Vivian was driving, however, at a speed in excess of 9 mph that a mishap occurred. The machine was running so happily that he and Trevithick joked of carrying on towards Cornwall. Vivian's concentration waned and he steered the vehicle into garden fencing in City Road. He was quick to remark, however, that it was his fault alone. Successful though his machine was, the ex-wrestler Richard Trevithick decided to concentrate on the development of tramroad locomotives

being produced'. So, Evans received an exclusive licence for the manufacture and operation of steam carriages within the State of Maryland for the fourteen years commencing May 1787.

He could not obtain financial backing for his steam carriage project – maybe his prophesies that one day people would travel in stage carriages moved by steam from one city to another almost as fast as birds could fly scared off prospective investors – so in 1801 decided to 'discharge his debt of honour to the State of Maryland by producing the steam waggons'. He had got no further than the preliminary stages of construction when he concluded that it would be more profitable to use his steam engine to drive mills. In 1805, however, he fitted wheels to a twenty-ton dredger he had built for the Board of Health of Philadelphia to convert it, albeit temporarily, to an amphibian; and the short, clumsy waddle of this 'Orukter Amphibolos' is generally accepted as the first successful journey by a steam carriage on American soil.

However, in Europe the first truly practicable steam carriage had already made its appearance, built by the Cornish mining engineer Richard Trevithick, who had devised a high-pressure steam engine of unprecedented efficiency, and had been building experimental models of steam vehicles since 1796.

Trevithick employed several workmen in Camborne for the repair and improvement of mining engines and pumping machinery, and in November 1800 they began work in their spare time on building a full-sized road locomotive to their master's design. Some of the larger components were finished in the workshops of Trevithick's cousin and collaborator, Andrew Vivian, while other parts had been made in the cradle of the British industrial revolution at Coalbrookdale.

The single vertical cylinder was recessed into the boiler, and its piston rod was attached to a crosshead which rotated the front wheels of the carriage by means of long connecting rods. The stoker stood on a platform at the rear; this apparently turned with the back axle, which had smaller wheels than the front, to give a reasonable steering lock before they fouled the tubby boiler. By Christmas Eve, 1801, the carriage was ready for its first trials, watched by a crowd of people, one of whom subsequently set down his reminiscences of the

event: 'I knew Captain Dick Trevithick very well. I was a cooper by trade, and when Trevithick was making his steam carriage I used to go every day into John Tyack's shop in the Weith, close by here, where they put her together. In the year 1801, upon Christmas Eve, towards night, Trevithick got up steam, out on the high road, just outside the shop. When we saw that Trevithick was going to turn on steam, we jumped up as many as could, maybe seven or eight of us. 'Twas a stiffish hill going up to Camborne Beacon, but she went off like a little bird. When she had gone about a quarter of a mile, there was a rough piece of road, covered with loose stones. She did not go quite so fast, and as it was a flood of rain, and we were very much squeezed together, I jumped off. She was going faster than I could walk, and went up the hill about half a mile further, when they turned her, and came back again to the shop.'

So, and apparently with very few teething troubles, the first successful self-propelled road vehicle in history took to the roads. Over the next few days, Trevithick and Vivian made a number of short journeys in the locality of Camborne, then the carriage broke down; conveniently, as it happened, outside an inn. The two young men pushed it under a lean-to and retired to the inn,

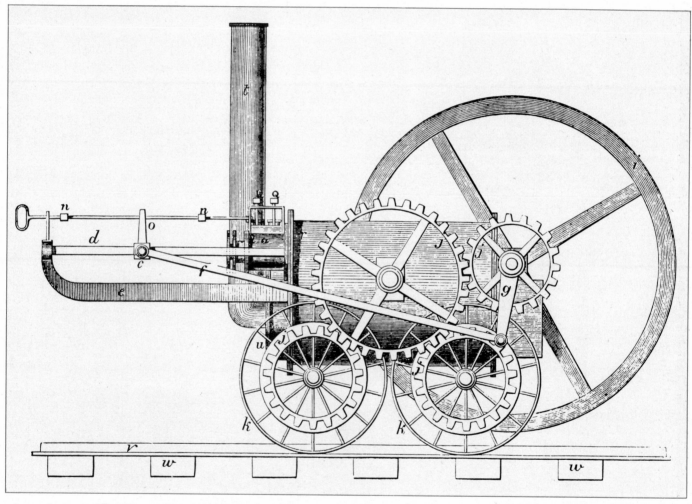

where the soporific efforts of an excellent roast goose plus appropriate drinks caused them to forget that they had failed to put out the fire in the carriage's boiler. Inevitably, the water evaporated, the iron of the boiler became red hot, and finally the wooden chassis smouldered and burned to ashes. So, too, did the lean-to . . .

Undaunted, Trevithick and Vivian journeyed to London where, on 22 March 1802, they secured a patent for high-pressure steam engines for propelling steam engines on common roads; in 1803, they built a carriage on the lines described in the London patent in Felton's carriage shop in Leather Lane. With the boiler and cylinder at the rear, and a coach body mounted between the large-diameter rear wheels, the London carriage was a far more sophisticated design than its predecessor, and its reported achievements were correspond-

Above: another of Trevithick's ventures was this tramroad locomotive of 1803. With a load of twenty-five tons behind, it could travel at a speed of 4 mph up various inclines. Running light, though, it could attain no less than 16 mph

Right: Trevithick's first carriage was this strange railway-looking device which was constructed in 1801. After successful trials, the vehicle was left outside an inn where its happy builders went to indulge in a little light refreshment. Unfortunately, they forgot to extinguish its fire and it burned up its chassis and the shed in which it was standing

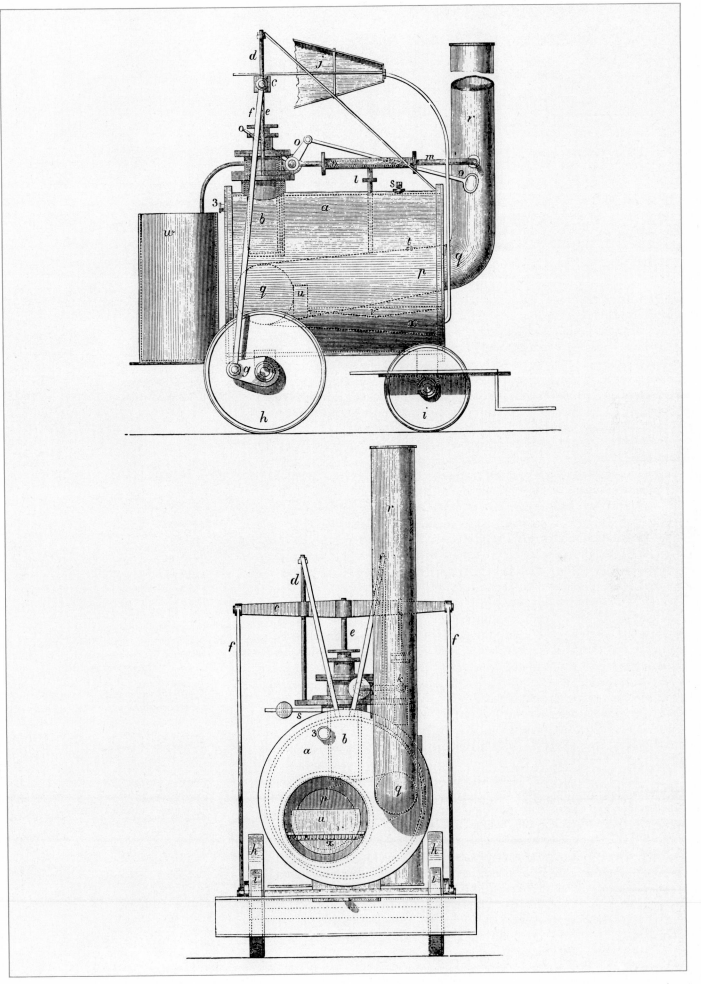

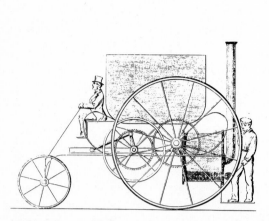

ingly greater. Vivian, for instance, is said to have made a journey of ten miles through the streets of London . . . from Leather Lane, Gray's Inn Lane, on to Lord's Cricket Ground, to Paddington, and home again by way of Islington.

Early one morning, Trevithick and Vivian were running along the City Road when Vivian, who was steering, became distracted, and allowed the carriage to run too close to the edge of the road, with the consequence that it tore down several yards of fencing. 'On one occasion, this steam coach ran through Oxford Street at a good speed, amid much cheering; no horses or vehicles were allowed on the road during the trial.'

It seems that the new carriage was a great success. The eminent scientist Sir Humphrey Davy saw it running: 'I shall soon hope to hear that the roads of England are the haunts of Captain Trevithick's dragons'. Trevithick, though, was already following a new star, and the following year he would build the world's first railway engine (he failed to persist with this invention, too). The London carriage was dismantled, and its engine sold to power a hoop rolling mill, which it continued to do for several years. Trevithick's inability to see his inventions through to perfection proved his downfall: when he died in 1833, his workmates at Hall's factory in Dartford had to club together to pay for the cost of his funeral, for he had spent all (and more) than he had.

However, he had opened the way to other inventors, although it must be admitted that for several years after the London Patent it was the lunatic fringe which predominated. Like the appropriately named John Dumbell, who in 1808 proposed an engine for drawing carriages along the highway propelled by an engine in which steam would be raised by dropping water on to a red-hot metal plate, causing 'vanes, or fliers, like the sails of a windmill' to revolve and rotate a driving shaft. Or John Tindall, whose 1814 patent described a three-wheeled vehicle pushed along the highway by four steam-driven legs attached to the 'hinder part of the carriage' and supplemented by the action of 'a species of windmill, driven partly by the wind and partly by the exhaust steam from the engine'.

Trevithick had long ago proved that the adhesion between carriage wheels and the road was quite sufficient to provide traction yet the obsession with articulated legs to circumvent wheelslip continued. In 1813, one W. Brunton patented a 'mechanical traveller' which had two legs at the rear of the boiler linked to the piston road in such a way that they performed a continuous 'walking' motion, pushing the carriage forward in a series of jerks. In the 1820s, David Gordon made trials with elaborate leg-propelled carriages, but they proved too complex and destructive of the road surface, and the project was abandoned. Gordon also patented another splendidly lunatic machine, in which a tiny railway engine running inside a nine-foot-diameter steel drum like a squirrel in a cage formed the tractive unit for a two-wheeled steerable fore-carriage. This project was also eventually abandoned.

However, practical inventors were appearing on the scene, like the Czech

Top left: Trevithick's Common Road Passenger Locomotive of 1803. Richard Trevithick was one of the few early steam pioneers whose products could be described as being truly practical

Top centre: Richard Trevithick's steam-powered *Catch-me-who-can* carriage of 1808; this, in fact, was a railway carriage. The engine was so heavy, however (it weighed about eight tons), that the timber underneath the rails sank into the ground causing the engine to overturn. Trevithick, having exhausted his finances by this stage, could not afford to have the project repaired

Above: Trevithick was one of the most successful of the early steam pioneers. Although he was a prolific inventor, his problem was that he seldom followed a project through to its end and when he died in 1833 he was virtually penniless

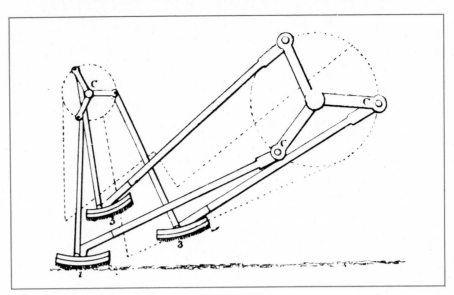

Above right : old traditions die hard, even among the most adventurous of inventors; so, the earliest designers built steam carriages, they refused to trust the wheel alone and insisted on fitting these mechanical legs called, appropriately, 'horses' feet'

Below : David Gordon's steam carriage of 1824; this monster used mechanical legs to move, but proved so heavy and destructive to road surfaces that the project was eventually abandoned

mechanic Josef Bozek, who in 1815 drove a little steam carriage, which would not have looked out of date eighty years later, through the streets of Prague. He also applied this engine to a small boat, but was ruined when the gate money taken during a demonstration of his inventions was stolen during a thunderstorm. Although his debts were later paid off by the local freemasons, Bozek destroyed his carriage and boats in disgust.

More successful was the English inventor Medhurst who, after dabbling with a 'new improved Aeolian engine' powered by compressed air, and even an artillery wagon propelled by a gunpowder engine, built a little steam carriage which, between April and July 1819, made several successful journeys along the New Road between Paddington and Islington at a speed of five miles an hour. A larger version of this machine could carry four people at a speed of seven miles an hour, but family pressures caused Medhurst to abandon his experiments in the mid 1820s.

However, he was the first of a series of inventors who, with varying degrees of success, would make the period between 1820 and 1840 the first golden age of the self-propelled vehicle.

Below: this cartoon depicting a steam-engined tricycle of 1818 can now be found in France's Conservatoire des Arts et Métiers in Paris. It seems that even in those days motorists had fuel-price problems because, in the cartoon caption, the driver is haggling over the price of a sack of coal. By 1818, of course, the Golden Age of Steam was well under way but the vehicles produced were still 'carriages' rather than 'motor cars' as we have come to know them

CHAPTER 2

The Golden Age of Steam

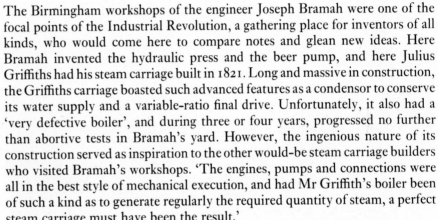

The Birmingham workshops of the engineer Joseph Bramah were one of the focal points of the Industrial Revolution, a gathering place for inventors of all kinds, who would come here to compare notes and glean new ideas. Here Bramah invented the hydraulic press and the beer pump, and here Julius Griffiths had his steam carriage built in 1821. Long and massive in construction, the Griffiths carriage boasted such advanced features as a condensor to conserve its water supply and a variable-ratio final drive. Unfortunately, it also had a 'very defective boiler', and during three or four years, progressed no further than abortive tests in Bramah's yard. However, the ingenious nature of its construction served as inspiration to the other would-be steam carriage builders who visited Bramah's workshops. 'The engines, pumps and connections were all in the best style of mechanical execution, and had Mr Griffith's boiler been of such a kind as to generate regularly the required quantity of steam, a perfect steam carriage must have been the result.'

In 1824, Timothy Burstall (ominous name!) and John Hill began work on a steam carriage, which underwent trials at Leith and Edinburgh in 1826, and in London in 1827. Again, this was a machine whose technical specification promised far more than the mediocre results of its test runs, for it was the first vehicle in history to feature four-wheel drive. A complicated system of bevel gearing permitted the front wheels to be steered as well as powered, and this was also the first shaft-driven road vehicle in history. Moreover, it had front-wheel brakes and a silencer and, according to an account in the *Edinburgh Philosophical Journal*, may well have had the first flash boiler. 'They proposed to heat (the boiler) from 250°F to 600°F and, by keeping the water in a separate vessel, and only applying it to the boiler when steam was wanted, they accomplished that desideratum of making just such a quantity of steam as was wanted; so that when going down hill all the steam and heat might be saved, to be accumulated and given out again at the first hill or piece of rough road when, more being wanted, more will be expended.'

Against all these advanced features were set the facts that Burstall & Hill's machine was powered by an archaic side-beam engine of the type normally used in paddle-steamers, and that it weighed an earth-shaking eight tons. Consequently, the carriage was incapable of moving at speeds greater than three or four miles an hour, and even that put so much strain on the boiler that it burst.

Undaunted, Burstall & Hill then announced a new project, for a two-wheeled 'power pack' to carry the boiler separate from the main body of the carriage, to allay the fears of passengers that there might be an explosion; a quarter-scale model of this machine, with six wheels, of which the centre pair drove, was demonstrated in Edinburgh and London. It seems that trials with a full-size version were unsuccessful, and that the boiler and engine were then removed and fitted in a railway locomotive, the *Perseverance*, which was entered for – and almost immediately withdrawn from – the Rainhill locomotive trials of 1829, where Stevenson's *Rocket* emerged victorious.

In 1824, William Henry James, of Thavies Inn, Holborn, London, a 'gentleman of superior mechanical talents', was the first steam carriage designer to attempt to give some positive form of differential action to the driving wheels, having realised that on a corner the outer wheel travelled further than the inner. Others, like Burstall and Hill, had arranged a sort of 'differential by default' in which ratchets in the hubs permitted the drive to the outer wheel to be overridden on curves (small wonder that their four-wheel-drive carriage was so troublesome!), but James proposed a far more commendable solution which, in model form at least, worked quite successfully. Each rear wheel had its own cranked half axle driven by a twin-cylinder engine working at high pressure; on the front axle were cocks which were opened and closed as the carriage turned, automatically controlling the amount of steam passing to each engine, so that when the carriage was running straight, both engines received the same quantity, but on corners the outer engine received more and therefore travelled faster thus adding to its efficiency.

Writing in the *Register of Arts* in 1829, Luke Herbert recalled that the model was 'so efficient that the carriage could be made to describe every variety of

Below: a painting of Gurney's steam carriage as it appeared at Hounslow on 12 August 1829; it towed a barouche containing, among other distinguished people, the Duke of Wellington. Goldsworthy Gurney was a prolific inventor who had the ability to promote his own products and was eventually knighted for his services in improving the heating and lighting of the House of Commons. Gurney's first steam carriage used both wheels and legs for movement. In 1825, he began work on a second carriage and this was used for a nine-mile trip from London to Edgware. By 1826, Gurney had produced a monstrous steam coach which attracted a lot of public interest and comment

Left: James' steam-carriage of 1824, built by William Henry James of Thavies Inn, Holborn, who was the first steam-carriage designer to give some form of differential action to the wheels, having realised that the outer wheel travelled further than the inner when cornering. Unfortunately, James had no capital to construct a larger and more advanced design. In 1829, however, he received a commission from Sir James Anderson to construct a new vehicle based on the 1824 design

curve; he has seen it repeatedly make turns of less than ten feet radius'.

James had not then the capital to construct his design on a larger scale, but eventually received a commission from Sir James Anderson, Bart, of Buttevant Castle, Ireland, and in March 1829 they carried out experiments with a steam diligence built on the lines of James's 1824 model. On every test, some fault in design or construction had to be altered, but eventually the machine was judged ready for road travel, and 'loaded with fifteen passengers and propelled several miles on a rough gravel road across Epping Forest, with a speed varying from twelve to fifteen miles an hour'. Then a boiler tube split, letting the water out of one of the boilers and extinguishing its fire.

'Under these circumstances', wrote Luke Hebert in *Galloway's Treatise on the Steam Engine*, 'with only one boiler in operation, the carriage returned home at the rate of about seven miles an hour, carrying more than twenty passengers, at one period, indeed, it is said, a much greater number; showing that sufficient steam can be generated in such a boiler to be equal to the propulsion of between five tons and six tons weight. In consequence of this flattering demonstration that the most brilliant success was obtainable, the proprietors dismantled the carriage and commenced the construction of superior tubular boilers with much stronger tubes.'

In fact, what emerged after the rebuild was an entirely new, and much less complicated, machine, intended to replace the team of horses in front of a stagecoach, and to which end the novelty of a two-speed transmission was provided.

In one of the very first road-test articles, which appeared in the *Mechanics' Magazine* in November 1829, the author commented: 'A series of interesting experiments were made throughout the whole of yesterday with a new carriage belonging to Sir James Anderson, Bart, and W. H. James, Esq, on the Vauxhall, Kensington and Clapham roads, with the view of ascertaining the practical advantages of some perfectly novel apparatus attached to the engines, the results of which were so satisfactory that the proprietors intend immediately establishing several stage coaches on the principle. The writer was favoured with a ride during the last experiment, when the machine proceeded from Vauxhall Bridge to the Swan at Clapham, a distance of two and a half miles, which was run at the rate of fifteen miles an hour. From what I had the pleasure of witnessing, I am confident that this carriage is far superior to every other locomotive carriage hitherto brought before the public, and that she will easily perform fifteen miles an hour throughout a long journey. The body of the carriage, if not elegant, is neat, being the figure of a parallelogram. It is a very small and compact machine, and runs upon four wheels.'

It seems that once again the workmanship of the day was not up to coping with the very high steam pressures used by James, though, for the new carriage rarely managed to run for more than three or four miles without one or other of its steam joints breaking.

James's last carriage was patented in 1832, and had a three-speed chain transmission, with the ratios changed by pedals. It seems that around the same time Anderson ran out of money, and this design was never built.

A carriage which attracted far less attention than that of James, yet which enjoyed far greater success, was constructed around the year 1827 by the young engineer James Nasmyth, who was then little more than a boy, being only some nineteen years old.

'Having made a small working model of a steam carriage,' he recalled, 'I exhibited it before the members of the Scottish Society of Arts. The performance of this active little machine was so gratifying to the Society that they requested me to construct one of such power as to enable four or six persons to be conveyed along the ordinary roads. The members of the Society, in their individual capacity, subscribed £60, which they placed in my hands as the means for carrying out their project. I accordingly set to work at once, and completed the carriage in about four months, when it was exhibited before the members of the Society of Arts. Many successful trials were made with it on the Queensferry Road near Edinburgh. The runs were generally of four or five miles, with a load of eight passengers sitting on benches about three feet from the ground. The experiments were continued for nearly three months, to the great satisfaction of the members . . . the Society of Arts did not attach any commercial value to my road carriage. It was merely as a matter of experiment that they had invited me to construct it. When it proved successful they made me a present of the entire apparatus. As I was anxious to get on with my studies, and to prepare for the work of practical engineering, I proceeded no further. I broke up the steam carriage, and sold the two small high-pressure engines, provided with a strong boiler, for £67, a sum which more than defrayed all the expenses of the construction and working of the machine.'

There were other experimenters active in the design of steam carriages around this time, but most faded away from lack of capital, or from attempting to construct over-ambitious projects. But one who did persist, and by dint of judicious self-publicity, managed to remain in the headlines for longer than most of the pioneers, was Goldsworthy Gurney who, most appropriately, could number the invention of the limelight among his many achievements (and was eventually knighted for his work in improving the heating and lighting of the House of Commons). Gurney, born at Trevorgus in Cornwall in 1793, gave a

Left: Goldsworthy Gurney's steam carriage is depicted struggling its way uphill to Barnet through Highgate Archway on 14 June 1828. It was on the descent that the carriage's brakes failed, sending the vehicle crashing off the road at high speed, to finish up in a ditch. Nevertheless, the fact that the Gurney reached the top at all was an achievement to be proud of

lecture on chemical science in 1822 in which he proclaimed that 'elemental power is capable of being applied to propel carriages along the common roads with great political advantage, and that the floating knowledge of the day places the subject within our reach. I consider that ammoniac gas is usable. This gas can be used in the normal mechanism of a steam engine, without its requiring any great modification.'

Having built a small carriage driven by ammonia, Gurney decided to construct a full-size steam carriage; like Brunton and Gordon before him, he was convinced that wheels alone would be insufficient to propel a carriage, and therefore included pusher legs in the specification of his machine. Despite this, the carriage managed to run on the roads, and is said to have ascended Windmill Hill, at Kilburn, in 1825; a second machine apparently made a nine-mile trip from London to Edgware. Quite a long trip in those days for what is now a small bus ride!

In 1826, Gurney began work on his most famous steam carriage, a monstrous coach intended for a regular London–Bath service; this, too, appeared at first equipped with 'propellers' to help it up hills, although in 1828 it managed to climb Highgate Hill without recourse to such superfluities. 'The wheels did not slip, nor was there need to use the mechanical legs for a single instant', marvelled Gurney (it seems, however, that on the descent of Highgate Hill, lacking adequate brakes, the carriage ran away at rather a high speed and eventually ended up in a ditch!).

In 1828, Gurney drove this carriage, which bore the proud inscription 'London and Bath, Royal Patent' on its sides, on its sole journey to the city of Bath, pausing every four miles to replenish the thirsty boiler (it may well be that the Bath Road was chosen because in Regency times Beau Nash had set up huge pumps at regular intervals so that the roads could be kept watered, thus laying the dust which would otherwise have been raised by the carriages of the elegant on their way to take the cure).

It seems as though the carriage broke down on the outward journey, and had to be hauled ignominiously to its destination behind a team of horses, but on the return it is said to have covered the 84 miles from Melksham to Cranford Bridge in ten hours . . . 'including stoppages'.

Gurney's 'London–Bath' carriage attracted much publicity, which must have gratified its inventor, but its design (the mechanism was scarcely accessible and very badly protected) was incapable of improvement. Although Gurney attempted to sell this type of carriage, there were no takers. At least, for the time being.

'At a sale in 1834,' recalled Francis Macerone, another bombastic steam-

Above: Goldsworthy Gurney (1793–1875) was responsible for many practical steam vehicles of the early nineteenth century

Right: Gurney's London and Bath carriage which he started to build in 1826. During its active service, it made but one trip to Bath, and unfortunately broke down *en route*, having to be towed the rest of the way by a team of horses. On the return journey, the large vehicle acquitted itself well, averaging 8.4 mph for the ten-hour journey between Melksham and Cranford

coach maker, 'a couple of those celebrated steam carriages, all but new (with a separate engine to work the pumps and blower), were sold for a mere trifle.'

By the end of the 1820s, Gurney was working on a more practicable design, a steam drag, a light four-wheeled tractive unit intended to pull a passenger-carrying trailer; he gave a number of public demonstrations of this machine. At Hounslow on 12 August 1829, the drag hauled a 'Barouche . . . containing the Duke of Wellington and other Persons of Distinction'. Robert Stephenson was another who rode behind the Gurney drag.

With its relatively modest dimensions, the new Gurney was the nearest thing yet marketed to a private car and, indeed, Sir George Cayley, the father of British Aviation, used one in this manner, contriving on one excursion to embed it in a Bond Street shop-front. In 1830, a Gurney drag was fitted with flanged wheels, and tested for its tractive abilities on a railway track, but could only haul six wagons, weighing a total of twenty tons at 5 mph. A little later, in 1831, the same machine, reconverted for road use, was sent to Scotland, where a man named Ward intended to use it for a regular passenger service in the Glasgow area. Its arrival was none too auspicious: 'Gurney sent a steam carriage to Glasgow, but instead of coming by road, he sent it to Leigh by barge. And when he attempted to go from Leigh to Glasgow, he had recourse to horses to climb the hills.' This, claimed the inventor, was the result of careless handling by the bargees, and proceeded to drive the drag from Glasgow to Paisley, a distance of some fourteen miles, at a speed of between nine and ten mph. Mr Ward thought better of his brave project, and Gurney and carriage returned home.

However, this orphan drag soon found a new owner, Sir Charles Dance, who proposed to inaugurate a regular steam-carriage service from Gloucester to Cheltenham, and ordered three Gurney drags (of which, apparently, only one was delivered). This ran for some four months until, on 22 June 1831, the engineer James Stone came upon a stretch of road which had been covered with large heaps of stones, and which was causing the horse-drawn traffic great difficulty. Twice the steamer managed to pick its way over the obstruction but, on the third attempt, the axle snapped.

'They say that it was the stagecoach proprietors who have damaged the road,' wrote Stone, 'but I am persuaded that there is no truth to this. These persons are too honourable to be capable of such an act. I do not think that anyone knows who is at the bottom of the affair.'

'At the time of this accident,' recalled Stone, 'we had completed 396 journeys in regular service, covering a total of 3644 miles' (this was, however, only about a third of the distance that should have been covered had the carriage fulfilled its advertised timetable of three round trips a day, pointing to other breakdowns than the broken axle which terminated the service).

The drag was sent back to London, where the celebrated engineers Maudslay and Field fitted it with one of their boilers (the standard item was prone to rupture) and improved the standard of its engineering. In September 1833, pulling an omnibus, the drag achieved a speed of 16 mph, and a few days later covered the 52 miles from London to Brighton in five and a half hours, carrying fifteen passengers in the omnibus. The return trip took only five hours. Then, Dance decided to prove the reliability of the rebuilt drag. 'About the middle of October the steam drag and omnibus were put upon the road between Wellington Street, Waterloo Bridge and Greenwich, where it continued to run for a fortnight, with a view of showing the public in London what could be done in this direction. The proprietor had no intention of making it a permanent mode of conveyance, and therefore kept the company as select as he could by charging half a crown for tickets each way.'

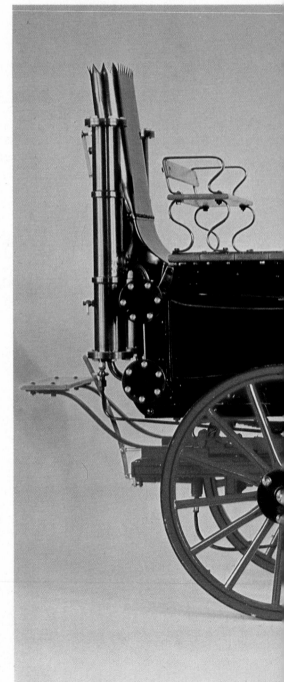

Already, however, there was evidence of some hostility to steam carriages. Commented Dance, 'Obstacles are always thrown in the way of a new invention, especially if it is likely to produce important results, by those who expect their interests will be affected by its success'.

The turnpike trustees, backed by the stagecoach proprietors, imposed swingeing tolls on those steam carriages that dared to attempt a long-distance journey, although there were few enough of these – and in 1831 a Parliamentary Commission was set up to investigate the situation, following a petition by Gurney.

It was, you might think, premature. After all, at that date Gurney's trip to Bath had been the only attempt at a true long-distance run, and even the Commission was forced to qualify its findings with a conditional statement. 'Tolls to an amount which would utterly prohibit the introduction of steam carriages have been imposed on some roads; on others, the trustees have adopted modes of apportioning the charge which would be found, if not absolutely prohibitory, at least to place such carriages in a very unfair position as compared with ordinary coaches.'

Of course, the main aim of calling the commission was to obtain some recognition – and hopefully, recompense – for Gurney, who had plenty of friends in high places. One of them was Sir George Cayley, who told Parliament: 'I consider Mr Gurney a very ill-used man. On the faith of our patent laws, Mr Gurney had given up, to pursue this noble invention, a very lucrative profession. Five years' toil and an expense of £30,000 brought it into practical use; yet he is now deprived of receiving any remuneration – not from any want of success in his experiments, not from any failure in his carriage, but by Act of Parliament: by our act and deed has he been wronged, and by our act and deed ought he to be, and I trust will he be, redressed.'

The act referred to by Sir George was the Turnpike Act, which empowered turnpike trustees to fix their own toll charges, and the Committee did indeed recommend the repeal of this act, as well as the payment of £16,000 to Gurney.

Left: Gurney constructed this small steam wagon for Sir Charles Dance in 1831; the vehicle is based on the barouche-hauling tractive unit built a couple of years previously

Below: a model of Gurney's London and Bath carriage with the engine cover removed. The steering mechanism seems to have been added as an afterthought, a steered 'bogie', at the front controlling the normal front wheels. This model was constructed in 1958, and can be seen at the Science Museum in London

However, the Chancellor of the Exchequer, starting a long tradition among those holding that office of unreasoning dislike of self-propelled vehicles, refused the grant; and the Bill to regulate the toll charges for steam vehicles – the so-called Steam-Carriage Bill – was twice rejected by the Lords.

Protested Gurney: 'When the repeal did not pass, I sold all my materials for manufacturing and gave up my factory, feeling that injury had been done to me.' He did well enough, however, out of his other inventions, and even today in the cloisters of Salisbury Cathedral can be seen an example of Gurney's other most famous invention, the Gurney stove. With typical grandiloquence, Gurney capped each stove with a Royal crown . . .

Oddly enough, after the death of the Steam-Carriage Bill, there came a decade or so in which, far from being driven from the roads, steam carriages actually multiplied and attained relative perfection. One of the first successful carriages to appear after the abortive Commission had ceased to exist was that of Summers and Ogle. It was in fact their second carriage – their first had broken its crankshaft near Basingstoke and been ignominiously shipped back to London on a canal barge. This new vehicle had three massive cylinders of 4 in

23

bore and 12 in stroke, was reputedly capable of reaching 32 mph and, according to a correspondent in the *Saturday Magazine*, was reliable enough to cover quite considerable distances without mishap. 'I have just returned from witnessing the triumph of science in mechanics, by travelling along a hilly and crooked road from Oxford to Birmingham in a steam carriage. This truly wonderful machine is the invention of Captain Ogle, of the Royal Navy, and Mr Summers, his partner, and is the first and only one that has accomplished so long a journey over chance roads and without rails. Its rate of travelling may be called twelve miles an hour, but twenty or perhaps thirty down hill if not checked by the brake, a contrivance which places the whole of the machinery under complete control. Away went the splendid vehicle through that beauteous city (Oxford) at the rate of ten miles an hour which, when clear of the houses, was accelerated to fourteen. Just as the steam carriage was entering the town of Birmingham, the supply of coke being exhausted, the steam dropped; and the good people, on learning the cause, flew to the frame, and dragged it into the yard.'

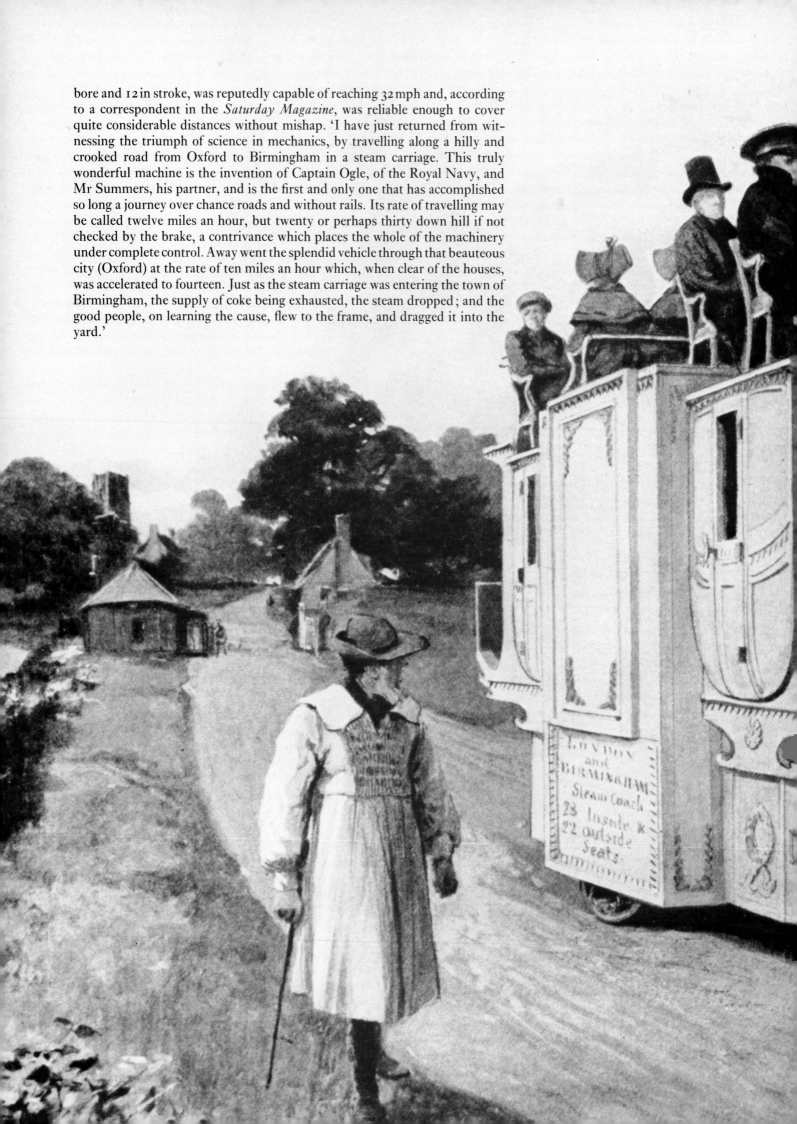

Like other pioneers, though, Ogle and Summers seem not to have persisted once they had achieved a long-distance journey. They were at least more successful than the notorious Doctor Church of Birmingham who, with backing from a group of optimists calling themselves the London and Birmingham Steam Carriage Company, sanguinely hoped to inaugurate a regular road service linking the two cities. If contemporary engravings are to be believed, Church's steam carriage was a massive rococo three-wheeler running on wheels with wide 'elastic rims' that 'bent into "flatted curves" as they came in contact with the ground, thereby preventing the wheels from sinking or sliding round'; it could carry fifty passengers.

The behemoth which was designed by one Doctor Church of Birmingham in 1833. This engraving depicts the fifty-seat vehicle travelling under its own steam in service, whereas in reality it only ran on two tests, and one of those ended ignominiously, with the carriage being towed by the horses it was supposed to replace

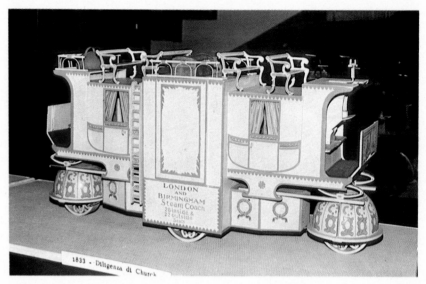

1833 - Diligenza di Church

Far left: a scale model of Doctor Church's steam coach depicted in the previous engraving; this miniature version can be found in the Turin Automobile Museum

Left and below: the steam carriage of Messrs Macerone and Squire, constructed in 1833. The builders were proud of their machine, and their works were always open to 'editors of newspapers, engineers and other scientific persons'. On one trip to Bushey Heath and Watford, the vehicle thundered downhill at the incredible speed of 30 mph. It was noted that Mr Squire, steering, 'never lost his presence of mind'

Even if the carriage was completed in this manner, its total public appearances were limited to two short test runs, one of which ended with the vehicle being hauled back to the works behind horses. However, within a few months, the London and Birmingham Steam Carriage Company optimistically advertised that 'all the difficulties of running steam carriages upon common roads were now overcome, and would be done to great profit to those engaged in it'.

'It was wisely suggested', noted one commentator, 'that instead of puffing and advertising, the company should put a carriage on the road at once for passenger traffic between Birmingham and London; but this scheme was never practically accomplished; the carriages were constantly brought out, and as constantly failed.'

Failure of a different and more tragic kind was the lot of Francis Macerone, an Anglo-Italian born in Manchester in 1788, whose early life was a series of wild adventures, culminating in his being appointed aide-de-camp to the King of Naples in 1814. Somewhere along the way he acquired the rank of Colonel and a taste for speed, fostered by the many breakneck horserides he had undertaken.

In 1825, he became assistant to Goldsworthy Gurney in London, but after four years he had become convinced that Gurney's efforts would never succeed, and left the steam carriage business to go to Constantinople to fight for the Turks against the Russians. He remained there until 1831, then returned to England. Then, recalled Macerone: 'Mr J. Squire came to me and informed me that he had built a steam carriage, which performed very well, and asked me to join him in the undertaking. Finding the little carriage much superior to any that Gurney had made, but unfortunately fitted with a very defective boiler, I undertook to join in the construction of another on my plan, for which a valid patent could be obtained, but I was without much money, having, through the "fortunes of war", returned from Turkey with even less than I went with. However, I mentioned my dilemma to a gentleman, the like of whom there are too few in this world, who provided me with the funds for taking convenient premises, purchasing lathes, tools, and establishing a factory on the Paddington Wharf. I placed Mr Squire in the house on the works as foreman, and we set to work on an enlarged scale.'

Macerone and Squire completed their first steam carriage in 1833 in a blaze of publicity; the works at Paddington were always open house to 'editors of newspapers, engineers and other scientific persons', who were encouraged to take rides on the vehicle, and its numerous trials were widely reported. It seems to have been a remarkable performer, with its turn of speed testified to by many accounts in the press.

One of the best descriptions of the machine appeared in *Turner's Annual Tour* for 1834: 'Drawn out of a hut on Bushey Heath by the appearance of an unusual commotion amongst the inhabitants of the village, we saw a steam coach which stopped there. The apparition of a vehicle of this kind, in such a place, was unaccountable. Bushey Heath forms the plateau of a mountain, which is the highest point of land in Middlesex and, although so far inland, serves as a landmark for vessels at sea. The access to it, from the London side, is by a difficult and steep road. Being accosted by Colonel Macerone, in whom we were glad to recognise an old acquaintance, he informed us that the journey had been performed with ease, adding that it was his intention to proceed to the town of Watford.

'Now, if the road from Edgware to Bushey Heath was steep and difficult, the descent from Bushey Heath to Watford was much worse. We told our friend that he might go by steam to Watford, but that we were quite certain that he would not return by the same means of locomotion. Nevertheless, at his pressing instance, we consented to hazard our own person in the adventure. We set off, amidst the cheers of the villagers. The motion was so steady that we could have read with ease, and the noise was no worse than that produced by a common vehicle. On arriving at the summit of Clay Hill, the local and in-experienced attendant neglected to clog the wheel until it become impossible. We went thundering down the hill at the rate of thirty miles an hour. Mr Squire was steersman, and never lost his presence of mind. It may be conceived what amazement a thing of this kind, flashing through the village of Bushey, occas-ioned among the inhabitants. The people seemed petrified on seeing a carriage without horses. In the busy and populous town of Watford the sensation was similar – the men gazed in speechless wonder; the women clapped their hands. We turned round at the end of the street in magnificent style, and ascended Clay Hill at the same rate as the stage coaches drawn by five horses, and at length regained our starting place.'

This was the high point in Macerone's career. In 1834, he quarrelled with Squire, who left the business. Finding himself short of cash, Macerone entered into a dangerously vague agreement with one D'Asda, an 'Italian Jew and audacious adventurer', who was anxious to exhibit the two steam carriages built by Macerone on the Continent. D'Asda promised that Macerone would be paid £1500 for a share of the patents he would take out in France and Belgium and, accordingly, the carriages were sent to Brussels and Paris for exhibition runs.

In Paris, D'Asda displayed the carriage in front of the King and Queen, who were much impressed with this 'French invention' which the audacious adventurer had shamelessly claimed had been built to his order by a French engineer named Clavière; their Majesties were so impressed that they gave D'Asda a gold snuff-box bearing the Royal Arms, and he subsequently sold his 'rights' in the steam carriage for £16,000, of which poor Macerone saw not a solitary penny.

Macerone's creditors stripped the Paddington factory bare, leaving the unfortunate engineer scarcely enough to exist on. Because he had no demon-stration vehicles, his attempts to form a new steam carriage company were doomed to failure. It was only in 1841 that a new Macerone carriage was built, for the General Steam Carriage Company. Macerone had contracted to supply the company with carriages for £800 each, but the engineer who built the prototype put in a bill of £1100 to cover the cost of alterations and experimental trips. Although the machine ran reliably and climbed Shooter's Hill, Black-heath, at a speed which 'delighted several shareholders', the Steam Carriage company refused to pay the engineer's bills; he, in turn, locked the machine away and refused to let it go on the roads again. Caught in the middle of this argument was the unfortunate Macerone, all of whose possessions were seized by his creditors.

He tried to sell his boiler patents to raise capital, but to no avail. The name of Macerone failed to figure in the subsequent history of steam traction, although his former collaborator, Squire, proposed an eleven-seater charabanc in 1843. The design of its boiler prompted an angry letter from Macerone in the *Mechanic's Magazine*, claiming that Squire had infringed his (obviously unsold) patent.

Around this time, a German engineer named Jean-Christian Dietz, who had come to France during the reign of Napoleon to build canals, was developing, along with his sons Charles and Christian, a series of improbable-looking

'The Progress of Steam: Alken's illustration of modern prophecy'. This illustration, with its cynical overtones, depicts White Chapel Road, East London, in 1830. The prophecy of mobile canteens and venders' vehicles is accurate, as is the pollution and smoke that is seen hanging low over the area. It was, however, left to the petrol-engine-powered vehicle to fit the bill. Road racing, represented by the *Infernal Defiance of Yarmouth* passing the *Dreadful Vengence of Colchester*, was also to be seen in later years *remorquers*, which were little more than road-going railway engines of great bulk and complexity, intended to draw great strings of carriages along the public highways.

In 1834, Charles Dietz gave a display of one of these *remorquers* in Paris, where it drew two three-wheeled carriages along the Champs-Elysees and out into the suburbs. Riding among the forty distinguished guests in the carriages was one Odolant Desnos, who effused: 'This glorious arrival of M. Dietz, since such results have hitherto not been achieved in France, was to the travellers a spectacle as brilliant as it was novel. No words can describe the magnificent picture afforded by the immense crowd which so covered the route that . . . the carriage could scarcely clear a passage. It was a triumphal progress . . .'.

On the spot, the Academie de l'Industrie awarded Dietz their gold medal. Other outings, though, were not so successful. In 1841 Christian Dietz attempted to run a regular service between Bordeaux and Libourn, but he was met with such open hostility from the local carriers that on one occasion he was forced to beat off attackers with his poker. Soon afterwards, the Dietz family ceased their experiments with steam traction.

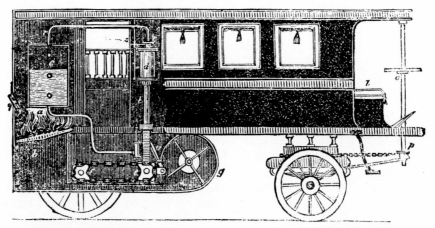

Left: the workings of Hancock's *Infant* of 1830, in its early, closed, form; after the machine blew up, it was rebuilt with a longer wheelbase, in an effort to improve it

Below: Walter Hancock produced these vehicles in his Stratford, East London, workshop; they are the rebuilt *Infant*, the *Era* and the *Autopsy*. *Infant* was 'the first steam coach that ever carried passengers for hire, or made the journey to Brighton, or passed through the City of London by steam'. *Autopsy* also made the Brighton trip and, like *Infant*, travelled 'thousands of miles'. *Era* was built for the London-to-Greenwich route, as opposed to that from London to Paddington travelled by the two other vehicles

However, the man who dominated this first steam age, and whose career successfully spanned it from start to finish, was Walter Hancock of Stratford, which was then a village on the eastern outskirts of London. Hancock had been born in Marlborough, Wiltshire, in 1799, and first turned his attention to the construction of steam carriages in 1824. His brother, Thomas, had pioneered the manufacture of vulcanised rubber goods, and this prompted Walter Hancock to devise an ingenious, if unsuccessful, power unit in which pistons and cylinders were replaced by rubber bags linked to a crankshaft; they were alternately blow up with steam and then deflated to rotate the crank. A carriage with this type of power unit was built, but refused to run.

Hancock's experiments really began to bear fruit in 1827, when he devised a new and more efficient design of boiler, which was installed in a little three-wheeled carriage which had a pair of oscillating cylinders of conventional design driving the single front wheel (which also steered). This carriage was really a mobile test bed for Hancock's ideas, and its design was altered many times; despite this, it covered several hundred miles, 'sometimes to Epping Forest, at other times to Paddington, and frequently to Whitechapel. On one occasion it ran to Hounslow, and on another to Croydon. In every instance, it accomplished the task assigned to it, and returned to Stratford on the same day on which it set out. Subsequently, this carriage went from Stratford, through Pentonville, to Turnham Green, over Hammersmith Bridge, and thence to Fulham. In that neighbourhood, it remained several days, and made a number of excursions in different directions, for the gratification of some of Hancock's friends, and others who had expressed a desire to witness its performance.'

Hancock's next design, which appeared in 1830, was a far more sophisticated machine. Named the *Infant*, it was a covered char-à-bancs with seats for ten passengers. Although it retained the oscillating engine, this was now placed at the rear of the machine, and drove the back axle through a chain.

In 1831, Hancock began running a regular service between Stratford and London with the *Infant*, which had already shown its merits in an assault on the 1-in-20 slope of Pentonville Hill. Hancock later wrote: 'A severe frost following a shower of sleet had completely glazed the road, so that horses could scarcely keep their footing. The trial was made therefore under the most unfavourable circumstances possible; so much so, that confident as the writer felt in the powers of his engine, his heart inclined to fail him. The carriage, however, did its duty nobly. Without the aid of propellers or any other such appendages (then thought necessary on a level road), the hill was ascended at considerable speed and the summit successfully attained, while his competitors with their horses were yet but a little way from the bottom of the hill.'

It was while *Infant* was operating its fare-paying service that its stoker (the French were already calling such men *chauffeurs*) decided that it would be an excellent idea to wire the safety valve shut and run the engine declutched from the transmission to get the fire really glowing with its blower fan, and thus build up a good head of steam for the restart. Unfortunately, it also created sufficient pressure to rupture the boiler, and the unfortunate stoker dropped dead with surprise! Hancock claimed, somewhat unbelievably, that none of the passengers noticed the incident . . .

In 1832, Hancock decided to remedy the many imperfections in the design of *Infant* by a rebuild, with the result that an almost totally new carriage was created, longer in the wheelbase and equipped with an extra row of seats. Most importantly, the power unit, which had previously operated in the full blast of the road dirt thrown up by the rear wheels, was replaced by a fixed twin-cylinder engine housed within the bodywork of the vehicle. The reborn *Infant* was used for the first-ever motorised seaside outing, in which Hancock took eleven 'scientific gentlemen' – including Alexander Gordon, who had just launched the world's first motoring magazine, *The Journal of Elemental Locomotion*, and would in 1833 form a short-lived 'motor club'.

A 'London & Brighton Steam Carriage Company' was formed, and Hancock constructed a closed carriage called *Era* for their projected London–Greenwich service (which, like so many steam-carriage promotions, failed to reach reality). In 1833, two more carriages, *Enterprise* and *Autopsy* were built – *Autopsy's* curious name meant, literally, 'see for yourself' in the original Greek, although passengers lacking the benefits of a classical education may have felt some apprehension . . .

In April 1833, *Enterprise*, which bore a closed omnibus body, began a short regular service between Moorgate and Paddington, over a route which had seen, only four years previously, the début of the first horse-drawn omnibus.

Announced Hancock: 'It is not intended to run this carriage more than about a week longer; partly because it was only intended as a demonstration of its efficiency, and partly because my own occupation will not admit of my personal attention to the steering, which I have hitherto performed myself, having no other person at present to whose guidance I could, with propriety, entrust it.'

So the service lasted only a fortnight, with *Enterprise* covering its ten-mile round trip within an hour. In that time, the regular and reliable working of the carriage aroused bitter opposition among users of horsed vehicles, who saw, somewhat prematurely, a threat to their livelihood. Complained a correspondent to the daily press: 'In watching, as I have done, the early operations of the new steam coach, the *Enterprise*, on the Paddington Road, I have been pained,

Hancock's *Enterprise* stayed in service for a mere
two weeks, between Moorgate and Paddington,
because Mr Hancock did not have time to do all
the driving himself, and would not let any other
person control the machine. Horse-drawn
vehicles tended either to get in the *Enterprise*'s
way or to chase it; one is seen here in full
pursuit of the Omnibus-bodied carriage

although not surprised, to see the malignant efforts of some of the drivers of the horse conveyances to impede and baffle the course of the new competitor. They must be taught not to endanger the lives of the passengers, who have entrusted themselves to their guidance, by a wanton courting of collision with a vehicle so vastly more weighty, more strong and more powerful than their own frail vehicles, and feeble, staggering, beasts of draught. One of these infatuated men, today, crossed about the path of the steam coach, palpably with a mischevious design, which was only rendered abortive by the vigilance and prompt action of Mr Hancock.'

Hancock's brief hour of glory was brought abruptly to a halt by the concupiscence of the proprietors of the London & Paddington Steam Carriage Company, under whose auspices the service was being run. The inventor had intended to prove, by conducting this trial service at his own expense, the abilities of his vehicle, in the hope of receiving orders for at least two more like it, and for which, indeed a contract had been signed.

However, under cover of a voluminous cloud of correspondence, the company encouraged its engineer, Redmund, to dismantle the *Enterprise* and copy

Left: this 22-seater, *Automaton* was yet another carriage built by Walter Hancock. Successful though this machine was, Hancock had too many problems to overcome with the steam vehicle

Above right: the first vehicle to be constructed with a final drive incorporating a differential was this 1840 vehicle, built by F. Hill of Dartford, Kent

Right: this 1829 'Patent Steam Carriage' of Anderson and James has a very curious steering system

its design; it took six months for Hancock to get his carriage back in one piece. Meanwhile, Redmund had built a Chinese copy of it which he named *Alpha*; he might just as well have called it *Omega* for the lack of success it had.

Walter Hancock continued to build steam carriages: in 1834, *Era* was rebuilt and, temporarily rechristened *Erin*, gave a number of demonstrations in Dublin in 1835. In 1836, Hancock launched another 'bus service' in London, using *Autopsy*, *Erin* and *Automaton*, a massive 22-seater char-à-bancs. Between May and October, the three carriages covered a total of 4224 miles and carrying 12,761 passengers (out of a total capacity of 20,420 seats available); 712 round trips were accomplished, 143 between the City and Paddington, 525 between the City and Islington, and 44 between the City and Stratford. After this apparent success, however, Hancock abandoned scheduled services for good, and contented himself with hiring his carriages out on special occasions.

Eventually, however, Hancock retired from the construction of steam carriages. Like his contemporaries, he had found the problems insurmountable. It was not hostile legislation, but the opposition of vested interests which drove the first steam carriages from the roads, plus the almost insuperable difficulties of trying to maintain high average speeds – *Automaton* was capable of well over 30 mph – on roads which were ill-surfaced and ill-maintained, in many cases in worse condition than the highways built 1500 years earlier by the Romans.

By creating their own iron highways, the railway engineers – who were, of course establishing the great inter-city network at the same time that Hancock was active – overcame this fundamental obstacle to rapid steam transit.

CHAPTER 3

The Shape of Things to Come

By the 1840s rail travel had become so cheap, fast and reliable that it had to be a special kind of masochist who would willingly subject himself to the rigours of journeys by steam carriage. Moreover, the railway companies attracted capital in unprecedented amounts, and spent a great deal of it on locomotives: for example, in 1839 the Grand Junction Railway possessed a total of 60 locomotives, and such a volume of production meant that technological advance was swift. Many of the faults which had bedevilled road carriages were soon found and corrected on railway locomotives, such as the replacement of the troublesome and fracture-prone wrought-iron crank-axle by crankpins on the wheels. And, impressive though the speeds of the steam carriages had in some cases been, they were soon totally eclipsed by the performance of railway engines; two Crampton locomotives built in 1846 for the Namur & Liége Railway could pull a 50-ton load at 62 miles an hour on the level and were capable of 51 mph with an 80-ton load.

Nevertheless, there were still the bold few who persisted with their experiments; F. Hill, of Deptford, Kent, whose 1840 carriage was the first to be constructed with a differential gear in the back axle, promoted the General Steam Carriage Company because he felt that it was desirable that road locomotion should counteract the exorbitant charges made by the gigantic railway monopoly for conveying goods short distances.

He made a number of demonstration runs, covering the 128 miles from London to Hastings and back in one day, but his proposed carrying company came to nothing.

Sir James Anderson, who had formerly financed the experimental carriages of W. H. James, now propounded an even more ambitious scheme, uniting steam transit by road, rail and sea. Railway trains would take passengers from London to Holyhead *via* Birmingham; they would then embark on a steamer to Dublin. From Dublin to Galway they would travel in coaches behind a steam drag and finally cross the Atlantic in a steamship which made landfall at Halifax, in Nova Scotia, and New York. Needless to say, nothing came of it.

There followed nearly twenty years of total inertia, during which the only steam road vehicles to appear were traction engines, apart from a couple of light steam carriages built by J. K. Fisher of New York in 1840 and 1853, and by Richard Dudgeon, of the same city in 1857.

The revival of the road-going steamer really dates from 1858, when Thomas Rickett, of the Castle Foundry, Buckingham, completed the first of several light steam carriages, a three-wheeler of which most of the body space was occupied by the boiler.

A similar machine was constructed towards the end of the year to the order of the Marquis of Stafford, who used it as a private car, though its individual excursions were obviously infrequent enough to be newsworthy. In March 1859, *The Engineer* reported: 'Lord Stafford and party made another trip with the steam carriage from Buckingham to Wolverton. His Lordship drove and steered, and although the roads were very heavy, they were not more than an hour in running the nine miles to Old Wolverton. His Lordship has repeatedly said that it is guided with the greatest ease and precision. It was designed by Mr Rickett to run ten miles an hour. One mile in five minutes has been attained, at which it was perfectly steady, the centre of gravity being not more than 2 ft from the ground. A few days afterwards this little engine started from Messrs Hayes's Works, Stoney Stratford, with a party consisting of the Marquis of Stafford, Lord Alfred Paget, and two Hungarian noblemen. They proceeded through the town of Stoney Stratford at a rapid pace, and after a short trip returned to the Wolverton railway station. The trip was in all respects successful, and shows, beyond a doubt, that steam locomotion for common roads is practicable.'

Ricketts built several more carriages, one of which was sold to the Earl of Caithness, who drove it from Inverness to his home at Borrogill Castle, a few miles from John O'Groats, climbing the notorious Ord of Caithness on the way. But it was not just the performance of his carriage which appealed to this thrifty laird from north of the border.

'It is cheap,' he gloated, 'and on a level I got as much as nineteen miles an hour.'

Lough and Messenger, of Swindon, built a neat two-cylinder carriage in 1858. It scaled only 8 cwt, and because of its excellent power-to-weight ratio, could run at a steady 15 mph on the level (though a claim of 'two years' constant running' was doubtless an exaggeration!). It was, for sure, a more practical design than that announced by a Mr Stirling, from Kilmarnock, in 1859, which had five wheels, of which one drove and the remainder steered.

As the 1860s dawned, there seemed to be a sudden flurry of activity in the steam carriage world, abated only slightly by the 1861 Locomotives on Highways Act. This Act placed certain limitations on the all-over dimensions, created the first road tax, and limited speed on the open road to 10 mph.

In 1861, W. O. Carrett, of Carrett, Marshall and Company, of Leeds, built a 'steam pleasure carriage' to the order of George Salt, of Saltaire, who must have been a gregarious fellow, for this little personal runabout seated nine and weighed five tons; it presented a generally ponderous appearance to the world, made faintly ridiculous by a dainty patent leather splash-shield which projected

Far left : the wide and short Rickett light carriage of Castle Foundry, Buckingham; this three-wheeler did not have much space for carrying passengers

Near left : two views of Virginio Bordino's 1854 steamer; this vehicle is now in the Biscaretti museum in Turin

Right : T. Cowan of Greenwich built this vehicle from a Yarrow and Hilditch design in 1862. It had a top speed of 30 mph, and was seen on one occasion to climb a 1-in-12 slope at a speed of 5 mph

forward from its elephantine prow. It certainly looked odd.

It was certainly capable of reaching 15 mph but, recalled a contemporary report, 'did little good for itself as a steam carriage'. Salt, tiring of his toy, presented it to Frederick Hodges, who ran a distillery in Lambeth and spent his spare time fighting fires as captain of his own private fire brigade (which was better clothed and equipped than London's official fire-fighting force).

'Captain' Hodges often ran the carriage after dark in an attempt to escape the attentions of stop-watch-happy policemen, but seems to have been unfortunate in that hope.

He christened it the *Fly-by-Night*, and it really did fly, and no mistake, through the Kentish villages when most honest people were in their beds. Its enterprising owner was repeatedly pulled up and fined, and to this day his exploits are remembered against him. Hodges ran the engine 800 miles; he had six summonses in six weeks and one was for running the engine thirty miles an hour.

Another notable design of the period was that of Yarrow and Hilditch, built by T. Cowan, of Greenwich, and exhibited at the Great Exhibition of 1862, at which a number of steam carriages appeared, and were seen by a young German engineer named Gottlieb Daimler, who was to make his mark in the development of the self-propelled vehicle in later years.

About this time, a teenager named Rookes Evelyn Bell Crompton was building a steam carriage during his holidays from Harrow; he completed this during the 1860s when he was serving with the 3rd Battalion of the Rifle Brigade in India and made a number of successful journeys on the Grand Trunk Road with it. The engine and some fragments of this *Blue Belle* are preserved by the Science Museum in London.

Oddly enough, India was a focus for steam traction experiments; in 1869 a Mr Armstrong of Rawalpindi made a neat little steam car, while Tangye of Birmingham, who had built a road carriage called *Cornubia* to act as a feeder to railway branch lines about 1862, became discouraged by the unhelpful legislation enacted by parliament and sold the machine to a resident of India.

The passing of the ludicrous Locomotives on Highways Act in 1865 restricted all self-propelled vehicles to 4 mph on the open road, and compelled them to be preceded by a man on foot with a red flag; even so, it is recorded that on 30 August 1867, two steam carriages indulged in the illegal sport of racing on the public highway. The carriages, one built by I. W. Boulton, of Ashton-under-Lyne, and the other by Daniel Adamson & Company, of Dukinfield, Manchester, started at 4.30 am from Ashton-under-Lyne for the Old Trafford Show Ground, eight miles away. Boulton's light carriage soon outdistanced its larger rival, and arrived at Old Trafford within the hour; at the show ground, both engines displayed their manouevring abilities, and thus the first motor race in history ended quietly.

Although development was stifled, it's interesting to note that, after the 1865 Act, private steam carriages in England began to shed their locomotive characteristics, and to be built lighter and styled more elegantly. This may have been an attempt to persuade the authorities that such vehicles should not be subject to a law intended to curb the road destroying propensities of heavy-weight traction engines; if it was, it did not have the desired effect. In any case, it was possible for the speed restrictions to be set aside, for R. E. B. Crompton was permitted to drive a Thomson road locomotive at speeds of up to 30 mph on a test run from Ipswich to Edinburgh and back to approve the vehicle before it was shipped to India.

It was in 1869 that one of the more remarkable light steam carriages of the period following the Locomotive Act made its appearance: it was built by a Scotsman by the name of L. J. Todd, and took the form of a compact tricycle with a vertical boiler set in front of the driver. Apart from the neatness of its appearance – it was only 8½ feet long – it was noteworthy for the fact that it employed worm and sector steering for its single front wheel rather than the inconvenient and potentially dangerous tiller steering which had hitherto been the commonplace on steam vehicles.

The year 1874 saw two more unusual machines on the roads of Britain – these were the first 'saloon cars' to be built.

The first of these was built by Randolph & Elder of Glasgow and the second by H. A. C. Mackenzie of Diss in Norfolk. Randolph's carriage had a high, glazed cab above the close-set front wheels, a lower centre portion like the body of a stage coach, and a sort of conservatory at the back which housed the mechanism, boiler and stoker. The Randolph carriage had two engines, one for each rear wheel, but could not exceed 6½ mph. Its driver had the consolation of an excellent view, for the high position of the cab gave him full all-round vision.

Quite the reverse is true of Mackenzie's steam brougham, in which the hapless passengers shared the interior with the boiler and engine, and also contrived to obstruct the driver's vision as they sat facing him in front of the vehicle's forward window. The driver, set almost in the centre of the vehicle, would hardly have had any exterior vision through the vehicle's tiny window glasses, and must have been a particularly brave man to venture onto the roads with this machine, even at its modest top speed of 10 to 12 mph.

Perhaps the most important step forward at this period was the adoption on some experimental carriages of liquid fuel instead of coke. Almost certainly the first to use this far more convenient method of firing the boiler – which eliminated the stoker – was the French engineer Ravel, who in 1868 built a neat little

The remarkable Bollées of Le Mans, Amédées *père et fils*. Father constructed the large and successful *L'Obéissante* and the smaller *La Mancelle*. His son built his first car in 1885, when he was a mere eighteen years old. There was one other famous member of the family (renowned for its bell foundry), who was to make a name for himself in the latter part of the nineteenth century; he was Léon

three-wheeled 'tilbury'. This machine had a little boiler mounted ahead of the driver and a two-cylinder oscillating engine mounted under the seat, directly linked to the cranked rear axle: water and fuel oil were housed in tanks which formed the framework of the seat.

Having obtained permission to carry out trials in the Rue de Revolté, in Paris, close to his workshop, between 7 and 8 am, Ravel first took this vehicle on the road early in 1870. He was accompanied by two policemen, who ran alongside the tilbury to make sure that no contravention of the traffic regulations took place; Ravel soon managed to persuade the panting gendarmes that they would be far better employed taking some invigorating refreshment inside a café, and proceeded on his way alone – 'merrily', according to some reports. His merriment was cut short at Saint-Denis, where the little carriage broke down, and took two hours to repair.

This, it seems, was the only journey that Ravel's tilbury was destined to make, for soon afterwards the Franco-Prussian War broke out, and the inventor fled to Spain.

When he returned, it was to discover that his workshop, and the steam tilbury along with it, had been buried in the foundations of a defensive earthwork raised against the invading Germans.

It was left for Ravel's son, Maurice, born a few years later, to make the family name famous – and he did so, not in the field of transportation, but in that of musical composition.

It was around this time that the bicycle began to make its appearance; by teaching engineers how to build structures that were both light and strong at the same time – the wire-spoked tangent wheel is a typical example – and by introducing thousands to the joys of touring by road (and thus prompting some improvements in the maintenance of highways which had fallen into neglect since the railway had ousted the stagecoach), the bicycle was to pave the way for the age of popular motoring. So it's odd that when the Michaux brothers, inventors of the velocipede, built themselves a private steam carriage, it should have been one of the old locomotive-type heavyweights, scaling $3\frac{1}{2}$ tons and designed to haul an eight-seater wagon in its wake.

Despite atrocious road conditions and, in Britain at least, increasingly hostile legislation, the search for a truly practicable self-propelled carriage went on.

Some of the vehicles which took to this period, however, showed that their inventors had failed to learn anything from those who had gone before: the 1875 Grenville, designed by R. N. Grenville and G. J. Churchward (who later became chief engineer to the Great Western Railway) was a hulking behemoth which would not have looked out of place beside the machines of Gurney and Hancock. Nevertheless, it has survived by a quirk of fate, and is thus one of the few tangible links with the prehistory of motoring in existence.

Also surviving is an American Dudgeon steamer of a few years earlier, which is little more than a boiler with wheels and bench seats added: it is hardly surprising that such appalling crudities failed to gain public approval, and one has to take with a pinch of salt Sir Richard Tangye's 1905 statement that 'but for the action of a bovine parliament, the manufacture of motor cars would have taken root in England forty years ago, and foreign nations would have been customers instead of pioneers, followed at a distance by ourselves'.

In fact, the only steam carriage builder of the 1870–90 era whose work deserved to succeed was the French engineer Amédée Bollée, descendant of an ancient line of bell-founders: his father, Ernest-Sylvain, originally from the Haute-Marne region, had established a factory at Le Mans in 1842, and it was here that Amédée was born two years later. In 1867 the young man visited the Paris Exposition, and saw a number of road locomotives: he was already an accomplished engineer, having temporarily taken over the running of the foundry at the age of 15, when his father was ill. He now decided to build himself a high-speed steam carriage. This decision may also have been prompted by the fact that he had recently acquired a Michaux velocipede, which was at that time the very latest thing in road locomotion: but it was not until 1871 that he was able to set up a little workshop within the family factory where he could realise his ambition.

Here, in the evenings, Bollée worked on the design of a steam carriage, which was ready for the road in 1873. He christened it *L'Obéissante* – 'The Obedient One'.

Although it had something of the air of a perambulating bandstand, *L'Obéissante* was a machine of great originality: its front wheels, pivoting in forks, were independently suspended, and the steering mechanism, which employed chains running over cams to give geometrically correct tracking, even on tight-radius curves, was well in advance of anything that had been done before. The rear wheels each had their own engine – this eliminated the need for a differential – and these power units, with their twin cylinders set at 90 degrees, were mounted under covers at each side of the vehicle, thus making minimum incursions into passenger space. The steersman sat at the front, the stoker at the back.

Bollée spent another couple of years experimenting with *L'Obéissante*, and then judged that it was ready for a trip to Paris. The Minister of Public Works gave Bollée permission to use his carriage within five designated *départements*, on condition that the local authorities were given three days' notice of the route to be followed by *L'Obéissante*.

Below: the vast *L'Obéissante*, now preserved in the Conservatoire des Arts et Métiers in Paris; the twin-engined vehicle has a novel steering system, which employs chains running over cams to give geometrically correct tracking, even on tight-radius curves; each engine has its own back wheel to power, so a differential was not needed

So, at dawn on 9 October 1875, Bollée began the 135-mile drive to Paris: as he entered each new *département*, an inspector of bridges and highways duly stopped him, and conducted a lengthy interrogation as to whether *L'Obéissante* was likely to damage the roads, and whether it could be allowed to proceed by the chosen route. After dark, eighteen hours after it had left its garage at Le Mans, *L'Obéissante* nosed into the capital, its single headlamp gleaming. Bollée later claimed that he had collected 75 traffic penalties *en route*; but after the Préfect of Police of Paris had made a triumphal progress along the Champs-Elysees aboard the steamer, there was suddenly no longer any question of prosecution.

L'Obéissante created a sensation in the streets of Paris: from its temporary garage on the Quai de Jemmappes, it drove through the Bois de Boulogne among the carriages of the smart set, encircled the Arc de Triomphe, and even climbed to the top of the Montmartre hill. Wherever it went, the passers-by applauded its passing.

Though Bollée received many enquiries from possible purchasers of replicas of *L'Obéissante*, all proved tentative, and none came to anything; next, a four-

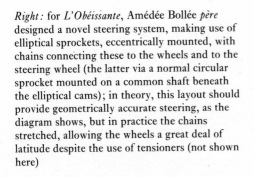

Right: for *L'Obéissante*, Amédée Bollée *père* designed a novel steering system, making use of elliptical sprockets, eccentrically mounted, with chains connecting these to the wheels and to the steering wheel (the latter via a normal circular sprocket mounted on a common shaft beneath the elliptical cams); in theory, this layout should provide geometrically accurate steering, as the diagram shows, but in practice the chains stretched, allowing the wheels a great deal of latitude despite the use of tensioners (not shown here)

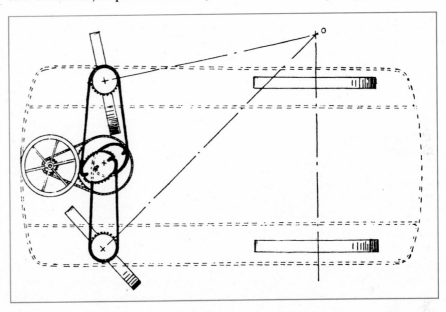

wheel-drive steam tram was built and tested. But again, the results were inconclusive.

Already Bollée was planning a new carriage, one whose appearance would conform more closely to accepted canons of coachwork design, and in 1878 he unveiled his *La Mancelle* – 'The Girl from Le Mans'.

If *L'Obéissante* had broken new ground, *La Mancelle* was a positive revolution, for it established the shape of the motor car for many years to come. Its three-cylinder engine was set at the front, under a bonnet, and drove the rear axle through a shaft, bevel gears and side-chains; only the gearbox essential to the petrol car would be added when this overall layout was re-invented 15 years later by Levassor (and, anyway, Bollée would soon produce a two-speed *Mancelle*).

Once again, the front suspension was something special. Parallel transverse leaf springs allowed each wheel independent movement, while the steering featured a pinion actuating an arcuate rack, with a separate track rod to each drag link, a layout which would not look out of place on a modern car.

La Mancelle was exhibited at the 1878 Paris World Exhibition, and attracted sufficient interest for Bollée to establish a workshop outside the factory, and to appoint a concessionaire general, a lugubrious individual named Lecordier. Replicas of *La Mancelle* with either *calèche* or *post-chaise* bodywork were offered, at a basic price of Fr 12,000, and Lecordier gave a number of demonstration runs along the banks of the Seine. These were, it seems, not without incident, for on one occasion he flattened a horse, and on another he trapped a wheel on the tramlines and snapped the front springs.

'Please don't let us go out with M. Lecordier again, sir', Bollée's mechanics wrote to their master.

But Lecordier had more unintentional mischief to work. A spinner of grandiose schemes, he managed to get Bollée embroiled in a fantastic business deal with a German banker, Berthold Aerons, who saw in Bollée's new design the salvation of the Wöhlert locomotive works, in which he had a considerable financial stake. He proposed setting up bus services in Germany, Austria, Russia and Sweden, and, though 22 vehicles were built in the Wöhlert factory, the scheme was far too ambitious for its day, and in 1883 the company collapsed, ruining the banker. Bollée, who had once written to Lecordier: 'The question of money revolts me – I'm first and foremost a worker', failed to receive any of the royalties due to him.

By then, he had bowed out of steam carriage construction: indeed, after 1880, the vehicles built at Le Mans – and these only amounted to a handful – were almost all for family use. In 1880 Ernest-Sylvain Bollée, aged 66 and newly appointed a Chevalier of the Legion d'Honneur, ordered a closed carriage, *La Nouvelle*, from his son; the following year, Bollée's brother, Ernest, commissioned a sporty six-seater, *La Rapide*, which was capable of 60 kph. Local residents appear to have ordered another two *Rapides*.

Then there was a vast mail-coach for the Marquis de Broc; this, which seems to have been largely the work of Bollée's talented elder son, also Amédée, was surely a tongue-in-cheek job. However, despite its outlandish styling, it was still in use 20 years later!

Thereafter, Amédée Bollée *père*, having sunk a considerable fortune in the building of steam carriages, decided that the time had come to call a halt and refused to take any more commissions: but he did not prevent Amédée *fils* from building a neat little two-seated steam car in 1885, when he was just 18 years old.

The truth was that the market was not ready for the motor car; only the most dedicated enthusiasts, like Gustave Koechlin, who bought a Mancelle in 1878, and was later a key figure in the development of Peugeot as an automobile manufacturer, were prepared to put up with its many defects.

The American inventor Lucius Copeland learned this lesson the hard way: he had grandiose plans for the production of three-wheeled steam 'Phaeton Moto-Cycles' around 1890, but failed to sell any, and retired from the as yet unborn car industry convinced that no-one would ever be persuaded to part with the equivalent of £100 for a motor vehicle.

Others were waiting in the wings: the late 1880s saw the first successful experiments with steam vehicles by De Dion, Bouton and Trépardoux, and by Leon Serpollet, but their time had not yet arrived. Nor was steam destined to be the motive power which would bring motoring to the millions.

With the discovery of illuminating gas by William Murdock in the eighteenth century, scientists began to wonder whether this inflammable gas had any use other than lighting urban roads. In 1791, John Barber, an Englishman, des-

Right: this 60 kph six-seater, *La Rapide*, was built for Ernest Bollée in 1881; like most other vehicles built by the talented Le Mans bell-founding family, this steamer was very successful and reliable; its success led to two more orders for similar carriages

Top left, above and right: the vehicle that was to set the trend for the design of the motor car for years to come, *La Mancelle*; although most mechanical parts seem to be at the rear, a three-cylinder engine is mounted under the front bonnet; first shown at the 1878 Paris World Exhibition, the wagon attracted great interest and replicas were offered at Fr 12,000

cribed a primitive form of gas turbine, fuelled by a mixture of air and paraffin oil, while three years later his compatriot Robert Street designed a simple gas engine operating on a straightforward two-stroke cycle.

Then, in 1801, Phillipe Lebon d'Humbersin, the Frenchman whom the French claim chauvinistically to have discovered illuminating gas, patented a curious gas engine with three cylinders of different diameters and a primitive form of electric ignition, but he died before he could exploit his invention.

On 30 January 1807, Isaac de Rivaz, formerly a major in the army of the Swiss republic of Valais, filed a patent 'On the manner of using the combustion of inflammable gases to impart movement to various machines and to replace steam'.

Commented De Rivaz: 'I had a cylinder made, six and a half inches in diameter and four and a half feet long, from laminated copper, bored out internally. Inside this cylinder fitted exactly the head of a piston, representing, as it were, a bullet, rendered airtight.'

The principle of De Rivaz's engine was extremely simple. The analogy of the bullet was not so far removed from the truth, for what the inventor had visualised was a machine rather like a vertical cannon mounted on wheels. Gas was admitted to the cylinder and ignited, thus firing the piston upwards to the top of the cylinder. The piston rod was linked by chain and ratchet gear to the wheels, and when a valve was opened to let the burnt gases escape,

the heavy piston fell and turned the wheels. The ignition, interestingly enough, was by electricity, provided by a Voltaic battery.

It seems that De Rivaz actually constructed a crude chariot on the lines described in his patent, and persuaded it to run the width of a room.

'The bother of putting the chariot back in position at the end of each trial persuaded me to have a fire engine built . . .'

In 1820 an English clergyman, the Reverend William Cecil, demonstrated a little model gas engine to the Cambridge Philosophical Society; running on hydrogen, it operated rather like a primitive steam engine, and turned at a leisurely 16 rpm. Its inventor suggested that illuminating gas, vaporised petroleum, turpentine or alcohol were possible alternative fuels. Although he did not apply his engine to any more exciting use than pumping water, Cecil directed the attention of those who were beginning to experiment with road carriages towards the use of gas engines.

David Gordon, indeed, proposed that vehicles could be propelled by compressed coal gas delivered to refuelling stations round the country in pressurised containers, but abandoned this scheme when he computed the operating costs to be prohibitively expensive.

Perhaps the most successful disciple of the Reverend Cecil was Samuel Brown, of Brompton, who in 1824 began experiments with a 'gas-and-vacuum' engine. In 1826 he mounted a developed version of this power unit, which had twin cylinders linked by a rocking beam, in a four-wheeled chariot. This was tested on the open road in May of that year, and climbed the slope of Shooters Hill, near Woolwich, 'to the astonishment of numerous spectators'. Once again, excessive operating costs were the rock on which this venture foundered, and Brown then turned his attention to employing his engine to drive canal boats; although he constructed a paddle steamer which ran on the Thames, Brown found that on water, too, gas power was too expensive.

Another form of motive power which was engaging the attention of inventors at this period was compressed air, and here the most ingenious suggestions were made by William Mann, of Brixton, who, after three years of experiment, published a pamphlet in 1830 in which he proposed a system of 'power stations' at intervals of 15 to 20 miles along the main carriage routes. Alternatively, he suggested a continuous iron main with power stations in the coal districts.

Mann intended that the carriages operating under his system should carry a supply of air in cylinders, each of around 5 cu ft capacity. Equipped with fifteen such cylinders, pressurised to 32 atmospheres, the carriage would, he claimed, run for 14 miles; at a pressure of 64 atmospheres, 34 miles could be covered at an average cost of a penny a mile.

'It would be well,' thought Mann, 'to make persons confined in Clerkenwell and other prisons earn their dinners by compressing air for the supplying of power for propelling His Majesty's Mails throughout the kingdom.' However, neither Mann, nor his contemporary, Wright, who patented a carriage powered by a combination of compressed air and steam, seems to have realised such designs in a practicable form.

It was not until the 1850s that a viable alternative to steam power for road vehicles became available. It had long been known that certain gases – notably oxygen and hydrogen – could be combined in certain proportions and ignited within a closed container to give a powerful explosion. The difficulty lay in harnessing the power of that explosion and turning it into useful work, as De Rivaz had found.

The first practicable gas engine was patented in 1853 by two Italians, Barsanti and Matteucci, who, ignorant of the attempts that had been made in earlier years to construct power units of this type, believed themselves to be the orignal inventors of the gas engine. The concept was actually that of Eugenio Barsanti, a priest who taught at a secondary school in Florence; he was the theorist and Felice Matteucci was the engineer who translated his ideas into metal.

Barsanti had conceived a twin-cylinder engine with free pistons carrying rack-rods which rotated a flywheel shaft as they operated on a complex three-

Barsanti, Matteuchi and a model of their first gas engine, patented on 13 May 1854; the twin pistons were set free in the cylinders and drove, via rack rods, a flywheel shaft; the unit's first public demonstration was in 1856 and Barsanti commented: 'This machine was enough to announce that before long the power of steam would be replaced by a perfect, inexpensive motive force'

cycle system, induction and explosion occurring during the same stroke of the piston, as opposed to the more usual arrangement.

In May 1856 the first public demonstration of this power unit was given in the workshops of the Maria-Antonia Railway Company in Florence, where it drove a drill and shears. Barsanti was overjoyed to see his brainchild at work: 'This machine was enough to announce that before long the power of steam would be replaced by a perfect, inexpensive motive force'.

Unfortunately, however, the inventor-priest was incapable of following one line of thought to a conclusion, and the following year he devised a new type of engine, which had two pistons working in tandem in each cylinder; this led, in 1858, to a third design with two opposed pistons, which was to have been installed in a boat but failed to work properly.

A company was formed to manufacture gas engines on 10 October 1860 and a new, more-complicated type of opposed-piston engine was made for them by the Escher & Wyss Company of Zurich. Again, it failed to perform in the expected manner.

The two partners quarrelled and Matteucci retired 'for reasons of health', while Barsanti returned to his tandem-piston design of 1857. Bauer-Elvetica of Naples built one of these engines, but refused to consider series production. However, a Belgian engineering company, John Cockerill of Liège, showed interest in manufacturing Barsanti's gas engine and the inventor travelled to Belgium to give a demonstration. Unfortunately, though, he caught typhoid fever and died . . .

Already Barsanti's temperamental engines had been supplanted by a superior design of gas engine devised by the Belgian inventor Jean-Joseph Etienne Lenoir, who was working as consulting engineer to Gauthier & Cie, of Paris. In 1859, they formed the Société des Moteurs Lenoir, with a capital of two million francs and workshops in the Rue de la Roquette, Paris Ile, to exploit the gas engine invented by Lenoir a year or so previously. This was a two-cycle engine in which the gas was ignited electrically at atmospheric pressure: it was thus quiet and extremely inefficient, needing some 18 litres to develop two horsepower, but it was also reliable, and within five years over 500 engines had been built and were in operation in France, Britain and America, with yet more being constructed under licence in Germany.

The young Gottlieb Daimler visited the Lenoir factory in 1860, and dismissed the new engine as too expensive to run, and operating at too high a temperature; but already Lenoir was attempting to adapt his power unit to the propulsion of a road vehicle. On 16 June that year, *Le Monde Illustré* published an engraving of 'a carriage recently built by M Lenoir', commenting: 'The casing which encloses the motor doesn't in any way encroach upon the passenger space. The gas is contained in the tank A. The rear wheels are driven by an endless chain running on two sprockets. The car is steered by a steering wheel on a vertical shaft placed in front of the driver. This shaft carries at its lower

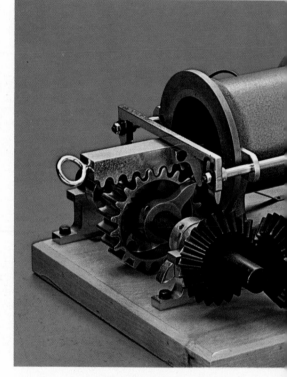

Far right: the Belgian Lenoir and, *right*, his carriage of 1860 as seen in *Le Mond Illustré*. Although Lenoir's gas engine was an unqualified success, the actual vehicle was less than a marvel, perhaps due to its primitive design

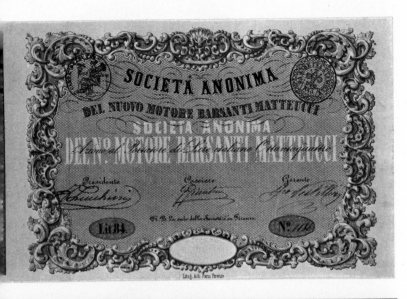

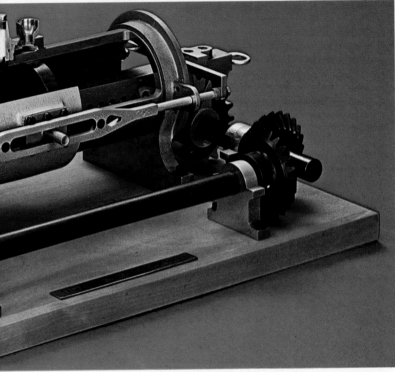

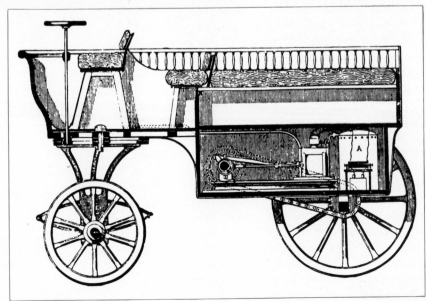

end a pinion acting on a semi-circular rack fixed to the forward wheel, which it obliges to swivel to right or left, thus changing the direction of the vehicle.'

It seems as though this report was a trifle premature, for Lenoir's carriage did not manage to make any sort of journey until 1863; indeed, this may have been an entirely new vehicle. Recalled Lenoir: 'With this, we went from Paris to Joinville-le-Pont (a village some 9 km from Paris); an hour and a half to get there, as long to return. The carriage was heavy; the motor, of 1½ horsepower, with a fairly heavy flywheel, made 100 revolutions a minute.' But those 100 revolutions a minute were hard-earned, for the journey was punctuated with breakdowns, and the consumption of fuel and water was 'considerable'.

Lenoir sold his patents to the Compagnie Parisienne du Gaz in 1863, although he seems to have retained the car; and in 1864 he received the world's first export order, from the francophile Tsar of all the Russias, Alexander II Nicolaevitch. The car was shipped to Russia . . . and vanished, its fate unrecorded. Documents relating to the sale were unearthed in Paris in 1906, but, although a search was made for the Lenoir in the Imperial Palace at St Petersburg, no trace was found of it. As for its inventor, he had died in poverty six years earlier.

It was the Lenoir gas engine which had inspired a German clerk, Nikolaus August Otto, to attempt to develop an internal-combustion engine which could be used in situations where steam power was impracticable. After numerous trials, he met a wealthy engineer named Eugen Langen, and together they developed a free-piston engine, which was patented in 1866, and which went into commercial production in 1872. Otto and Langen's company was reorganised as the Gasmotoren-Fabrik Deutz, and a 38-year-old engineer named Gottlieb Daimler was appointed factory manager, with his protégé, Wilhelm Maybach, as chief designer. They reorganised the factory, creating an efficient production system, and by 1875 had increased annual sales to 634 engines with a total of 735 horsepower; the workforce had increased to 230, and Maybach was now receiving a bonus of one thaler for every engine delivered satisfactorily.

Already, however, the free-piston engine was reaching the limits of its development potential: although, by the standards of the day it was reliable, it was also noisy and inefficient. Output was limited to about three horsepower, and at that rating the engine needed an overhead clearance of around thirteen feet to allow for the movement of the piston rod. Inspired by the early success of the engine, the Deutz company began an overambitious programme of expansion, and when sales began to tail off, the board ordered Daimler to start development of a 'petroleum engine'.

Eventually, Otto returned to the four-stroke engine, a line of development which he had abandoned in 1861–2; in 1876 his new chief engineer, Franz Rings, drew up an engine of this type for the first time, and this was running in prototype form that autumn. Otto attempted to gain a monopoly of the gas-engine industry by patenting the four-stroke cycle, forcing other experimenters to concentrate on the two-stroke or risk prosecution. But in 1886, after two years of litigation, Otto's patent was overthrown on the grounds that an obscure French civil engineer, Alphonse Beau de Rochas, had, in a long-winded and rambling leaflet which he had distributed in 1862, described the four-stroke cycle and patented the concept.

Although this was, naturally enough, a matter of some chagrin for Otto, it was a vital step in the development of the motor car: inventors, who had been diverted into developing engines which avoided the Deutz patents, could now concentrate on the relatively simpler task of making engines which would run reliably.

Leading the field were Gottlieb Daimler and Karl Benz. Daimler had broken with Otto in 1881 and he was working with Wilhelm Maybach in the shed of his house in Cannstatt to develop a rapid-revolution motor, suitable for vehicle propulsion, using Maybach's patented hot-tube ignition system, which was cruder – but more reliable – than existing electric ignition systems. Benz, who had been operating a machine shop in Mannheim, Germany, since 1871, had hoped to overcome his financial problems by mass-producing tin-working machinery; when this plan had failed, he decided to develop an engine.

48

Far left: pioneers of the petroleum-engined motor car, Karl Benz, *above*, and Gottlieb Daimler, *below*

Left: Daimler's single-cylinder, half-horsepower engine, constructed in 1885; this was first fitted to a boneshaker bicycle, but was later tried in a 'horseless carriage'

Overleaf: a scene in Daimler's Bad Cannstatt workshop, with the Daimler-powered boneshaker on the workshop floor

Below: completed in 1885 and first run in early 1886 was this Daimler wagon built by Wimpff and Son of Stuttgart. As Daimler wanted to keep this project secret until the wagon was fitted with his 1.1 hp engine, he told the builders that it was merely a present for his wife; they thought the carriage would be horse-drawn

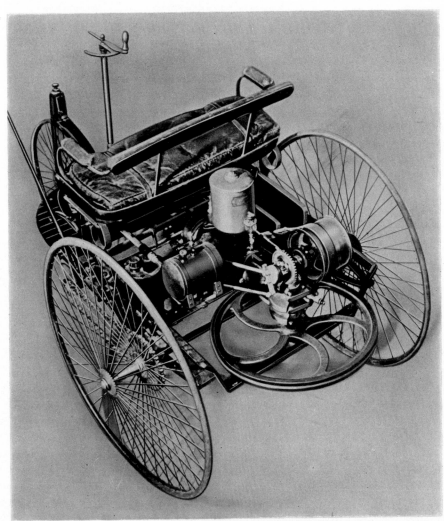

Above: beating the Daimler into manufacture by a couple of months was the famous Benz three-wheeler, generally acknowledged to be the world's first successful petrol-powered motor car

49

He was successful in building a two-stroke engine, which first ran on New Year's Eve, 1879, and received backing for this project from Emil Buhler, the court photographer, who encouraged Benz to form the Gasmotorenfabrik Mannheim in 1882. After only three months Benz resigned from this company, found new backers, and again began producing internal-combustion engines. Already he was considering the manufacture of a motor vehicle, so when, in 1884, it became evident that Otto would almost certainly have his four-stroke patent cancelled Benz started to build a four-stroke engine as part of the 'vehicle with gas-engine drive', which appeared in 1885–6.

The Benz car was one of the great highwater marks in the development of the motor car, for it was the first successful machine designed as an entity, and not just as a horse-drawn carriage with a motor added. The 0.8 hp four-stroke engine was mounted at the rear of the tubular chassis, which obviously owed much to bicycle technology in its construction. There was only a single front wheel, freeing Benz from the necessity of developing the geometrically accurate steering which would have been necessary with two wheels, and the engine drove the big, cycle-type rear wheels through a flat belt, a cross-shaft, fitted

Left: Gottlieb Daimler is seen here sitting back and enjoying being driven by his son, Adolf; this is Daimler's first vehicle, on trial in 1886

Above: an example of early Benz advertising

with a differential, and side chains. The power unit had its heavy flywheel mounted horizontally; this was because Benz feared that the gyroscopic action of a vertical flywheel might upset the steering.

Ignition was by coil and battery, with a spark plug made by Benz; the carburettor was a simple affair, a tank in which the volatile petroleum spirit gave off its rich fumes, which were then sucked, together with the requisite volume of air, into the cylinder. The engine speed was controlled by regulating the amount of air taken in, thus altering the fuel's ignition characteristics.

By the summer of 1886, the Benz car was sufficiently reliable to be able to make its trial runs in public. On 3 July, a local paper noted: 'A velocipede driven by Ligroin gas, built by the Rheinische Gasmotorenfabrik of Benz & Cie, already reported in these pages on 4 June, was tested this morning early on the Ringstrasse, during which it operated satisfactorily'.

Benz's partners found his preoccupation with the car an annoyance, for it prevented him devoting all his energies to the manufacture of gas engines, on which the company relied for its somewhat precarious existence. But he persisted, no doubt encouraged by press reports like the one which appeared in the Mannheim *Generalanzeiger* on 15 September 1886: 'The very first time that we saw it we were convinced that Benz's invention had solved the problem of

Top: after experimenting with steam four-wheelers, Albert, Comte de Dion built a succession of these three-wheelers in the 1880s; however, it was with quantity-produced petrol vehicles that he was later to make his name

Above: the boneshaker, with stabiliser wheels, used as a testbed for Gottlieb Daimler's first single-cylinder engine

building a road vehicle driven by a basic power source. However, as was to be expected, many deficiencies came to light which will have to be corrected by further experiments and improvements. The difficult task of inventing it may now be considered over and done with, and Benz intends to proceed with the manufacture of these vehicles for practical use. This motor vehicle is not meant to have the same purpose and characteristics as a velocipede, which one could take for a pleasurable spin over a smooth, well kept country road; rather, it is conceived as a cart or peasant's wagon, suitable not only for travelling fairly good roads, but also for carrying heavy loads up steep inclines. For example, it would enable a commercial traveller to take his samples from one place to another without any difficulty . . . We believe this wagon has a good future, because it can be put in use without much trouble and because when the speed is made sufficient, it will be the most inexpensive promotional tool for travelling salesmen, as well as a way for tourists to get around.'

Despite such eulogies, the car was not yet ready for sale, but by 1888 Benz judged that the time was ripe to put the new, sturdier version of his three-wheeler on public display. That September, he took it to the Munich Engine

Above: another view of Karl Benz's three-wheeler of 1885; note the massive flywheel, which is placed horizontally in the chassis; Benz thought that the gyroscopic precession of a vertical wheel would upset the steering on corners

Left: Enrico Bernardi, born in Verona on 20 May 1841

Below right: one of Bernardi's tricycles of 1896; it was powered by a single-cylinder engine of 624 cc, which produced 2.5 hp at 800 rpm

Exposition, and gave a number of demonstration runs in that city.

'Seldom, if ever,' ran one newspaper report, 'have passers-by in the streets of our city seen a more startling sight than on Saturday afternoon when a one-horse chaise came from the Sendlingerstrasse over Sendlingertorplatz and down Herzog Wilhelmstrasse at a good clip without a horse or shafts, a gentleman sitting under a surrey top, riding on three wheels – one in front and two behind – speeding on his way towards the centre of town. The amazement of everyone on the street who saw him was such that they seemed unable to grasp what they had before their eyes, and the astonishment was general and widespread.'

To temper such uncritical praise, the *German Yearbook of Natural Science* growled: 'Benz also has made a petrol car which caused some stir at the Munich Exposition. This employment of the petrol engine will probably be no more promising for the future than the use of the steam engine was for road travel.'

And certainly there were no buyers. Benz advertised his car as 'an agreeable vehicle, as well as a mountain-climbing apparatus', but the truth was that when

Above left: Bernardi's single-cylinder engine of 1882 was named *Motrice Pia* after his daughter; the 126 cc power unit produced 0.024 hp and was used mostly on a sewing machine

Left: built in 1884, this Bernardi engine could power the designer's son Lauro's bicycle at 7–8 kph

Right : the Serpollet steam tricycle of 1888. The French military authorities were interested in the design and asked for a trial; all went well until an army captain asked Léon Serpollet to test the vehicle's brakes; he pulled on the brake lever while the steamer was travelling at 15 mph and although the steamer stopped the captain did not, and he somersaulted over the dashboard

his family borrowed one of the first cars for an impromptu motor tour, they found that its single-speed transmission was sadly deficient in hill-climbing powers. There were perhaps a couple of Benz cars in private hands; one was owned by the Parisian agent for the Benz gas engine, Emile Roger, another survives today in London's Science Museum, possibly the first motor car to have been imported into Britain.

Benz had conceived his power unit as an integral part of a purpose-built motor vehicle; Daimler, on the other hand, saw his engine as a universal power unit, for industry as well as for vehicles, and made his preliminary tests in November 1885 with a 0.5 hp engine mounted in a boneshaker bicycle frame. Only when this had proved itself capable of driving a vehicle did he consider fitting an engine in a carriage; and even then it was installed in a four-seater phaeton made by a firm of coachbuilders who were ignorant of the fact that it would not be drawn by horses.

Daimler, indeed, made no special stipulations when ordering the vehicle save that it should be 'handsome, but very solidly built', as it was to be a birthday present for his wife; he wanted, it seems, to keep the secret of his engine as long as possible.

When the carriage arrived, the power unit and transmission were installed by the Esslingen Engineering Works. The upper part of the engine protruded through the floor ahead of the rear seat, while final drive was simple, a two-ratio belt drive rotating a countershaft with pinions at each end engaging in toothed rings attached to the rear wheels.

Despite its crude design, the Daimler car seems to have performed successfully, but it was just an interlude in the production of engines for all kinds of uses, from firepumps and saw benches to primitive airships. Demand for these power units grew to such an extent that Daimler and Maybach had to move into larger premises, taking over an old nickel-plating works. It was here that the partners developed one of the crucial power units of the pioneering days of motoring, the V-twin; this 565 cc engine, with its cylinders set at 20 degrees, possessed an excellent power-to-weight ratio and turned at the rapid rate of 630 rpm, far faster than any contemporary gas engines. It was to remain the most advanced power unit available to car constructors for several years. Wilhelm Maybach designed a car round the V-twin engine; this 'steel-wheeler' followed, like the Benz of four years earlier, contemporary bicycle practice, and was a much neater design than the original Daimler car. It was shown at the 1889 Paris World Exhibition, where it attracted much attention. One of its keenest passengers was Réné Panhard who, together with his partner, Emile Levassor, and Levassor's lady friend, Louise Sarazin, a widow whose late husband had represented Deutz in France since 1874 (and had told his wife on his deathbed to continue the business association with Daimler), planned to build Daimler engines for stationary use; after the Exposition, Mme Sarazin signed an agreement giving her the French and Belgian rights for Daimler

petrol engines. In 1890, Levassor married Louis Sarazin, and Panhard and Levassor began manufacturing Daimler engines. They could see no future for the horseless carriage, however, and transferred their rights to use these power units in a carriage to Peugeot, who were already established as bicycle manufacturers, and who, although keen to build automobiles, had just decided against making Serpollet steam cars.

While these men were stumbling towards the beginnings of series production, others were still groping for the secret of making an engine that would drive a carriage. Most notably the Austrian Siegfried Marcus, who was said to have fitted a crude atmospheric engine to a wheelbarrow in 1870, the whole confection, with its tall guide rods for the piston, looking remarkably like a portable guillotine. Little more advanced than the 1805 De Rivaz, it ran only 200 yards before breaking down.

Siegfried's idyll had started in the mid 1860s, when this dilettante inventor had devised a 'carburettor' in his first-floor workshop in the Mariahilfstrasse in Vienna. Intended to vaporise petroleum spirit for lighting purposes, this device was scarcely suitable for adaptation to a road vehicle: for one thing it

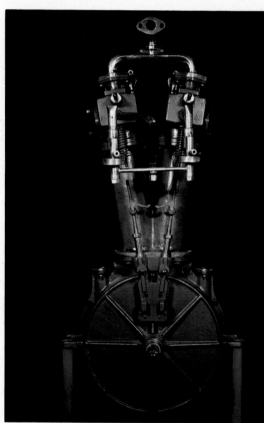

Above left: an 1891 Panhard & Levassor which ran quite successfully; later cars had front engines (as opposed to the rear-mounted unit of this car) and featured the first 'modern-style' gearboxes

Above: a Daimler V-twin engine of 1892, with hot-tube ignition; although seemingly crude, this form of ignition was better than the electrical units of that early period

Left: part of the extraordinary Millet tricycle of 1887; the power unit is a five-cylinder rotary engine

was so big it virtually filled the room . . .

Marcus was one of those typical Victorian inventors who, scarcely having proved that an idea might work, was immediately away in pursuit of another chimera. He seems to have built another motor carriage in the late 1870s, which was reported, somewhat unreliably, to have made a 12 km journey to Klosterneuberg, and about 1888–9 had a third vehicle built which, with its strange 3–4 hp 'grasshopper' engine and rudimentary construction, looked a good deal older than it was. And so it was, when the Nazis celebrated the fiftieth anniversary of Benz's first patent, that the Austrians chauvinistically claimed that the Marcus car, which was still preserved in a Viennese Museum, preceded Benz by a decade – and added that its inventor had been Jewish . . . This so incensed the Germans that during the war they sought to destroy the Marcus car, thinking that this would eradicate any claim on Benz's priority . . . but the Viennese had foreseen such a move, and hidden the car away safely. The '1875' dating, however, stuck for many years afterwards.

Another experimenter whose work promised more than it delivered was Edouard Delamarre-Deboutteville, of Fontaine-le-Bourg, younger son of the

Top: even in 1891, this steam tricycle was looking very outdated; it was built in Italy by Enrico Pecori

Above: a two-cylinder petrol engine provided the power for this 1883 wagon built by Delamare Deboutteville; unfortunately, on its first run, the chassis broke in two. This model is now in the Budapest transport museum

Right: electric vehicles came thick and fast around the time of this Hautier cab of 1889; development of the clean and silent power of electricity has progressed little, however, even to this day

owner of a weaving works. In 1884, he drove through the town on a heavy tricycle powered by compressed gas. Passing over a crossroads, the rubber tube linking the gas containers burst with a terrifying explosion and Delamarre-Deboutteville decided to try some more amenable motive power.

Aided by his mechanic, Malandin, he fitted a twin-cylinder petrol engine into his father's old horse-break. It seems to have made one short test-run, which terminated in the chassis coming in two, after which the two experimenters converted their engine to a stationary power unit, and later marketed a developed version of this. Indeed, one of Delamarre-Deboutteville's descendants probably contributed more to the progress of motoring in his position as marketing manager of Ford-France in the 1930s . . .

CHAPTER 4

The Birth of an Industry

Left: the Scotte steam carriage of 1892, which had a top speed of 12 kph; for what is really a very late design in the steam-vehicle field, this performance seems pathetic; this was, after all, at a time when there were far more sophisticated petroleum-powered vehicles on the road

To its fond parents, the motor car was now a commercial proposition, but, for a prospective purchaser, to buy one would be an awfully big adventure. When, in 1888, Emile Roger took his new Benz away from the works, he had been personally coached in its care and maintenance by 'Papa Benz' himself. After it had been duly transported back to Paris, however, the car refused to start, and Benz had to follow it, to instruct a mechanic in its handling. Curiously enough, Roger had garaged his car in the workshop of Panhard & Levassor, who also manufactured Benz two-stroke engines under licence, in addition to their Daimler activities. They showed as little interest in the vehicle as did the rest of the public, and no sale was forthcoming.

To Benz's partners, Rose and Esslinger, his preoccupation with the motor vehicle was becoming a threat to the business. 'Herr Benz', Rose would complain, 'we've now made a nice pile of money, but you had best keep your fingers out of that motor car or you'll lose everything'. Then he would sigh and add 'My God, my God, where is this all going to end?'.

It ended for Rose and Esslinger in 1890, when they resigned from the company, to be replaced by two more accommodating businessmen, Von Fischer and Ganss, who had useful experience of selling in foreign markets. From then on, progress, if not swift, was at least positive.

On New Year's Day 1891, a postmaster named Kugler wrote to Benz, intrigued by the latter's suggestion that the motor car might prove useful to the postal authorities. 'I am positive that your ingenious and most practical invention will be crowned with a great success, I am not only thinking of its usefulness to the postal services, but I am utterly convinced that it would be most excellent for a country doctor. Not every doctor in a small village has box stalls, horses and a farm to maintain them, yet some kind of a cart is essential for a doctor who has to make calls in a number of places distant from each other. How often is a doctor called on during the night, and how else is he meant to get where he has to go? Before he has roused the sleep-drunk peasant from his bed and got him to put the bridle and harness on the horse, a lot of valuable time has been lost.

'There is another thing about your vehicle: it comes to a halt and turns off and that's it. It doesn't need any feed, or any groom, no blacksmith, no danger of having a horse shy; it just moves along as though a ghostly hand were pushing it—and one stroke of the brakes and it stops. That is what makes it so inexpensive to operate. Even the stupidest blockhead must be able to see such an immense advantage as this.

'The vehicle in motion does have something comical in its appearance from the aesthetic point of view, and someone who did not know what it was might think it was a runaway chaise he was looking at. That is because we have not yet grown used to it.

'But here also, in my opinion, a lot of minor changes and adjustments can artfully be made to improve its appearance without in any way losing sight of the characteristics that serve its purpose. If this were done, the lack of an

Two examples of the 1893 Benz Viktoria, the
first four-wheeled car built by the company. The
cars' single-cylinder engine produced 3 bhp at
700 rpm and could propel the vehicles at 25 kph.
The world's first production car, the 1894 Benz
Velo was based on the Viktoria design

exactly trouble free, and he only kept note of his progress as far as Gondorf, where he computed that he had used 140 kg of gasoline to travel 939 kilometres, and that the radiator had consumed 1500 litres of water. Von Liebig, though, concluded that the journey had revealed 'the delight of passing through beautiful landscape by an entirely new means of transportation', and had thus been well worth while.

By now, Benz was attempting to popularise the motor car, groping his way towards a primitive form of assembly-line production. And, on 1 April 1894, he delivered the first 'Velo', a smaller, lighter version of the Viktoria, with a 1½ hp engine, which cost only 2000 Marks in its most basic form.

In 1895, out of a total output of 135 cars, 62 were Velos and 36 were Viktorias, the remainder being made up of various larger models like the Phaeton, the eight-seat Jagdwagen (shooting break), the eight passenger Landau and the stage-coach-like Omnibus. Developments of the Velo were to maintain the popularity of the Benz marque into the 20th Century, while the simplicity of the design ensured that it was widely copied by British and French manufacturers. Yet, even when it appeared, the Velo was a somewhat passé design. The truth

Left: the first vehicle to be fitted with Georges Bouton's high-speed petrol engine was this tricycle of 1895; the air-cooled engine, of 137 cc, featured non-trembler coil ignition, and could spin at 2000 rpm

Right: development by Karl Benz progressed by way of the Velo, first produced in 1894

of the matter was that, like so many innovators, Karl Benz was strictly a one-note man, and all the cars produced under his aegis were recognisably descended from the original 1885/6 model, with rear-mounted engine and belt-and-chain final drive. Having created what he was convinced was the ultimate design of motor car, Benz stuck doggedly to it, even when it proved commercially foolhardy. This form of shortsightedness was not unique to Benz, as can be seen from inventions as diverse as the Wright Flyer, the Edison Phonograph and the Ford Model T, all of which were produced long after progress had rendered them obsolescent.

However, compared with the cars being turned out by Gottlieb Daimler, the Benz Velo was the height of modernity. Daimler had signed contracts with a gunpowder manufacturer named Max Duttenhofer and another industrialist, W. Lorenz, to gain the necessary capital for expansion of his engine-building activities, a move which resulted in the formation of the Daimler-Motoren-Gesellschaft on 28 November 1890. Daimler and his new partners soon fell out, though and, at the end of 1892 he and Maybach broke away from the company to set up their own experimental workshop in the great summer hall of the

Left: the Velo was what Karl Benz called the ultimate design of motor car and he continued to market developments of the one basic theme right into the 20th century; the success of the vehicle, however, was enough to ensure respect for the company for years to come

Below: Karl Benz on his Viktoria follows another Benz family member driving a Velo. This photo was taken on a family outing in 1895

defunct Hotel Hermann in Cannstatt. Here they developed the successor to the V-twin power unit, an equally outstanding engine which they called the Phönix. This had two cylinders in line, and was fitted with Maybach's new invention, the spray carburettor, which adjusted the gas/air mixture according to the engine speed and the load imposed on the power unit. This seems to have been an excessive amount of refinement for the inflexible tube-ignition system, which was happiest running at a constant speed.

Having developed an excellent power unit, Daimler and Maybach then totally nullified their achievement by fitting it in a belt-driven car of unbelievably retrograde design, which remained in production even after Daimler and his partners had resolved their quarrel, in 1895. It is hard to comprehend how Maybach could have produced this clumsy vehicle, with its centre-pivot steering, in 1893, when only seven years later he was to conceive the most advanced car in the world.

In fact, it could be argued that the principal effect of all this hard work by the Germans was to establish the French as the world's leading motor manufacturers for the ensuing decade, for the French were willing to experiment and

Left: an 1894 Peugeot tourer, with trimmings characteristic of that company; as with most early Peugeots, it used handlebar steering, a tubular chassis (in which the cooling water passed) and a Daimler V-twin engine mounted at the rear

Below: two V-twin Peugeots, four and three-seaters respectively, triumphant after the 1894 Paris–Rouen reliability trial. It was this race which led to the great Paris races in latter years

alter, while the Germans seemed content to progress along the lines that they had established several years earlier. And the French seemed far more confident of the potential of the motor vehicle, too: in 1891, Peugeot dispatched one of their earliest cars on an ambitious foray, following the competitors in the 2047 km Paris–Brest–Paris cycle race. It covered the distance in 139 hours, 'without a moment's trouble', a feat which helped Peugeot to sell five cars to private owners that year, and to boost output to 29 in 1892.

The cars which Peugeot were making echoed the company's long experience in cycle manufacture, with tubular chassis (through which the cooling water for the engine circulated) and spindly spoked wheels. The rear-mounted Daimler engines were purchased through Panhard and Levassor until Peugeot developed their own power unit in 1896.

Having seen the results obtained by his friend Peugeot, Levassor decided to build a horseless carriage for himself, prompted, it seems, by his go-ahead wife, the former Mme. Sarazin.

The first Panhard & Levassor car appeared in the late summer of 1890. It was a dogcart with the engine mounted between the seats, similar in conception to the original Daimler carriage of 1886. It was not, apparently, an unqualified success, and Levassor would grumble gently: 'If Daimler can make a carriage run at eighteen kilometres an hour, so can I . . .'

After building a couple of cars with the engine at the rear, Levassor settled on a front-engined layout, with the unit contained under a square bonnet, driving through the famous '*brusque et brutale*' gearbox (which had four speeds forward, four speeds in reverse, and operated completely *al fresco*, devoid of any protective—or oil-retaining—casing) to the countershaft and side chains which gave the final drive.

'Build heavy', said Levassor, 'and you build strong!'. He also, it seems, built reliable, for with his second car (still rear-engined) he was the very first Parisian to make the summer drive that is now an annual ritual, from the capital to the coast, covering the 225 km from his works in the Avenue d'Ivry to his summer home at Etretat in a total running time of 23 hours 15 minutes on 31 July/

Not looking that much more advanced than the
Viktoria and the Velo is this Benz Comfortable
of 1898

1 August 1891. The greatest annoyance he found was the need to stop every so often and refill the surface carburettor, which also acted as a fuel tank, and only held 1.3 litres. 'It's true', he philosophised, 'that I made use of the halts to fill up the water tank and grease the car'.

This journey, however, was eclipsed less than two years later when his partner's 23-year-old son, Hippolyte Panhard, set out from the factory bound for Nice, driving the 2 hp car which his father had bought at a specially reduced price of 4318 francs on 28 August 1892, as a present for the young man. Leaving Paris via the Bois de Vincennes, Hippolyte drove the solid-tyred vehicle gingerly over the cobbled quais at Alfort, which had last been paved during the reign of Louis XIV. Once he reached the smoother roads beyond the city, though, he engaged the third speed, and allowed the carriage to reach a heady seventeen kph. 'It's possible to attain twenty kph, but such great speeds require considerable attention on the part of the driver, and are not always advisable', warned the company's catalogue. Pausing for an excellent lunch at Fontaine-bleu, Hippolyte, who was accompanied by his uncle Georges Méric, covered 140 km in the day, noting in a letter to his father that 'some undulations of the

terrain often compelled the use of second gear'.

Their progress was also impeded by the fringed canopy attached to the car, which caught the wind, so they abandoned it the next morning. Obtaining fuel was another problem, and they had to search for sources of supply: at Pouilly they were given 23 litres of gasoline by the owner of an 'oil-engined plough', while in another town, Hippolyte had to buy his fuel in a grocer's shop.

'Unfortunately, I had stopped behind the grocer's handcart. As I got down from the car, I pushed the clutch lever and the car jerked forward, overturning the handcart. Cost: 10 francs . . .'

As the car stuttered through villages, it attracted a vast amount of attention: 'Urchins, dogs, cats and chickens all rushed after us, each making their own distinctive noise. It was a dreadful racket . . .'

The important factor was that Hippolyte and Georges Méric were not making a test run: they were touring, and touring in a relatively relaxed manner. 'Yesterday at dinner there were five exquisite courses, much appreciated by Uncle Georges. Dinner, two rooms, stabling for the car and breakfast cost us a total of 10 francs. It's really not expensive . . .'

There were few mechanical annoyances on the road. Descending the steep Col de la République, they free-wheeled, and the car ran 'silently, like running on velvet', but the brakes overheated badly, and Georges Méric had to hold a bucket of water between his legs and cool the brakes with a wet rag. Nearing

Right: an 1898 Decauville *Voiturelle* built by a French railway locomotive firm. This vehicle featured sliding-pillar front suspension, although the designer has ignored any springing at the rear. As with most vehicles of this type and age, the manufacturers went to De Dion for their power units, in this case it was a twin of 489 cc

their destination, the travellers paused at Hyères, where Belhomme, a mechanic from Ivry, replaced Méric. It seems that a few components had dropped from the car during the eight day run (the French still call spares 'detached pieces'!) and a request for replacements was telegraphed to Levassor.

In Cannes, Nice and Monaco, the Panhard was the centre of attention, and Hippolyte showed it off at the best hotels, theatres, casinos and promenades, in front of prominent personalities.

However, the clutch (which was Levassor's eccentric 'brush' design) was beginning to play up: 'M. Levassor will say that I drove the car very badly, but I assure you that I took every possible care of it and did not try to climb hills more quickly by slipping the clutch'. And there were demonstration runs to be given to important prospective customers . . . 'a whole heap of Englishmen and the Grand Duke of Mecklembourg, cousin of the Grand Duchess Michael'.

The Grand Duchess Michael was keen to buy a car and drive it herself, and asked Hippolyte to drive her party to the Golf Club of which her husband was president.

'There will be three or four of them', wrote Hippolyte to his father, 'and it seems that they are all big and fat . . .' The reason for his anxiety was that misbehaving clutch. 'I'll try and put a wedge behind the clutch spring which, by the grace of God, will make it engage better. It would be awful to fail in front of all those grand people.'

The clutch did not fail, luckily, and the car continued to attract attention during Hippolyte's stay at Nice. On the way home, though, the young man tempted fate by driving into the mountains beyond Grasse and, sure enough, the clutch packed up, and the car had to be hauled to the next village behind horses. 'Anyway, it's been a picturesque journey', said Hippolyte philosophically.

It had been a journey, too, which could hardly have been made anywhere else but in France and emphasised that country's lead in the construction and use of motor vehicles.

In America, for instance, the number of successful gasoline carriages which had been built up to that date could be counted on the fingers of one hand, even though George Baldwin Selden had made his first patent application for a 'reliable road locomotive, simple, cheap, lightweight, easy to control and powerful enough to climb any ordinary hill' in 1879, and on the basis of this patent (which was not published until 1895!) attempted to gain a monopoly of the nascent American motor industry.

The first American motor vehicle appears to have been the unsuccessful Schank tricycle exhibited at the 1886 Ohio State Fair. This had an engine 'as big as a kitchen stove', and was chiefly important in having inspired young Charles Duryea, a cycle manufacturer from Peoria, to start experiments with an 'atmospheric engine'. Curiously enough, American pioneers seem to have almost wilfully ignored the fact that perfectly good power units were readily available to them on a cash and carry basis as early as 1891, when Gottlieb Daimler's friend William Steinway (of piano fame) began building Daimler engines under licence in his Long Island factory, a venture which lasted until 1896.

It seems that the first successful American car was the three-wheeler built by John W. Lambert, of Ohio City, which was running—and photographed—in January or February 1891. The same year, Henry Nadig of Allentown, Pennsylvania, built a four-wheeler vehicle with a single-cylinder power unit, which does not seem to have been too successful, for it was replaced two years later by a twin-cylinder engine, in which form the car was operated until 1903 (it still exists, as does the 1892 Schloemer from Milwaukee).

In September 1893, Charles Duryea and his brother Frank made their first successful trials with a horseless carriage in the streets of Springfield, Massachussets. However, Frank recalled fifty years later 'because of its friction transmission, the car was barely operative, and I was never able to give a demonstration to a prospective client'.

More success and a measure of financial backing were forthcoming eventually, and in 1895 the Duryeas founded America's first motor-manufacturing firm,

Top: by the mid 1890s, the motor car was becoming an accepted form of reliable transport, as shown by these two young ladies who have ventured out in their 1895 Panhard & Levassor

Above: advertising for the 1896 Duryea, said to be America's first motor car. Frank Duryea was so impressed with a Benz he saw in 1895 that he based his design on it

Left: the Honourable Evelyn Hills proudly displays his Panhard & Levassor to a gathering in England in the 1890s

Below: another example of Enrico Bernardi's three-wheeler design; perhaps it is fortunate that these vehicles had a very modest performance with the hood looking like a horizontal parachute

Apart from keeping other manufacturers well
stocked with engines, De Dion were, themselves,
building complete cars. This is a four-wheeler of
1897, complete with exposed transmission, which
must have caused a great many problems in
wet or dirty conditions. At one time, De Dion
were providing engines for over 140 different
makes of car; on top of this, their power units
were copied by several companies, such as
Humber and Pierce-Arrow

the Duryea Motor Wagon Company, in Springfield. The following year they set up an agency in London, under the aegis of one J. L. McKim, but this pioneering venture was short-lived.

In any case, Britain was far from being an ideal market for would-be motor magnates: successive Governments had compounded the asininities of the Locomotives on Highways Act to the point of absurdity by insisting that lightweight motor cars should be subject to the same regulations as adipose traction engines, especially with regard to having a crew of two aboard to attend to the mechanism, plus a third to walk ahead to warn of the vehicle's approach. Thus, those who wished to experiment with self-propelled vehicles had to behave like clandestine criminals, and some of the most able, like Edward Butler, of Newbury, who built an ingenious petroleum tricycle in 1888, abandoned their vehicles in disgust. Frederick Bremer, of Walthamstow, a young cycling enthusiast, who had conceived the idea of fitting a gas engine to his cycle during the 1880s, began building a tiny, Benz-inspired car in 1892, which he completed a couple of years later. He ran it very little, and always after dark, to avoid infringing the law, and eventually abandoned it in his

Left: a Delahaye *vis-a-vis* of 1898 is, again, a fairly conventional design of small car, with a rear-mounted 'slow-running' engine

Above right: an example of the first Daimler to be built in Great Britain; a two-cylinder machine, it was constructed on contemporary Panhard lines and had a four-speed-plus-reverse transmission. Prices ranged from about £360 to £420

Right: an example of original thinking in the motor-car world is shown by this 1898 Egg. The car, which was built in Zurich features variable-ratio belt transmission, which was later to appear in the DAF cars of the 1950s

garden shed, from which he disinterred it some forty years later and presented it to the local museum. It was restored during the 1960s and successfully completed the London–Brighton Veteran Car Run.

John Henry Knight, of Farnham, Surrey, who had built a steam car in the mid 1860s, and who now owned the Reliance Motor Works, builders of stationary engines, had a three-wheeled car constructed there in 1895; in its later, four-wheeled form, it is now preserved in the National Motor Museum at Beaulieu. Knight was understandably bitter about the anti-motoring attitude of the British Government: 'It is this prejudice which has allowed England to be flooded with French and German motor cars, and the sum of money that has crossed the Channel for the purchase of these cars must have been very considerable', he wrote in 1902. 'Money lost to this country, because our legislators refused to allow motor cars to run on English roads! Had it not been for these restrictions, we might have taken the lead in self-propelled carriages, instead of leaving it to the Germans and French. A lost trade is seldom if ever recovered. French-made cars are now to be found in most foreign countries and our colonies, and we may be sure that these makers will do all they can to keep the trade they have obtained—partly through the want of foresight on the part of our House of Commons.'

78

Certainly, the manner in which the Daimler patents were handled in Britain in the early 1890s compared very unfavourably with the situation in France. Frederick Richard Simms, a young mechanical engineer from Warwick, had met Gottlieb Daimler at an exhibition in Germany at the end of the 1880s, and had acquired the Daimler rights for the United Kingdom and its colonies (except Canada). However, he found it difficult to popularise this power unit, due to the restrictive laws which dissuaded most people from attempting to go motoring. So, the first public demonstration of the Daimler engine in Britain took place in 1891 with a motor launch brought to London from Cannstatt, with which trials took place on the Thames at Putney.

Nevertheless, Simms formed the Daimler Motor Syndicate Limited, to handle Daimler products, and an arch was rented at Putney Bridge Railway Station, where the Syndicate's main activity consisted of converting launches to petrol power (around this time three young brothers called Lanchester were also experimenting with a petrol launch powered by their own engine).

In 1895, Simms imported the first Cannstatt-Daimler car to be seen in Britain, and was approached by a syndicate which saw the possibility of vast

profits in the new invention, and were willing to pay a considerable sum of money to acquire the Daimler rights. Prominent in this syndicate was Harry J. Lawson, an engineer turned company promoter. He had received his training in raising large amounts of cash for dubious projects during the bicycle boom of the early 1890s at the hand of the notorious Terah Hooley, whose name had become synonymous with the securing of capital for companies whose potential never quite managed to match the glowing terms of the share prospectus.

Lawson's training as a cycle engineer, and his experience of the cycle boom, convinced him that once the law with regard to motor vehicles was relaxed, a similar boom in self-propelled transportation could occur, and he intended to be the one to profit from such a situation. To which end, he set about systematically acquiring the British rights to all the leading Continental patents (although he also acquired a considerable amount of costly dross along the way), and then launched a manufacturing group to exploit them.

In January 1896, he floated the Daimler Motor Company, and set about publicising the 'new locomotion', especially through the columns of *The Autocar*, one of the very first motoring journals, which had been founded in

November 1895 as the mouthpiece of the Lawson organisation (and which was to prove infinitely more durable than its sponsor).

By continued lobbyings, Lawson persuaded Parliament to change its attitude to the motor car (the Marquis of Salisbury, whose Conservative administration was then in power, subsequently became a keen motorist himself) and to bring in a new Act which freed motor carriages weighing less than three tons from the need to carry two people, and abolished the peripatetic harbinger altogether, raising the overall speed limit to 12 mph.

To commemorate the 'throwing open of the highways', Lawson organised a run from London to Brighton, on 14 November 1896—'Emancipation Day'.

The administration of the event was maybe a little dubious—at least one of the vehicles which reached Brighton did so by courtesy of the Southern Railway Company—but at least Britain was now on the way to being a country with its own indigenous motor-manufacturing industry, and could begin to make up the ground which had been lost to it by the Law.

A policeman casts a wary eye over a red-flag bearer in 1895. The Red Flag Act caused many problems for motorists at that time and, judging by the size of the flag, it is a wonder that anyone noticed it

CHAPTER 5

The Veteran Years of Motoring

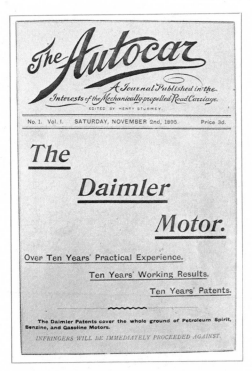

'What is it?

'It is an Autocar.

'Some people call it a motor car.

'It is worked by a petroleum motor.

'The motor is of four horsepower.

'It will run sixty miles with one charge of oil.

'No! It can't explode – there is no boiler.

'It can travel at 14mph.

'Ten to eleven is its average pace.

'It can be started in two minutes.

'There are eight ways of stopping it so it can't run away.

'It is steered with one hand.

'Speed is mainly controlled by the foot.

'It can be stopped in ten feet when travelling at full speed.

'It carries four gallons of oil and sixteen gallons of water.

'The water is to keep the engine cool.

'It costs less than three-farthings a mile to run.

'The car can carry five people.

'It can get up any ordinary hill.

'It was built by the Daimler Motor Company of Coventry and cost £370.

'We have come from John O'Groats House.

'We are going to Land's End.

'We are not record-breaking but touring for pleasure.'

These words, printed on little cards which were handed out to members of the public along the road from John O'Groats to Land's End, were the bare facts behind the first epic drive on British soil. It was, after all, less than a year since 'Emancipation Day', and the infant British motor industry had done little except relieve credulous investors of a considerable amount of money. Indeed, when Henry Sturmey, founding editor of *The Autocar*, set out on this marathon drive in his newly delivered Daimler on 2 October 1897, the Daimler company had been building cars for only a few months. During 1896 and most of 1897, they had been importing Daimler and Panhard cars from the continent, and their first production models were, indeed, straight copies of the contemporary Panhard. They constructed the frames and engines. Their associates, the Motor Manufacturing Company, produced the carriagework, and it was a toss-up whether the finished vehicle was sold as a Daimler or an MMC.

Sturmey's long drive, on which he covered a total of 1600 miles, and took seventeen days (including three days' rest) to cover the 939 miles from furthest north to furthest south, showed the basic reliability of the design. He had no trouble apart from clutch slip brought on by a howling gale which drenched the entire car, its occupants and its mechanism, and the total failure of the inadequate braking system on the descent of the Kirkstone Pass. The car ran away, attaining the suicidal velocity of 30mph, Sturmey avoiding disaster by

sitting tight and steering like a demon. He rammed a bank when the car attempted to repeat the episode a few miles further on!

However, not all the pioneers enjoyed such little trouble – after all, Sturmey was a director of the Daimler Company, and his car had doubtless been assembled with more care than a less-exalted order would have received. Among those who suffered from the awkward temperament of the early tube-ignited motor cars was the author Rudyard Kipling, who in a letter written in 1904 looked back over his motoring experiences with wry amusement: 'I like motoring because I have suffered for its sake. I began seven years ago in the days of tube ignition, when 6 hp was reckoned fair allowance for a touring car, and fifteen miles an hour was something to talk about. My agonies, shames, delays, rages, chills, parboilings, road-walkings, water-drawings, burns and starvations – at which you laughed – all went to make your car today safe and comfortable. If there were no dogs there would be no vivisection, and people would still be treated on the lines of Galen and Avicenna. Any fool can invent anything, as any fool can wait to buy the invention when it is thoroughly perfected, but the men to reverence, to admire, to write odes and erect statues to, are those Prometheuses and Ixions (maniacs, you used to call us) who chase the inchoate idea to fixity up and down the King's Highway with their red right shoulders to the wheel . . .'

However, it was not just mechanically that the pioneers suffered. Harry Lawson's house-of-cards empire started running into trouble within two years of its inception. Most of the components of that empire were housed in the Motor Mills, a converted four-storey cotton-mill building on a thirteen-acre site near the Coventry Canal, which had been acquired in 1896 (and advertised as 'the largest autocar factory in the world . . . for the manufacture of autocars under the Pennington, Daimler and Bollée systems . . . 200 highly skilled workmen' before the Lawson companies had even moved in!). Here at various times were housed Daimler, the Motor Manufacturing Company, the Great Horseless Carriage Company, Humber & Company, the British Motor Syndicate, the Beeston Pneumatic Tyre Company, the Coventry Motor Company . . .

These companies lived, for the most part, a curiously incestuous existence, robbing Peter to pay Paul by complex financial double-shuffles like the 1898 acquisition of the Great Horseless Carriage Company by the British Motor Syndicate, where some £300,000 did a now-you-see-it-now-you-don't vanishing trick to, it seems, the complete satisfaction of 4000 out of 4070 shareholders who did not realise they had been comprehensively gulled . . .

The British Motor Syndicate, indeed, does not appear to have actually *built* anything. True, it issued some very handsome brochures, although half the vehicles in these were total improbabilities and the other half consisted of imported Panhards (which, Lawson generously conceded, with somewhat less than a regard for the truth, had been 'built under British Motor Syndicate Patents'). It did, however, rigorously pursue those hapless individuals who

Another example of Peugeot's early *vis-à-vis* design, albeit with more ornate bodywork than that shown previously. These vehicles had engines of 1018 cc and could attain a speed of 30 kph. This particular example was built in 1892, along with 28 other cars

Left: a scene in Billancourt in 1898; Marcel Renault, on the left, is in the front of a contemporary quadricycle, his brother, Louis, is at the wheel of the car in the centre and Paul Huge is in the prototype Renault. The Renault's power unit is a De Dion 273 cc air-cooled 1¾ hp engine, driving through a three-speed-and-reverse gearbox. In the first six months of trading, the Renaults sold over sixty cars

Above: an early Georges Richard of the late 1890s; it was built on Benz lines and featured belt drive and three forward speeds

Left: this De Dion Quadricycle of 1898 is thought to be the original prototype from the Paris factory
(Château de Grandson, Switzerland)

were presumed to have trespassed against those expensively bought patents.

Take the case of the would-be motor manufacturer from Birmingham against whom the Syndicate took action in 1896: 'An order was immediately made restraining the defendant from proceeding further with the infringement, and a wholesale order was made for the destruction of the parts produced'.

Added Lawson, casually: 'I am sorry to say that the man committed suicide . . . in the circumstances, and on representation being made to me, the directors accepted £150 instead of £600, due under one head of the infringement . . . The case proved that the patents are the absolute property of the Syndicate, and as much property as freehold land'.

This, when the Syndicate was little more than a squatter on the freehold of other men's ideas, was rankest hypocrisy. However, one gets the impression that Lawson was so puffed up with vanity that he could not see the dubiousness of the premises from which he was arguing. His father had been a Methodist minister, and it seems as though Lawson regarded himself as a prophet sent to lead the faithful into the promised land flowing, if not with milk and honey, at least with unlimited share capital.

For all his ridiculous posturings and grandiose schemes, Lawson did attract some able men into his organisation, among the charlatans like E. J. Pennington, the American inventor who matched Harry J. at his own game by selling him the rights to some pretty amazing vehicles, none of which was capable of running more than a short distance without mishap.

Among the gems in Lawson's dross were a young man named Percival Perry, who was later to head the Ford organisation in Europe, and a brilliant electrical engineer, Walter C. Bersey, who had built an electrical omnibus as early as 1888, while he was still in his teens.

Silent and elegant, Bersey's electric carriages caused a great sensation in London (where, indeed, he was issued with the last summons under the old Locomotives on Highways Act). In 1896, a correspondent from the *East Anglian Daily Times* was a passenger on one of Bersey's many demonstration runs: 'Observing a crowd assembled by the Northumberland Avenue entrance of the Grand Hotel, our correspondent found that it was occasioned by a very smart yellow-wheeled Landau, driven by a gentleman whom he afterwards found to be the inventor of the carriage, which it appeared was owned by the Great Horseless Carriage Company . . . our correspondent was at once recognised and invited to take a seat . . . The carriage, therefore, amidst a dense crowd which had already assembled, started with a living freight of no less than seven persons, who anticipated that their driver would take them along the less frequented Thames Embankment. On the contrary, the intrepid Mr Bersey sharply turned round, and with *coeur leger* dashed into the thick of the Strand traffic and into the thick of the light badinage in which the London bus man and cabby are so gifted and fluent.

'Onward we sped, amid cries of "A penny all the way", "Whip behind" and "Where's your 'osses?" – and very instructive it was to observe the sudden surprise of the foot passengers as they realised that the handsome carriage which whisked past them was propelled silently and swiftly without the aid of the patient, nervous, skating quadrupeds to which they were accustomed. As we sped past them, we could easily have thrown one of the early Christmas oranges which were offered us into the gaping mouths of the startled foot passengers.

'Instructive was it to see the problems which the jealous Jehus set our driver by pulling their clumsy buses and cabs across his path, but calm and unmoved our skilful coachman brought his obedient motor carriage to rest within a few inches of the adversary, and when they gave him the slightest chance, flew, without apparent movement, swiftly and resistlessly past every vehicle, all the while having his machine under absolute control.

'Our correspondent, having no business instincts, had no thought beyond the absolute comfort of being propelled with the touch of the tiny lever at will, without effort, and without work or suffering to dumb, patient animals, wheresoever he wills. In his mind's eye, he beholds the streets of the 20th Century free from the crack of the cruel whip, the struggles of terrified animals, with traffic swiftly and silently passing through comely and cleanly streets, emancipated from the tyranny of the merciless "friends of the horse" . . . To show the docility of the electric carriage of towns, our driver assured us he had driven his chairman (the Earl of Winchelsea) and six other directors of the Great Horseless Carriage Company, from Westminster to Ludgate Circus and back (eight miles), through the thick of the Strand traffic, in thirty minutes. Welcome the motor car!'

Certainly, in the early days of motoring, it was the electric car which appealed most to the non-motoring classes. Bersey, who had invented a new type of dry battery which promised a longer service life than the lead-acid type, was obviously convinced that the electric vehicle was superior to its rivals, as he told the *Gentleman's Journal* in 1896: 'The petroleum motor carriage inevitably subjects its occupants to annoyances from which its electric rival is entirely free. The former is subject to excessive vibration, smell, noise and heat. From all these defects the electric car is free. Moreover, the petroleum motor requires an engineer to drive it, that is, if the danger of explosion is to be reduced to a minimum. The electric car is so simple that any coachman may learn to

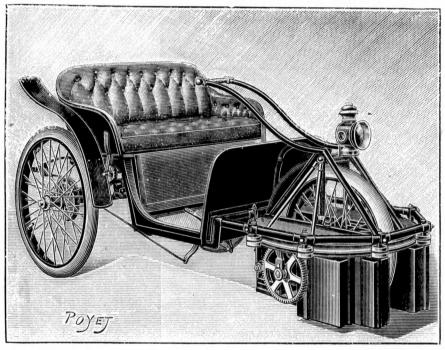

manipulate it in less than half-an-hour!'.

However, although Bersey attempted to popularise the electric by operating a fleet of cabs on the streets of London, the venture was short-lived. Right from the beginning, the major drawbacks which have always bedevilled the electric vehicle were apparent: the cabs could run no more than fifty miles on one charge, and then had to return to a generating station, either to take on fresh batteries (which weighed fourteen cwt!) or to be recharged (which took several hours). And, when the batteries reached the end of their service life, replacements were costly. With this constant need to return to base, no wonder that Americans nicknamed electric vehicles 'homing pigeons'!

The failure of the London Electrical Cab Company was one of the first cracks to appear in the elaborate corporate set-up of the Lawson organisation. Once one component had collapsed, however, the rest were not far behind; it was the affair of the Electric Tramways Construction and Maintenance Company which was to prove Lawson's ultimate downfall. In this instance, Lawson was acting as nominee for his old mentor, Terah Hooley, who, as an undischarged bankrupt, was debarred from trading. This company attracted official attention, however, with the result that Lawson and Hooley were committed for trial, charged with fraudulently creating a 'paper' company for the sole purpose of extracting large sums of money from the public, most of which had found its way into Lawson's pocket. Hooley, accustomed to nothing

Below left: even when most manufacturers had set about building cars which were mostly of a standard form, there were still small companies who carried on building original, and mostly unworkable, designs. Charles Mildé's works built a great deal of electric vehicles, this being a voiturette with 'a detachable power unit'

Below: the first Wolseley four-wheeler; it was built in 1899 and had a 3½ hp engine. A car of this type successfully competed in the 1000 Miles' Trial of 1900

but the best, had hired the brilliant Rufus Isaacs as his advocate, and was eventually acquitted after a three-week hearing, but Lawson was found guilty of false statements and sentenced to twelve months hard labour. So the 'Father of the British Motor Industry' passed from the scene.

In any case, his hold on that industry had been too tenuous to be maintained for long. By persuading the Government to ease the restrictions on the use of motor vehicles on the roads of Britain, Lawson had prised open the floodgate to release a tide of imports and home-produced cars too strong to stem. Brilliant engineers like the Lanchesters were operating outside his organisation, using concepts which were years ahead of those costly 'master patents'.

Only Daimler ultimately survived out of Lawson's original companies, and prospered greatly under its new 'far-seeing and practical Board of Directors'.

Oddly enough, the most popular car of the era, the little belt-driven Benz, did not fall under Lawson's aegis, but was imported into Britain by a wealthy industrialist named Henry Hewetson, who had been one of the first owners of this marque in England, and had turned his hobby into a profitable business. The car was popular because it was relatively cheap, and simple enough to be

worked on by someone who knew absolutely nothing about motor cars. And that was a very necessary thing, as the author Max Pemberton, who first rode on a Benz in 1896, recalled: 'Whenever we met a motor "hung up" by the roadside – and that was uncommon occurrence – be sure that it was a Benz in difficulties with its ignition. Carrying the engines aft, and access to them being by a door which let down in the manner of the flap upon a butcher's cart, the proprietor invariably wore the air of a man who was looking for a mutton chop he had mislaid, and would take some three weeks to find it'.

Despite this reputation for temperament, the Benz was still the world's most popular car. From 67 cars in 1894, output rose steadily until, in 1899, the year in which Benz delivered its 2000th car, production reached a record 572. The basic Benz design was now available in several variants, ranging from the little 3 hp Velo and Comfortable to the twelve-passenger Break, powered by the 15 hp opposed-twin Kontra-Motor announced in 1897. Demand reached its peak in 1900, when 603 cars were delivered, but collapsed the following year, when only 385 cars were ordered, as more modern designs began to undermine the popularity of the Benz.

Karl Benz would not – or could not – come up with a modern design to replace the old faithful, and so his directors first commissioned the company's chief design engineer, Georg Diehl, to produce an up-to-date car with shaft drive and a vertical-twin engine at the front, and then, when this had proved a disappointment, called in the French engineer Marius Barbarou, and commissioned him to design a whole new product range, from single-cylinder runabouts to a 60 hp, four-cylinder racing car. These were not an unqualified success, either, and Barbarou and his assistants resigned in 1904, but a pooling of the lessons learned from these German and French designs created a new range, called the Parsifal. Bitterly offended by the unsurpation of his powers, 'Papa Benz' had already left the company, although he returned briefly to help guide it through a sales crisis. He retired finally in 1906 and, with his sons, set up a little, limited-production car factory in nearby Ladenburg.

However, while it had been current, the belt-drive Benz had been an import-

Above: de Riancey of Levallois-Perret, Seine, built cars between 1899 and 1901. This is their 1899 twin-cylinder model, one of only eleven built
(Château de Grandson, Switzerland)

ant factor in the creation of enthusiasm for motoring. Because it was simple, it was widely copied. Among the legions of Benz imitations were numbered the Star, the Georges-Richard, the Marshall, the Arnold, the Popp, the Hurtu, the Orient Express, the Hewinson-Bell . . .

Some ten years ago, an octogenarian survivor of the earliest days of motoring, who had carried a red flag for the North Oxfordshire Steam Ploughing Company in the late 1880s, and whose cycle repairer father had owned one of only six Hewinson-Bells ever made, recalled that the first time that a car stopped in the little Berkshire town where he lived, such a crowd gathered that he thought a circus was coming!

With so very few motor vehicles in existence, it was hardly surprising that the sight of one caused a sensation. And, right from the very beginning, motor shows were a popular form of public diversion. At the first indoor exhibition of motor vehicles in Britain, at the Stanley Cycle Show in November 1895 (there were five cars on display), visitors were also regaled with another technological sensation, in the shape of a moving picture show on the Edison Kinetoscope. More shows followed, and soon became annual fixtures. One of the best of the

Above: based on the original Renault, this 1899 car has a slightly longer wheelbase than that machine and is powered by an aircooled 1¾ hp De Dion engine, driving the rear wheels via a three-speed gearbox, propeller shaft and differential
(Skokloster Museum, Sweden)

early exhibitions, the Cordingley Show in Islington's Agricultural Hall, got away to a very curious start, for it was originally a sideshow at the Fourth Annual Exhibition of Laundry Machinery in 1896; two years later, the Laundry Exhibition still featured a 'moto-car section', although now this part of the display now contained almost one hundred vehicles instead of the half-dozen or so at the first show. The august *Automotor and Horseless Vehicle Journal* rather sniffily looked down its nose at what it considered a vulgar display: 'If, however, the projectors of this Exhibition are going to continue to hold exhibitions of moto-vehicles, we would suggest the propriety of entirely dissociating them from any purely trade display such as the so-called Laundry Exhibition, because from the public point of view there is nothing in common between the automobilist and the laundry worker . . . we then utterly fail to see how it is possible that any good can result to the cause of automobilism by the association indicated. Moreover, we are by no means satisfied that the time is at all opportune for exhibition of moto-vehicles. It is not two years since the Locomotive on Highways Act was passed, and hence much progress is not to be expected'.

In passing, it should be observed that Stanley Spooner, who edited the *Automotor Journal*, did not learn to drive a car until 1926, when his colleague Edgar Duffield convinced him that the editor of a motor paper really should know how to drive, and persuaded him to buy an Austin Twelve. And that Charles Cordingley, who organised the Agricultural Hall Show (which was soon to rid itself of its bagwash associations, and to survive another decade), also happened to be the publisher of the rival publication *Motor Car Journal*, and that therefore Spooner's barbs might have been loaded with more venom than strictly necessary . . .

However, exhibitions and demonstrations still tended only to reach a localised audience, most of whom were already motoring enthusiasts. There were still millions of people in Britain who had never seen a motor car, and there was still much opposition to the new locomotion from those who made their living in one way or another from horses, and saw the motor vehicle as a threat

to their livelihood. It was, thought Claude Johnson, the go-ahead secretary of the Automobile Club of Great Britain and Ireland (founded in 1897, and elevated to the title of Royal Automobile Club ten years later), time that some concerted demonstration was made to 'advance the automobile movement in the United Kingdom' and, accordingly, set out in November 1899 to survey the route for what would be the greatest trial of motor vehicles ever held in Britain, following a 1080-mile route linking most of the major towns and cities of England and Scotland. At Buxton, recalled G. F. Hodgkinson, Johnson's Daimler began playing up. 'My father gave the car some attention. By that time we had got a supply of petrol from Carless, Capel and Leonard, Limited, which used to arrive four two-gallon tins in a case, and come by rail. Claude Johnson stayed the night with us and then proceeded on his journey,

The 1000-Miles Trial of 1900 was contested by 65 cars, representing most of the leading manufacturers of the day. Here the Hon C. S. Rolls and S. F. Edge contemplate Edge's 8 hp Napier. Edge was the company's first distributor and the 8 hp was their first complete car. It featured a front-mounted 2.4-litre twin-cylinder engine, four-speed gearbox, armoured wood chassis and chain drive

The Decauville 'Voiturelle' was a huge success at
the turn of the century. The four-wheeled car
was powered by a rear-mounted, air-cooled,
$3\frac{1}{2}$ hp, vertical-twin engine. It is memorable as
the first petrol-driven production car to use
independent front suspension

and my father was appointed chief marshal and timekeeper for that section
of the trial.'

Young Hodgkinson, who seventy years later was still an active participant
in Veteran Car Club events, had a part to play in the 1000-Miles Trial, too.
'These "engines of death" were not permitted to come through the main
street of Buxton, because Buxton was a town which really catered for ailing
people – rheumatism, arthritis, sciatica and all the other complaints – so it
was my job to marshal the cars at the entrance to Buxton by a secondary road
so that they did not come through the main part of the town. This I was doing
with a $\frac{3}{4}$ horsepower Werner motor cycle with the engine mounted on the
handlebars and driving the front wheel by a flat belt. It was very high and very
liable to skid, and you could quite easily come off . . . When the Werner went
out of commission, then it was my duty to pilot the cars on a pedal cycle.'

A total of 83 entries was received for the Trial, and 65 of these actually
competed in the event, setting off on their trip round Britain from Hyde Park
Corner on 23 April 1900.

Most of the leading designs were represented, with a preponderance of
English Daimler and MMC cars; there were several Panhards, notably the
new 12hp model belonging to the Hon C. S. Rolls. This was the most powerful
vehicle in the Trial, capable of some 40mph on the flat, although it was run
pretty close by the 8hp Napier, the first complete car built by this London
engineering firm, and driven by S. F. Edge, a former racing cyclist, whose

bombastic flair would soon put Napier in the forefront of the world's motor manufacturers. Other British car makers represented were Wolseley (makers of sheep-shearing machinery, whose chief engineer, Herbert Austin, was investigating the possibilities of motor-car manufacture) and Lanchester. There was, too, a representative cross-section of imported models: Panhards and De Dions from France, Benz and Orient Express cars from Germany, Locomobile and Brown-Whitney steamers from America.

The crowds who turned out to watch the event more than met the organising club's expectations. 'In the cities and towns, the footpaths and roads have been so densely crowded with spectators that only the narrowest passage remained through which the motor vehicles had to pass. At every cross road in the country there were knots of on-lookers from the neighbouring villages, the parson and his daughters on bicycles, the country squire on his horse, the old dowager safely ensconsed in her landau, coaching parties enjoying champagne lunches at the road side, and cyclists in legions. In villages, the children were given a "whole holiday", and were ranged on the school walls and cheered each motor as it passed. The confidence of the spectators in the control of their

Gottlieb Daimler is justly acknowledged as the father of the petrol engine. Daimler's early research culminated in his first high-speed engine in 1883 and his first purpose built car in 1889. His early cars were the basis for a multitude of copies throughout the world. The car below was built in 1899, the year in which Daimler introduced his first four-cylinder engine

vehicles was, although flattering, decidedly embarrassing, for the crowds
assembled at the bottoms of hills left a lane of barely seven-feet wide through
which the vehicles had to pass at high speed. The police seemed to share with
the public a keen enjoyment in seeing vehicles at thirty miles an hour, and
sympathised with the rebukes which the crowd addressed to drivers who failed
to go at top speed. Generally, the public looked on the passage of the motors
as they do the passage of a fire-engine, namely, as a fine inspiring sight which
makes the pulse beat faster and satisfies a craving for excitement.'

Seventy years later, one of the mechanics on the run recalled. 'Even if you
broke down on a remote road, while you were doing a repair crowds of people
would appear apparently from nowhere and gather round you so closely that
you could not get on with the job.'

Breakdowns (at least of a major sort) were remarkably rare, although some
of the more eccentric vehicles on the run proved somewhat accident prone.
'At Bath and Bristol, the Simms Motor Wheel skidded in the tramlines and
upset, the man being thrown out. He got things right to a certain extent and
arrived at the Bristol Drill Hall in good time. After a somewhat adventurous

journey, during which the driver behaved with great courage and pertinacity,
the vehicle disappeared after Carlisle.'

Some of these less successful vehicles, too, finished in much the same
condition as the legendary Irishman's shovel: 'Motor Manufacturing Co's
tricycle . . . new frame and wheels were substituted at Manchester, and a
new motor was fitted to frame at Nottingham. This tricycle has since been
withdrawn from Competition by the makers'.

Most of what a contemporary writer referred to as 'a legacy of annoyance
and expense' was caused either by the imperfect design of the vehicles or by
the sheer mechanical ignorance of their drivers, although some of the contestants
in the Trial displayed a remarkable ingenuity, as one of the last survivors of
the event, E. A. Rose, recalled at the end of the 1960s. 'Just before the speed
trials in Welbeck Park, the car I was on as mechanic, the Marshall Dogcart
driven by J. J. Mann, broke the drive to the water pump. It was driven by

friction from the flywheel, and we carried out a wonderful repair. We got a cork and two pennies, drilled a hole through the cork and the pennies, shoved them on the spindle in some way and were able to get drive to the pump. We were hours getting the pump going, and we did a rotten time in the speed trials . . . The Marshall was a belt-driven car, and you got this terrible slip on the belts. They stretched when they got wet, and you spent your time cutting and rivetting and putting resin on them to make them grip!'.

Later in the Trial, Rose transferred to Alfred Harmsworth's Daimler Parisian Phaeton, driven by Sir Hercules Langrishe. Although 'Herky's' mount was a better-engineered machine than the little Marshall, it was obviously not entirely trouble-free: 'It had two cylinders, four seats and six horsepower. It was listed as weighing 16 cwt, but it felt more like two tons when you were pushing it! It was an unusual car; it had about ten lubricators on the dashboard, and the mechanic had to sit on the floor, with his feet just off the ground, ready to jump out if the car stopped on a hill. It was his job to see that the drip-feed lubricators did their work – so many drops per minute.

'Those Daimler cars were devils . . . for ignition, they had a platinum tube

In 1900, 'Voiturettes', a name coined by Léon Bollée for his own small car, proliferated. The open car below is a Quérey and the elegantly fringed model is a Levenn. The Levenn, of which this was the only style available, used an early example of friction disc transmission

The French Clément-Bayard company was founded by one of the motoring world's great early promoters, Adolphe Clément, who made his fortune from bicycles and pneumatic tyres before moving into car manufacture. The car shown is a rear-engined voiturette of 1900. It was powered by a $2\frac{1}{4}$ hp de Dion engine driving the rear wheels. The cars were also known as Clement-Gladiators
(Château de Grandson, Switzerland)

inserted into the cylinder head, and below the part protruding from the cylinder was a sort of metal cup which you filled with methylated spirits or petrol, put a lighted match to, and when the tube became red-hot, you then started your car. People often used to set the damned thing on fire!'.

C. S. Roll's Panhard had both tube and electric ignition, but because the tube system was, although crude, more reliable than the primitive electric ignition, which at that stage relied on temperamental dry batteries (Bosch had only just invented the magneto), it was more frequently in use. Unfortunately for Rolls, 'Misfortunes seldom come singly, and it was therefore in the correct order of things that when Mr Rolls, between Keswick and Carlisle, had finished wrestling with a spiteful horseshoe which had punctured his front tyre, he should find the bonnet of his car in a blaze through a defective burner'. But this was nothing to Rolls's earlier escapade on the descent of the notorious Cat and Fiddle Hill when, taking a corner at high speed, he contrived to lose both his passenger and most of the luggage over the side of the car! Fortunately, Rolls managed to stay on board.

Climbing Dunmail Raise, the clutch of the 8hp Napier failed, and the car

Even the world's first mass-produced car, Ford's legendary Model T, relied on the advertiser's art to sell it to the public. This romantic scene appeared in 1915. The Trafford Park, Manchester, works where the 'T' was advertised at £135 closed in 1931 when production moved to Dagenham

A hybrid from the early part of this century was this Dumont. It featured an ingenious form of transmission, which employed a varying diameter drum and belts. Initial power is by a large single-cylinder engine

ran away backwards, as the brakes did not work in reverse. Pushing his passengers out of the car, S. F. Edge steered the car to safety, no mean feat when you considered the undulating nature of the old road up Dunmail.

Quite the equal of this remarkable act was the ingenious way in which Monty Grahame-White overcame what could have been disastrous damage to his car. 'While attending to an adjustment, the tiller being temporarily in the hands of a passenger, Mr Grahame-White's car tried to jump a ditch and a hedge, resulting in the steering gear being broken. This occurred fourteen miles north of Alnwich, with 52 miles still to cover before reaching the Newcastle control. Towing or pushing would, with most people, have been an easy(?) solution to the difficulty, but Mr Grahame-White would have none of either, and determined to steer the vehicle with his foot, which he successfully accomplished by standing on the offside step, guiding the wheels with the hollow of his right foot on to the outside axle box, and thus wise did he travel right through to Newcastle, making his average speed for the day ten miles per hour. The only person who seemed to think nothing of the feat was Mr Grahame-White.'

Difficulties of quite a different kind were experienced by the journalist A. J. Wilson, who wrote for the cycling press under the pseudonym 'Faed' (he was stone deaf, and merely spelt his disability backwards as a penname). Much of the power of his Ariel tricycle was lost through an improperly closed compression tap. He could not hear the tell-tale hissing that indicated this fault, and just pedalled harder on hills to supplement what seemed to be a particularly unenthusiastic engine. He must have had legs like piston-rods, for the Automotor Journal reported: 'The time of Mr A. J. Wilson on his Ariel for Taddington Hill is remarkable, but it must be borne in mind that Mr Wilson's skill in pedalling is a factor in the case, which an ordinary flabby mortal under like conditions would have to allow for. When the longer hills had to be negotiated, Mr. Wilson's state of collapse was a thing to be seen, and not easily forgotten'.

For the record, Wilson pedalled up Taddington at an average speed of 18.91mph, compared with Rolls's Panhard, which achieved 17.77mph under full power . . .

Eventually, the competitors returned to London, and the Thousand Miles' Trial was brought to a successful conclusion. Then, as now, some manufacturers treated a minor class win as the occasion for vast, shrieking headlines in the motor press, a trend which offended the Automotor Journal: 'The public will be induced, by misleading assertions, to purchase vehicles which will disgust them once and for all with automobilism. The natural argument will be that if this is the sort of car that was able to be "first everywhere", a day spent in assisting an itinerant knife grinder now and again by way of relaxation would be equally exhilarating and less expensive'.

The Trial had done immense good in promoting goodwill for the motor car throughout England, although a few entrenched diehards still fulminated against it. At least one bastion of the Law was a staunch automobilist, though – Lord Kingsburgh, the Lord Justice Advocate of Scotland, who was a passenger in one of the competing cars. Summing up the achievements of the Trial, he concluded: 'One of these vehicles, going twelve to fourteen miles an hour, could be absolutely pulled up in less than its own length. That was an element of safety unattainable with horses . . . there have been several breakdowns, and some cars have been dropped, but in almost every case – indeed, in every case – the fault was not with the motor machinery, but because the coach-builder had not understood the proper strength of wheels or axles or springs to provide for such vehicles. Automobilism, in my opinion, is not only a sport, but provision for locomotion in this country which is needed and will be efficient'.

If in England motoring was just beginning to throw off the shadow of the Lawsonian era, American manufacturers were now faced with a far more pernicious patent monopoly, which was to create news, not only in the motoring world, for a long time to come.

Below: Britain's first motor race took place in 1900 on the Welbeck Abbey Estate of the Duke of Portland. The private roads of the estate provided a perfect location for the early competition, away from the restrictive laws of the day. The fastest car managed an average speed of 42 mph, while the slowest trailed home at 25 mph. The competitors are seen here preparing for the start.

Right: the Type One Vinot et Déguignand built in Puteaux, Seine, in 1901. This car featured a 1½-litre vertical-twin engine rated at 5½ hp. An unusual feature of this car was its vertical gearchange gate

George Baldwin Selden, having neatly bided his time until the first experimental cars were running on American roads, published his 1879 patent in 1895, and then claimed that all gasoline-driven vehicles developed since 1879 were infringements of that patent. He had not, let it be added, actually built a car to prove that his invention was practicable, although he had at one stage attempted to raise the capital to do so, only to frighten off the potential investor with the remark: 'Jim, you and I will live to see more carriages on Main Street run by motors than are now drawn by horses'.

However, the delay had proved fortuitous for Selden. By waiting until 1895, he had gained the maximum effective life for his patent, although at first he lacked the money to enforce it. In 1899, he began negotiations to raise the necessary capital, and was on the point of closing negotiations with five Wall Street bankers who were prepared to put up $250,000 when fate – and a gullible patent aιorney named Herman Cuntz – stuck a far bigger fish on his hook, in the shape of the Pope Manufacturing Company, America's leading cycle manufacturer. They were considering going into car manufacture, and asked Cuntz to investigate any patents which might affect this multi-million-dollar venture. He had already come across the Selden patent, and attempted to proclaim its merits to his employers . . . whose engineering experts dismissed it at once. But ex-Navy Secretary William Whitney, head of the consortium which was providing the capital for the Pope venture, proved a more receptive audience for Cuntz and, on learning that Selden would rather his patent be administered by a car company than by investors, decided to make a deal, and took an option on Selden's patent until January 1900, in which the Pope-Whitney interests were given a 'definitive licence' – in effect an assignment of the patent – in exchange for $10,000 plus a percentage of any royalties collected.

The patent's validity having been attested by a British 'expert' named Dugald Clerk (who, although he knew a great deal about two-stroke gas engines, was far from being an authority on motor cars), the Pope-Whitney group – the Columbia and Electric Vehicle Company – was reformed as an $18,000,000 corporation, the Electric Vehicle Company, and set about prosecuting the manufacturers who were, in all innocence, transgressing against Selden's patent.

With its vast finances, the Electric Vehicle Company had little difficulty in steam-rolling the token resistance put up by most American manufacturers into the ground, and by September 1902 the motor manufacturers were ready to negotiate. An Association of Licenced Automobile Manufacturers was set up, which paid 2/5 of 2.5 per cent of the retail price of each car to the EVC, retained 2/5 of that amount for its own coffers, and paid the remaining 1/5 to Selden (who seems to have paid half his share to the manager of the ALAM!). Not all the Association's concerns were monetary, however, for it made a genuine attempt to create uniform standards throughout the motor industry, establishing standard sizes for screw threads, copper and steel tubes, and many other common fittings. Moreover, association members could obtain access to all the latest technical information free of charge, enjoyed a standardised system of contracts, guarantees and agreements, and had their products featured in the ALAM's annual *Handbook of Gasolene Automobiles*, which claimed that 'each manufacturer or importer conducts his business entirely independent of the other and, of course, in open competition (although the ALAM also seems to have existed as a price-fixing ring)'. Customers were assured, too, that buying a car manufactured under the Selden Patent was a 'guarantee . . . that secures to the purchaser freedom from the annoyance and expense of litigation because of infringement of this patent'.

However, as ALAM also chose who could be licensed, its activities represented a brake on free enterprise, and Henry Ford (who had founded the Ford Motor Company in the summer of 1903 after a couple of false starts) decided that it had nothing to offer him. His aim, after all, was to produce a $500 motor car which anyone could afford, and the average price of ALAM-built cars was $1382.

The first truly popular American car had been the little Locomobile steamer, designed by the Stanley brothers, which had enjoyed a great vogue – despite

Below left: There are few more famous names in the history of motoring than that of Henry Ford. Ford's vast manufacturing operation is based on a background of inspired innovation which was Henry's best known personal characteristic. The company began operations, shakily at first, in 1903 and by the end of that year they were firmly established. Ford himself died in 1947, aged 84, but the company carries on to the present with a strong family involvement

Below: The 1901 Oldsmobile Curved Dash is regarded as the world's first mass-production car. It had a single-cylinder 1.6-litre engine and chain-drive. In 1903, Whitman and Hammond drove a Curved Dash from San Francisco to New York
(Skokloster Museum, Sweden)

its many design shortcomings – in the period 1900–1903; it had been followed by the 'curved-dash' Oldsmobile, but even this fairly basic single-cylinder gas-buggy sold for $650 (and its makers were members of the ALAM).

At first, Ford found it impossible to rival these prices – his first car, the twin-cylinder Model A, sold for $850 – and production got off to a shaky start; soon, the company was courting bankruptcy. Then came the first order, from a Chicago doctor named Pfennig, which was followed in quick succession by a flood of sales. On 11 July 1903, the Ford Motor Company had been down to $223.65, and could not meet its obligations, by 20 August there was a balance of $23,060.67 in the bank.

Said Henry Ford: 'The business went along almost as by magic – the cars gained a reputation for standing up'. In its first year of operation, the company sold a million dollars' worth of cars, establishing itself high in the ranks of the Detroit motor-manufacturing companies, which included Cadillac, Olds and Packard. Already, the city was becoming the motor capital of America, with fourteen companies assembling 11,180 cars in 1905, as well as component and coachwork manufacturers.

The growth of the American car industry had been phenomenal: in 1899, an estimated 57 companies employing a total of 2241 people had been involved in the manufacture of motor vehicles. By 1904, the total number of companies had risen to 178, employing over 12,000 workers, and producing over thirty million dollars' worth of automobiles.

At the end of 1904, Ford began to transfer production to a new, purpose-built factory on Picquette and Beaubien Avenues, and by the following spring, output had risen to a peak of 25 cars a day, although prices still remained at the $800–$1000 mark for the best-selling Fords, while the $2000 Model B, produced at the insistence of Ford's wealthy coal-merchant backer, Alexander Malcomson, was selling rather badly (Ford, wanting the freedom to make his own decisions, would eventually buy out all the other partners in his business, thereby achieving complete control).

F. L. Smith, who provided the backing for Oldsmobile, was also convinced that there was a future for the expensive car, even though sales of the little Olds runabout had risen from 4000 in 1904 to 6500 in 1905, and forced R. E. Olds and the team who had made the runabout successful to resign. He then

promoted the high-priced models, with the inevitable result that the company sank deep into debt.

There was a shadow over the Ford success, however, for in 1904 the ALAM had begun proceedings against the company for infringement of the Selden Patent. The young company confidently stated, however: 'To dealers, importers, agents and users of our gasoline automobiles . . . we will protect you against any prosecution for alleged infringements of patents'.

Furthermore, Ford was confident of victory: 'The Selden Patent is not a broad one, and if it was, it is anticipated. It does not cover any practicable machine, no practicable machine can be made from it, and never was, as far as we can ascertain. It relates to that form of carriage called a FORE Carriage. None of that type have ever been in use; all have been failures'.

And, indeed, the Selden case did end in victory for Ford, but the hearing dragged on until January 1911, and involved legal costs of over a million dollars. Selden's patent, although judged valid, was ruled to apply only to vehicles powered by the obsolete Brayton engine: everything else was exempt. By that time, too, the patent had nearly run its course, and would have expired anyway

Left: A 1901 Rochet-Schneider. The French company had a tendency to copy other manufacturers' designs, the model here being a Panhard type, but made up for a lack of originality by sound engineering (Château de Grandson, Switzerland)

Right: A 1902 CGV (Charron, Giardot et Voight) 3.3-litre. After 1906, the cars were called simply Charrons

Above left: A 1901 Baker Electric with a ¾ hp motor giving a top speed of 17 mph over a fifty-mile range

Below: The makers of the very handsome 1903 Prunel Phaeton proudly boasted that, apart from the engine, every part of their cars was made by themselves

Below right: Vera Francis Nicholl stands proudly by her single-cylinder 1903 Renault. The car was given to her as a wedding present by her father, F. H. Butler

within eighteen months. The case established Henry Ford as a popular folk hero: the David who had slain a monopolistic Goliath, and further enhanced his reputation as a builder of cars for the masses.

Both in Europe and America, manufacturers were paying increasing attention to the 'motor for the man of moderate means'; on the forefront of this movement was the De Dion-Bouton Company, of Puteaux, near Paris, whose proprietors, the Comte de Dion and Georges Bouton, had originally collaborated, in the 1880s, in the production of light steam vehicles. Since the mid 1890s, however, they had become increasingly interested in the high-speed petrol motor, initially used on lightweight tricycles and then, since 1899, in voiturettes, starting with the rear-engined Type D, with its curious *vis-à-vis* coachwork, and then in more orthodox models with the single-cylinder power unit at the front, under a coal-scuttle bonnet. Additionally, engines were produced in unprecedented numbers for other manufacturers all over Europe, the speed of operation being so rapid that any engine which failed to perform properly on the test bench was not rebuilt but simply dismantled to give spare parts for other units.

'In point of numbers', wrote Roger H. Fuller in 1902, 'the firm of De Dion-Bouton et Cie, of Puteaux, Seine, are the largest manufacturers of the modern light automobile, there being over five hundred of their voiturettes and light cars now in use in the British Isles, and the firm have sold 26,000 of their motors from ¾ hp to 10 hp. It is, therefore, not surprising that dozens of motor-car manufacturers have adopted the De Dion-Bouton motors for their cars, thereby being undoubtedly assisted over one of the most difficult problems of automobile manufacture. I counted no fewer than fifteen exhibitors at the recent Automobile Show who had adopted the De Dion-Bouton motor . . . A De Dion is generally admitted to be the easiest of all cars to learn, and is very suitable for ladies to manage. A beginner can hardly do much damage to the mechanism by ignorance and incompetence; in fact, I have often heard the remark made that the De Dion 4½ hp car is almost "foolproof"'.

However, at a selling price of 300 guineas, the 4½ hp De Dion was, although popular, still only within the reach of a fairly well lined purse; nor was it, as a 1902 diary proves, entirely 'foolproof'. 'Left Menai 9 am. Called at Bangor for a new tyre, could not get one; ran over a sheep; at Bethesda changed gears so rapidly that I broke the connecting rod of the steering gear; being at the top of a long hill there was nothing for it but to go down the hill backwards in the hope of getting to the bottom alive and finding a blacksmith; this was done; slate quarry workers on strike and much interested in car; after wait of 2½ hours blacksmith finished his job; but the product of his labour was 1/16th of an inch too small; waited another 2½ hours; this time successful result. Going round a sharp corner nearly ran into a big lake; down a steep hill in Bettws-y-

Coed skidded on slippery surface and ran into front steps of hotel on my right; fielder suggested the back yard would be a cheaper and quicker way of entering. It was getting dark and I was getting so fed up and weary that I determined to sleep in the next available building, it was at Pentre Voelas, and it was a good thing for me that I did so. The next morning I had not gone more than a mile before I came to an absolutely rectangular corner going up a steep hill; there was a little wooden notice with the word "Danger" on it; had I continued in the dark of the night before I never could have seen it, and we should have been precipitated over the edge to the bottom of the ravine. Total distance accomplished – twenty-five miles'.

Part of the trouble, of course, was that the men who were adopting automobilism were, for the most part, mechanical illiterates, with absolutely no idea how their machine worked; it is on record that the owner of a De Dion living in North Wales telegraphed the company's London depot in some distress, saying that he was quite unable to start his car. Fortunately, a friend's mechanic diagnosed the trouble, otherwise De Dion would have had to have sent a man on a two-and-a-half day, 480-mile round trip just to discover that

the motorist had forgotten to turn on the petrol tap of his car!

An additional hazard in Britain was the attitude of the police, who enforced the open road speed limit of 12 mph with severity, often prosecuting motorists on the flimsiest of trumped-up evidence . . . *The Autocar* published a road map each week, showing the location of all the latest speed traps, and a cycle patrol operating on the Brighton road by the London motor agents Jarrott and Letts in the summer of 1905 grew into the Automobile Association, whose scouts warned motorists of looming police traps by failing to salute and by wearing their lapel badges red side out instead of white. In many cases, prosecution of motorists was totally unjustified, but there was a hard core of 'scorchers' who antagonised the public by the speed with which they hurtled along the dusty highways. These adventurers not only took their own lives in their hands, but those of other roadusers, too, and they usually deserved the punishment they received.

They had been encouraged by the introduction of cars that were increasingly powerful and expensive. The manufacturers of such vehicles at first gained extra power by adding more cylinders, doubling up from two to four, then by

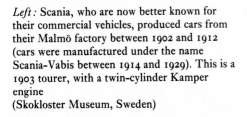

Left: Scania, who are now better known for their commercial vehicles, produced cars from their Malmö factory between 1902 and 1912 (cars were manufactured under the name Scania-Vabis between 1914 and 1929). This is a 1903 tourer, with a twin-cylinder Kamper engine
(Skokloster Museum, Sweden)

Right: The first company to successfully market a six-cylinder motor car was Napier. This is an example of their 1903 24 hp

increasing the capacity of those cylinders. In an age when there was no testing of drivers' abilities at the wheel, small wonder that the owners of such juggernauts often succeeded in reducing their vehicles to a heap of metallic flinders. But, wrote the famous artist, Sir Hubert von Herkomer (who instituted an international reliability trial which bore his name) in 1902: 'The real weak point in the present state of motoring is not to be found in the car, but in the present supply of drivers. You see mere boys driving – boys who can have had no training or experience . . . the present law insists on a licence, but does not insist on any qualification for which this serious licence is granted. Anyone, blind or lame, can get it. To prove which, *The Autocar* obtained a licence for a blind beggar, whom they then photographed, sitting in a car, with a card labelled 'blind' hung round his neck.

The epitome of high-powered cars was the Mercedes, originally developed by Wilhelm Maybach out of the succession of rapid Cannstatt-Daimlers evolved for the rich Herr Jellinek and put into limited production (and mainly sold by Jellinek to his wealthy acquaintances, one of whom, Baron Henri de Rothschild, recalled: 'I drove to Stuttgart to take over the car, and found it by no means elegant, but the price was certainly proportional to the weight, its great size creating anything but a favourable impression amongst people who preferred the light carriages of 8–12 horsepower constructed by the French makers'). Out of this ponderous machine, Maybach evolved the lithe and elegant Mercedes; the contract to produce for Emil Jellinek the first batch of this 'car of the day after tomorrow' – thirty cars worth over half-a-million marks – was signed less than a month after the death of Gottlieb Daimler in March 1900, and the new model made its début at Nice the following year, causing an immediate sensation with its advanced technology – pressed-steel frame, mechanically operated inlet valves, low-tension magneto ignition and selective 'gate' for gear-changing.

Within a few years, there was a considerable market for such expensive machinery, as the motoring author A. B. Filson Young noted: 'One would think that there cannot be a great many people anxious to spend from £1500 to £3000 on a motor car. Nevertheless, the number of cars of this type bought in England and America is astonishing, and when one considers the complaints of "bad times" which seems to have become habitual with a certain class it is not a little surprising to realise that more and more money is being spent daily on luxuries – among them that most elaborate and costly form of luxury, the high-powered, sumptuously fitted motor car, which as a means of travel has in the few years of its life eclipsed the railway train in speed, comfort and convenience'.

Provided then, that you had the money, this was the dawn of the first golden

Below left: A scene at the Daimler factory in 1900 with a whole range of cars in various stages of completion. It all looks rather haphazard and, indeed, it must have been difficult working out which car was where. Henry Ford was to later make things easier with his mass-production techniques

Below: 1904 saw the production of this tricycle, the Larroumet et Lagarde 'Va Bon Train' (Château de Grandson, Switzerland)

age of motoring, especially, as Filson Young remarked, in France, with the 'vista of roads that lie visible before you for five or six miles, straight as a gun barrel, empty as the blue sky – these are conditions at which a speed of fifty or sixty miles an hour can be kept up through mile after mile, not only with pleasure and convenience, but with perfect safety'. In direct contrast were the rolling roads of England, where, as you went to Birmingham by way of Beachy Head, you would find 'every mile had its score of lurking dangers, its sudden corners, high hedges, crowded villages, busy farmhouses, sheep and cattle, hens and dogs, children shouting and playing in the roads, heavy wagons creaking along on the wrong side, with the driver dozing on his load. Obviously, the English roads could be very dangerous and the British driver had to be far more aware than any in France.

'On the French road there was nothing to do but open wide the throttle, advance the spark and sit and sing like a bird while the engine sent you swooping and skimming as fast as a swallow over the world . . .'

It must have been exhilarating driving in the early part of the century with just you, the car and the open road . . .

CHAPTER 6

Edwardian Elegance and Excellence

Left: The American Cameron company had no less than eight changes of identity in its nineteen-year history. This is a 1904 example built by the James Brown machine corporation of Pawtucket
(Château de Grandson, Switzerland)

Within a decade the motor car had progressed from a stuttering novelty into a reliable means of transport, and the underpowered creepabout of the 1890s had been supplanted by vehicles that were high-powered, fast, well appointed . . . and expensive, both to buy and to operate.

'I heard', confided Max Pemberton in 1907, 'of the owner of a 100 hp Rochet-Schneider who offered a great firm of tyre makers £1000 a year to keep his car supplied in tyres, and met with but a chilly response . . . If men will drive engines of 60, 80, or 100 hp, they must foot the bill and foot it cheerfully. Even the possessor of a 40 hp car, should he make considerable use of it, will find himself £400 or £500 out of pocket at least at the end of his first year . . . Motoring in its speedier phase is one of the costliest pursuits we can follow – racing and yachting apart.

'I have taken the account books of three careful friends of my own – each owner of a 40 hp car – and I find that their expenditure upon tyres for the year just ending has been £580, £667 and £700.'

Or, in 1970s terms, an annual tyre bill of around £7000 . . . and that, as a 45 hp Hotchkiss proved on an observed Royal Automobile Club trial in mid 1907 could be over a mileage as low as 15,000, during which the Hotchkiss devoured the astonishing total of 46 tyres costing £12–£13 each.

Ironically enough, the Hotchkiss had a six-cylinder engine, a pattern claimed to be easier on tyres than big four-cylinder models – and a pattern, moreover, which had been established by the British motor industry, which was at last able to compete in terms of quality with the leading Continental manufacturers.

'In December of 1904,' recalled a correspondent to *Country Life* two years later, 'I wandered in the Grand Palais inspecting many motor-cars with an interest and delight to which there was but one drawback. Many cars were present from many countries, but to an Englishman, commercially as well as sentimentally patriotic, it seemed that not nearly enough of them were of English origin. Still wandering, I came across rather an insignificant little stand occupied by two gentlemen, a two-cylinder voiturette chassis of 10 hp, three sets of two cylinders of the same casting mounted on a base chamber, and a handsome body mounted on a frame, but lacking the organs or mechanism essential to life and motion. The gentlemen, it seems, were more interesting than the machines, for they were the Hon. C. S. Rolls, already well known as a racing driver, and Mr Claude Johnson, who, as the first secretary of the Automobile Club of Great Britain and Ireland, had, by universal consent, proved himself to be an organiser of the most remarkable ability . . . I ventured to ask what the special and characteristic features of that car might be, whether it contained any new and striking departure, and so forth. The answer impressed itself deeply on my memory. It was to the effect that this was an effort to combine in one engine all the best features of many engines, which seemed an eminently sensible if not very original method of reaching a good practical result . . . It was with some pleasure, but not with any high anticipation, that I accepted an offer from Mr Rolls to try a similar two-cylinder car then and there on the Champs-Elysees. It was, in a single word, a revelation . . . Never before had I been in a car which made so little noise, vibrated so little, ran so smoothly, or could be turned about so easily and readily in a maze of traffic. Indeed, the conclusion that I almost reached there and then was that the car was too silent and ghostlike to be safe . . . When, wandering again through the Grand Palais in 1906, I came across a six-cylinder Rolls-Royce in one of the galleries, the extraordinary measure of progress which had been achieved in the interval, and the shortness of the interval, came upon me in a flash, and struck me "all of a heap", as the saying goes'.

In 1906, the 30 hp Rolls-Royce six-cylinder model defeated a four-cylinder Martini in a reliability trial which received the popular title 'the Battle of the Cylinders'.

Shortly afterwards, J. E. Vincent drove from London to Norfolk in the victorious Rolls-Royce: 'There was no reason in life against a good spin at top speed except that superstitious regard for the letter of the law which not one man in a thousand really has. The car simply flew forward; the speed indicator

marked 25, 30, 35, 40, 45 and even 50 miles an hour; the road seemed to open wide to our advent, to stretch out its arms, so to speak, to embrace us; the motion, smooth, swifter and swifter still, even as the flight of the albatross, that stirreth not his wings, and absolutely free from vibration, was, in a single word divine'.

And the 30 hp Rolls-Royce was supposed not to have been a particularly successful model . . . In fact, after only half-a-dozen had been produced, the 30 hp was replaced by the illustrious 40/50 hp six, which was soon christened the 'Silver Ghost' after the most famous of the early examples produced, which in 1907 was subjected to a 15,000 mile trial by the RAC. It had already travelled from Bexhill, in Sussex, to Edinburgh and Glasgow, using only direct-drive third gear and overdrive top, at an average fuel consumption of 20.8 miles per gallon – not bad for a 7.4-litre engine!

On the sixth day of the 15,000-mile test, a petrol tap vibrated shut, bringing the Silver Ghost to its only involuntary stop (apart from tyre trouble) of the entire run. At the end of the 15,000 miles, the RAC officials stripped down the car to see which parts, in their opinion, should be renewed in order to return the

Left: Peugeot's type 818 torpedo of 1906; this four-cylinder, twelve-horsepower machine was built in the same year as Robert Peugeot began building his Lion-Peugeot machines, having previously constructed motor cycles; the two companies were reunited in 1911, although the 'Lion' part of the name survived until 1913

Right: An experimental Peugeot quadricycle of 1905, in which the driver sat on a saddle behind the passengers and on top of the rear engine
(Peugeot collection)

Rolls-Royce to 'as-new' condition: 'The engine was passed as perfect; the transmission throughout was passed as perfect; one or two parts of the steering details showed very slight wear, perhaps one-thousandth part of an inch, and the committee condemned these as not being "as good as new"; they also required the small universal joints in the magneto drive to be replaced, and the water-pump to be repacked; and this was all that was required for making the car equal to new after a mileage which many cars do not cover in three years' work'.

Some of the credit, however, should be given to the car's mechanics and chauffeur, for during the trial, it spent 40 hours 'in the motor houses . . . for repairs, replacements, and adjustments'. Concluded the RAC: 'The running of the car was excellent, except for a slight tendency to misfiring at low speeds during a part of the trial. The car (as a whole) and the engine (in particular) were exceptionally quiet (especially on the third speed, direct drive) and free from vibration. The springs, however, at the back of the car were scarcely stiff enough for the load carried. The front footboards became uncomfortably warm'.

The results of the Trial proved the built-in durability of the 40/50 hp Rolls-Royce (due mainly to Henry Royce's early training as a locomotive engineer), and established this well-constructed, if scarcely innovative, car as a claimant for the coveted title of 'The Best Car in the World'.

But the Rolls-Royce hadn't started the six-cylinder trend; that honour belonged to the British Napier company. Although Spyker in Holland and Automotrice in France had constructed six-cylinder cars before Napier, it was the British firm which had established the configuration as a production model, thanks to the remarkable selling powers of Selwyn Francis Edge. As a motoring writer with the pen name 'Auriga' noted in 1907: 'Mr S. F. Edge has shown, indeed, a rare and almost unique combination of the abilities, mental and physical, and of the spirit of enterprise tempered by prudence, which is exactly calculated to carry a man to the highest place with the automobile movement'.

Above: A 1904 Argyll 10/12 hp two-seater; in this picture, taken in 1907, the car is being driven by its then owner, a Mr Hill

Right: A Stanley Steamer of 1906, with the 'coffin' bonnet over the boiler, which characterised Stanleys from 1906 on; it was in 1906, that the famous Stanley called *Wogglebug* exceeded 127 mph with its specially developed streamlined body before taking off on a bump and crashing heavily
(Château de Grandson, Switzerland)

'Auriga', apparently, had ridden on one of the very first Napier sixes in 1904 (the first, built in 1903, was sold to a Mr W. Bramson . . . his purchase was 'rather a brave thing to do', thought Edge) and noted: 'A good six-cylinder car is perceptibly and unmistakably more comfortable, more luxurious, less vibrant, less noisy than the best four-cylinder car that ever was built. Some say she ought not to be; but the fact remains that she is and she can be built to what power one pleases. She is easy on tyres, too, and as for her petrol consumption, I am afraid it does not worry me. It is the sort of thing which troubles an omnibus company desirous of making a profit, but it does not cause any anxiety to the rich men and women, of whom the supply is seemingly unlimited, who buy Napier six-cylinder cars. To such people also the argument that the extra luxury is not worth the extra money has no meaning. Like the difference between first and third classes in a railway train, it is worth buying for people who like comfort, and there are many to whom the cost is a matter of no moment'.

At first, though, there seem to have been other considerations than luxury, as Edge recalled over twenty years later: 'I read a paper at the RAC on the advantages of six cylinders over four, and I remember Rolls said that one of the

Right: A Mors of 1905, photographed while competing in the Coupe des Pyrenées of that year

Below left: A Ford Model N, built in 1906 to undercut a similar Oldsmobile; this was the direct predecessor of the Model T (Château de Grandson, Switzerland)

Below: A 1906 De Dion-Bouton, with interior trim of silk and basketwork paintwork, executed by a Chinaman living in Paris (Château de Grandson, Switzerland)

advantages was, you had six strings to your bow instead of four, which rather goes to show the kind of straws we clung to in the early days of motoring. What was in Rolls's mind was that you were more likely to have one cylinder left firing if you had six of them than if you had only four!'.

Those early sixes had one major drawback, for the crankshaft damper had not yet been invented, and so they had critical engine speeds at which unpleasant vibrations occurred. Edge tried to explain the phenomenon away as the 'Power Rattle' . . . but whatever you called it, it could still snap a crankshaft.

Nevertheless, the overall performance of the Napier was so good that the six-cylinder layout was widely copied: by the end of 1906, claimed Edge, there were 141 different makes of six-cylinder car on the market.

Some, of course, were awful – it wasn't every engineer who could make one carburettor feed six-cylinders with the requisite smoothness, as gas-flow was, at best, an imperfectly understood science – but others were worthy to vie with Rolls-Royce and Napier for quality. Like the Delaunay-Belleville, introduced at the 1904 Paris Salon in four-cylinder form, and first available as a six-cylinder in 1906 in the shape of the monstrous 70hp, which had a swept volume of 11,846cc. The distinguishing feature of these cars was the circular radiator and bonnet, which recalled the company's origins as marine engineers, and, indeed, the excellent system of high-pressure lubrication incorporated in their power units had been developed as early as 1897 for the Delaunay-Belleville high-speed steam engines, which were built with power outputs of up to 7000hp. The quality of the engineering fully justified the company's

slogan 'The Car Magnificent', and the President of France and the Tsar of Russia were both enthusiastic users of the marque; the Tsar, in fact, was such a regular customer that one of the firm's more ostentatious sixes – a development of the 70 hp – was named the 'SMT' ('Sa Majesté le Tsar') in his honour. From 1910, Delaunay-Bellevilles could be fitted with a particularly refined form of self-starter, *Le Démarreur Barbey*, which operated by compressed air generated by a four-cylinder pump mounted between the dumb-irons; 'The driver, sitting in his seat, need exert no strength to operate the Starter. A tiny lever within the reach of his hand allows him, with two fingers, in one simple movement, to effect, almost instantaneously the engagement of the starter with the engine, its withdrawal and replenishment'.

Of similar quality to the Delaunay-Belleville – and, indeed, also endowed with a circular radiator and bonnet (which *Country Life* thought 'peculiarly ugly') – was the Hotchkiss, built by the famous armament factory founded in 1867 by a Connecticut Yankee called Benjamin Hotchkiss. Coincidentally, both the Hotchkiss and the Delaunay-Belleville were built at St-Denis-sur-Seine, 6 km north of Paris.

Below: A 1912 Delaunay-Belleville 70 hp six-cylinder machine, complete with compressed-air starter; unless otherwise specified, the chassis for the cars sold in Britain were sent to Aberdeen by sea to be clothed by the Shinnie Brothers, a subsidiary concern of the Burlington company

However, if such cars showed the luxury aspect of the big six, others merely represented it taken to absurd lengths, with cylinders like cannon bores and sumps the size of hip-baths – even a comparatively common model like the Napier 60 had a sump getting on for six feet in length! Imagine then, the sheer bulk of the power unit of the 50/60hp Ariel-Simplex of 1907–8, which had a swept volume of 15,904cc, making it the second-biggest car ever catalogued, and surprisingly good value for cubic centimetres at a chassis price of £950 – Napier's biggest, the 14,565cc 90hp of 1909–12 cost £1500. Surprisingly, the most cubically capacious car ever catalogued was the four-cylinder 200hp Benz of 1913–14, with a 21,504cc engine, or well over five litres per cylinder!

Only Fiat could do better, and their 300hp was a one-off record-breaker which boasted a 28,353cc four-cylinder engine which made infrequent appearances on the speed tracks from 1911 onwards, and managed to clock 132·37mph at Ostend in 1913 (bigger engines have subsequently been used, but only in 'straight-line' land-speed-record contenders).

Reverting to road cars, wealthy megalomaniacs could also toy with such volumetric inefficiencies as the 60hp Leader, one of the first production V8s,

Above: a 1906 Benz four-cylinder machine, similar to the car that gained an impressive second place in that year's Herkomer Trial

which had a 15,505cc engine and cost £1500 complete with bodywork in 1906 (its maker, Charles Binks of Nottingham, subsequently became better-known as a manufacturer of carburettors, including the celebrated 'rat-trap' pattern favoured by sporting motor cyclists). Contemporary with it was the 40hp Adams V8 built in Bedford; although its engine was only half the size (7274cc) of that of the Leader, it had a more lasting claim to fame, for its power unit was a French Antoinette, designed by Léon Levavasseur, a power unit more often found in early flying machines, for which its compact construction and relatively light weight made it admirably suitable. Adams also built V16 Antoinette engines under licence, but does not seem to have succumbed to the obvious temptation of installing one of these in a car . . .

Although the rich Edwardians loved a long bonnet, surprisingly few straight-eights made their appearance, and almost all were exclusively racing machinery. However, at the 1902 Paris Salon the firm of CGV (named after the triumvirate of racing drivers – Charron, Girardot and Voigt – who had founded it) showed a prototype touring eight-cylinder power unit. At the end of March 1903, the motoring correspondent of *Country Life* sampled the finished car: 'Her quietness and smoothness was almost astounding. The engine is a comparatively slow one, running at only 900 revolutions a minute when accelerated, while, of course, the mechanically operated valves make it very quiet at low speeds. The noisiest items of the engine are the gearwheels on the half-time shafts, but when cogs of fibre are substituted for the present metal ones, everything about the motor will be practically inaudible. Its elasticity is

Left: Unic's were popular in London during the early part of the century as taxis. This is a 1908 12/14 hp which was in production for no less than twenty years
(National Motor Museum, England)

Left, centre and bottom: a 1906 Renault 20/30 hp town carriage. The bodywork on this particular example is by Windsor of Hounslow. This impressive machine has a top speed of 50 mph and it can return 16–18 mpg
(National Motor Museum, England)

Below: De Dietrich started building cars with Bollée engines made under licence; then they concentrated on building Turcat-Méry designs. They even copied the Marseilles company's six-wheeler. This is the De Dietrich 40 hp seen in London in 1907. Drive was by chain to the centre pair of wheels

delightful to experience in actual use. M. Voigt, who drove the car, was able to thread his way through Piccadilly blocks at a mile an hour, yet the car is capable of travelling up to fifty times that speed. Only one speed is fitted, and inasmuch as it is possible to start on this, although geared to fifty, it is obvious that if a low speed were fitted for starting purposes and steep hills, the present gear could be considerably raised. A reverse is also needed, but we understand that both the items named will be embodied in the next eight-cylinder vehicle, the present one being regarded only as an experiment which must be pronounced as highly interesting and in a large measure successful'.

It failed to reach production status, though maybe the prospect of devoting over half the vehicle to the engine was too daunting, even for the most megalomaniac motorists!

Nearly every manufacturer of note succumbed to the craze for engines of vast capacity; Gobron-Brillié, famed for their opposed-piston engines, built a vast six-cylinder 70/90 hp of 11,404 cc between 1908 and 1910. As its combustion chamber was formed by the crowns of the opposing cylinders, and thus varied in size as they approached and recoiled, the giant Gobron was

apparently particularly smooth-running.

Of course, the ostentation of the chassis had to be matched by similar excess in the coachwork department. The growth in the demand for luxurious coachwork can be traced in the rise of the Rothschild coachbuilding company of Levallois-Perret, which traced its origins back to horse-carriage days, but which had since the turn of the century devoted itself to building high-class motor-bodies, setting a long-lasting fashion by the creation, in 1902, of a particularly voluptuous body on the 40 hp Panhard belonging to the King of the Belgians. Coming at a time when the sinuous curves of *l'Art Nouveau* were all the rage, the *Roi-des-Belges* body was widely copied by coachbuilders everywhere, as Rothschilds had neglected to patent the design.

Even so, Rothschild bodywork had an extra flair that most other coach-builders could only envy; it was partly due to the fact that while the elders of the company's proprietors, Rheims, had been a carriage-builder for many years, the younger, Auscher, had been a sporting motorist since the 1890s, even riding in motor races so that he could better appreciate the stresses put on automobile coachwork.

The Rothschild factory had to be doubled in size in 1904, by which time the company held one-sixth of the coachwork market; the new factory employed 600 men, of whom 180 were employed in the blacksmiths' shop alone. The varnishing shop could hold thirty cars at a time, and was equipped with ovens to hasten the drying of the final colour and varnish coats. Output of new bodies was two per day in 1905, plus repair and conversion work on existing coachwork, and the manufacture of wooden wheels, in which the company held a monopoly in the French industry; they even deigned to build the odd horse-drawn carriage, although these were regarded as very much out-of-date!

Perhaps the most sensational bodies of all were the *limousines de voyage* built for the automotive grand tour, but they had nothing in common with modern GTs, with their smooth lines and low headrooms. These were machines complete with every possible luxury – one wealthy American even specified a built-in flush toilet in his 75/90 hp, 12,868 cc Charron – and one of the most sybaritic was built around 1907 for the rich Parisian Count Boni de Castellane, who had married Anna Gould, daughter of the American Millionaire Jay Gould. Boni de Castellane's 40 hp Panhard Pullman Limousine de Voyage was built on a chassis with a wheelbase stretched to 12 ft 6 in, and its coachwork was panelled throughout in satinwood, with polished mahogany mouldings inlaid with silver. In the panel which divided the front and rear seats were a folding table, a small electric heater concealed in a frame of polished copper and a silver washbasin. This was fed with hot or cold water from two tanks concealed in the roof, hot water being provided by the engine. And on either side of the central division were cabinets equipped with cocktail, toilet, manicure and vanity-case requisites.

Left: three views of a 1907 Napier 60 hp, built as a replica of the car with which S. F. Edge averaged 65.91 mph for 24 hours at Brooklands in that year. The engine is 'square' with 127 mm × 127 mm bore and stroke; this, in six cylinders, gives a displacement of 7724 cc (National Motor Museum, England)

Below: a 1908 Lanchester 20 hp landaulette. Although Lanchesters were way ahead of the rest of the industry in some respects, *ie*, live axles, worm drive and foot accelerators by 1895, models up to 1909 still had lever steering. This vehicle had a disc brake, which operated on the transmission

In the rear compartment were two adjustable armchairs, upholstered in Rose Dubarry silk brocade, and capable of being transformed into a comfortable bed. The windows, of bevelled glass, were fitted with roller blinds and curtains to match the upholstery, and the interior was lighted by four electric corner brackets and a countersunk ceiling light, all silver-gilt.

The exterior of the body was finished in de Castellane's racing colours, and all exterior metalwork was of silver-plated copper, except for the doorhandles, which were of solid silver. On the dashboard, the usual controls were augmented by a barometer, altimeter, route indicator, speedometer, clock and thermometer. And the final touch to this extraordinary car was added by de Castellane's companion, a pedigree-bred bulldog with a silver-mounted collar two-inches wide, studded with diamonds and rubies, and hung with an 18-carat gold St Christopher medallion.

The appearance of this flamboyant vehicle incensed de Castellane's rival, the Baron von Eckhardstein, who swore to eclipse its magnificence at the forthcoming Concours d'Elegance Automobile at Nice, and ordered himself an even more exotic vehicle. Like the Panhard Pullman, this vehicle was furnished throughout by the Paris branch of Maple & Company. The centre portion of the body resembled a stagecoach, and once again featured silk chairs which could be turned into a bed. Between the seats were sliding doors leading to the rear of the body, which housed a fully equipped kitchen, in which the Baron's corpulent chef, Emile, cooked meals for his master *en route*. There was also a 'tradesmens' entrance' to the kitchen at the rear of the car.

However, the most remarkable feature of Von Eckhardstein's car, which was reputed to have cost £4000 (or £3300 more than the standard 35hp De Dietrich on which it was based), was its chasses, which had six wheels, with the front and rear axles steering, and the central axle drove. This curious layout, which also incorporated an unorthodox disposition of the springs, was the invention of a military engineer named Lindecker, who had persuaded De Dietrich to take it up around 1905. It was supposed to soak up all the unevenness of the road, enable the vehicle to run smoothly over potholes and humpbacked bridges, and to provide 'comfort, sweet running, positive steering and safety'.

The Baron had wagered de Castellane that the De Dietrich would 'knock the feathers out of his blasted cocked hat at the Concours', but in fact both cars won high awards.

Perhaps the most consistent of all the concours set was the wealthy Englishman Montague Grahame-White (the same man who had steered his Daimler in the Thousand Miles' Trial by kicking the hub after the steering had broken, and whose brother, Claude, was the most famous British aviator of the day). Grahame-White loved big motor cars, and loved nothing better than to take an already huge vehicle and make it even more eye-catching by lengthening the wheelbase to absurd proportions.

In 1911 Grahame-White owned the biggest of all the pre-war Mercédès, the six-cylinder 75/105hp model, of 10,179cc. This was a chain-driven behemoth with canework panelling round the top of its tourer body. Fitted spanners were concealed in the hinged upholstery of the doors and plate glass panels in the top and sides of the bonnet displayed the gun-barrel finish of the cylinder blocks and the highly burnished pipework. A spectacular enough machine, you might think, but it was not enough for Grahame-White. In December 1911 the Mercédès was returned to the coachbuilders, who lengthened the wheelbase to 15 ft 6 in, fitted an aggressively pointed radiator of special design, giant Rushmore acetylene headlamps and new mudwings.

'Monty' was still creating such vehicles during the 1920s; but most of them had long since vanished. Let the epitaph of the Edwardian monsters be Grahame-White cruising down the long, straight avenues of poplars in Burgundy at a steady 90 kilometres an hour on his way to Monte Carlo, pausing only to sample the superb cuisine and the occasional bottle of Chateau Mouton Rothschild '99 – 'no more costly than a Beaujolais in many West End London hotels before the 1914 war'.

Below: in 1907, Clément-Bayard announced a 1.6-litre light car, with a monobloc engine in unit with the gearbox; this was the first example of the marque to feature a dashboard radiator, *à la* Renault, complete with sloping bonnet, which subsequently became a Clément-Bayard characteristic. This example was built in 1909, by which time the small car was the company's main offering
(Château de Grandson, Switzerland)

Below right: a 1909 Humber 8 hp; this represented an early British attempt to market an inexpensive runabout, but it failed, because the vertical-twin power unit was rather noisy and was far from smooth; one useful feature of this car was that it had quickly detachable wheels – and with the poor roads and primitive tyres of the day this must have been a blessing
(National Motor Museum, England)

CHAPTER 7

Mass-production for the Motor Car

'There will always be snobs willing to pay Fr10,000 (£400) for the name on the bonnet of their car,' wrote Comte Pierre de la Ville-Baugé in 1905, 'but wouldn't it be interesting, in the cause of furthering the spread of motoring, to enable us to avoid this by listing conscientious firms who give value for money?

'What purchasers want is a reliable car comfortable and commodious enough for their needs, at a reasonable price; it's too much to ask for if you want one of these snob's cars, but not impossible to find, I reckon, outside this aristocracy of motordom... The interests of tourists are becoming more and more divorced from those of racers, for whom cost is nothing, and the leading marques are wrong to make so much of these attention-grabbing vehicles to promote their ordinary cars.

'If you haven't Fr20,000 or more to invest in a car before taking four passengers on a tour in hilly country, should you give up this mode of transport... or make your will before leaving? I don't know...'

It was a difficult problem to resolve, for there was still an immense gulf

between the *voiture de grande luxe* and the light car: if you bought cheaply, you usually bought a vehicle in which everything had been pared to the bone. And perhaps the most successful example of minimal motoring was the Sizaire-Naudin, introduced at the Exposition des Petits Inventeurs in March 1905. Commented *La Vie Automobile*: 'New ideas are plentiful in this little car; almost everything about it is original, and, even better, properly carried out. The main aim of the designers is extreme simplicity. In this voiturette, everything possible has been omitted; the remaining parts have been so designed

that the costs are reduced to a minimum without, however, neglecting the quality of construction.

'Apart from the chassis and wheels, the voiturette consists of: a 6 hp single-cylinder motor mounted at the front of the chassis, a multi-ratio final drive and irreversible steering.' It also had independent front suspension, but not even the makers realised the advantages of this. They had done it for lightness, using a transverse spring.

The rear axle was an ingenious affair, for it gave three speeds forward and reverse through the medium of a crown wheel and four pinions of differing sizes, which were engaged by a curiously-contoured cam, which moved them both laterally and longitudinally.

'This system presents not only the advantage of a great simplicity, but also that of efficiency, for in every one of the forward gears there is only one intermediary between the engine and the wheels.' It also presented the disadvantage that a silent gearchange was virtually impossible . . .

Even the electric wiring was reduced to a minimum: the coil and batteries were housed in a box in front of the engine (helping to fill the aching void under

the ample bonnet) so that only a few inches of wire were needed to link coil and contact breaker, while the 'plug lead' was a length of metal spring from the box to the sparking plug.

Although the Sizaire enjoyed several years of popularity and even achieved a number of sporting successes, its formula was obviously a sterile one, for, having reduced a vehicle to the absolute basics, its designers could only elaborate it as customers demanded extra refinement; and the Sizaire-Naudin would end up as a staid – and rather corpulent – light car of conventional design.

What then was the answer to the problem of designing a car for the masses? Already Henry Ford was practising the economies of scale, by raising production and reducing prices. In 1906, for example, he replaced the old Model F, with its twin-cylinder engine beneath the seat, with the four cylinder Model N, a far more sophisticated machine. Model F had cost $1000; Model N was only

Previous page: an early 7 hp Austin, not to be confused with the famous car of the 1920s; this 1910 machine was really a Swift, made in Coventry and sold under two names and it was equipped with a single-cylinder power unit (National Motor Museum, England)

Left: Peugeot and Lion-Peugeot were separate entities when this VC2 one-cylinder phaeton was made in 1909; however, the two amalgamated in 1911 (Peugeot collection, France)

Below: two views of the 1909 twin-cylinder Turicum from Switzerland; this model was very short-lived, being preceded by single-cylinder models and succeeded by a four-cylinder machine, but like its predecessors it had a friction-drive system (Château de Grandson, Switzerland)

$600 ('It carries no equipment, it is "just automobile – all automobile"', announced the company) and was exported to Britain where it sold for around £125, a price which caused the deepest suspicion among the home industry. 'Nothing so cheap can be any good,' they said . . . and were duly surprised by the model's success, with annual British sales of 600. But Ford had even greater things in mind . . .

'The automobile of the past,' said Ford at that time, 'attained success in spite of its price because there were more than enough purchasers to take the limited output of the then new industry. Proportionately few could buy, but those few could keep all the manufacturers busy, and price, therefore, had no bearing on sales. The automobile of the present is making good because the price has been reduced just enough to add sufficient new purchasers to take care of the increased output. Supply and demand, not cost, has regulated the selling price of automobiles.

'The automobile of the future must be enough better than the present car to beget confidence in the man of limited means and enough lower in price to insure sales for the enormously increased output. The car of the future, "the

133

car for the people", the car that any man can own, who can afford a horse and carriage, is coming sooner than most people expect.

'A limited number of factories can supply all the demand for high-priced cars, but the market for a low-priced car is unlimited. The car of the future will be light as well as low in price. This means the substitution of quality for quantity, even to the use of materials not yet discovered.'

Sometime early in 1907, Ford began development of his own personal vision of that 'car for the people'; already, despite the relatively high price of automobiles, America was becoming a nation of car-owners at a spectacular rate. In 1902 there had been one car to every 1,500,000 citizens of the USA; by 1905 the proportion was one to every 65,000, and in the spring of 1907, one American in 800 owned a car. Now Ford was after the remaining 799/800ths of the market . . .

In the little experimental room, only 12 ft by 15 ft, at Ford's Picquette Avenue plant (which the company had occupied for only a couple of years, yet was already outgrowing) Henry Ford and his associates, C. H. Wills, C. J. Smith and Joseph Galamb were working on the successor to Model N. Models R and S had been de luxe versions of the N, so the new car was to be called the 'Model T'.

Joseph Galamb, a young Hungarian engineer who had worked with the F. B. Stearns company before joining Ford, would draw up Ford's ideas on a blackboard, while Henry Ford, sitting in a big rocking chair that had belonged to his mother, would watch and comment. Then the ideas were translated into metal and tested. Much use was made of vanadium steel and special heat treatments of the metal, which gave the new design lightness combined with durability. Transverse springs fore and aft, combined with three-point suspension of the power unit, gave the car a unique ability to cross uneven ground without undue chassis distortion, while a pedal-operated epicyclic transmission developed from that of the Model N gave clash-free gear-changing (a notable boon in those pre-synchromesh days) though it only possessed two forward speeds. This wasn't such a disadvantage as it might have seemed, for the Model T had a 2892 cc engine, which, while its power output was restricted by narrow gas passages, had ample low-speed torque.

When news of the Model T was released to Ford dealers – especially its price of $850 – some of them informed the factory that they had hidden the advance catalogues of the car as its low cost and improved specification would render all the old model Fords still in stock quite unsaleable.

'High priced quality in a low priced car!' shrieked the advertisement which announced Model T to the public on 3 October, 1908, adding: 'We make no apology for the price – any car now selling up to several hundred dollars more could, if built from Ford design, in the Ford factory, by Ford methods, and in Ford quantities, be sold for the Ford price if the makers were satisfied with the Ford profit per car'.

In fact, by the standards of the Model N, the Model T got away to a slow start, only 309 were built in the first three months of production, while Model N output had been running at an average of 70 to 80 cars *a day* during the summer of 1908, reaching a peak of 101 a day as the final orders were met, before the changeover to the T.

But by the summer of 1909 output was nudging 2000 cars a month, and the Ford company was claiming 'the largest shipment of motor cars in one consignment in the history of the trade . . . a train of 41 cars, loaded with three motor cars, 123 motor cars in all . . .'. Already, however, it was becoming uneconomic to ship built-up motor cars over long distances, and Ford began to set up branch assembly plants, to which components were shipped in knocked-down form; by 1912 they owned sites in Kansas City, St Louis, Long Island City, Los Angeles, San Francisco, Portland and Seattle, while the first overseas assembly plant had just been established in a former railway carriage works on Britain's first industrial estate, at Trafford Park, Manchester. The plant produced 1485 cars in 1911 and 3081 in 1912, which put it in the front rank of British car manufacturers in terms of volume.

It was just a drop in the ocean against Ford's total output that year in its

Left: a 15 hp Model N Ford of 1907, passing the more usual form of road transport of that period; maybe the two drivers are arguing about who should have had right of way

Below: one of the first of Renault's 1100cc, twin-cylinder machines, the AX; this particular example was constructed in 1910, although the type was introduced in 1905. The AX was a forerunner of Renault's famous *Taxis de la Marne* (Château de Grandson, Switzerland)

135

Right: the 1912 Hispano-Suiza Alfonso was named after the King of Spain, who was an enthusiastic driver

Far right: the famous Hispano-Suiza emblem (National Motor Museum, England)

Below: the 1912 Scania-Vabis was built in Sweden. The body is mostly mahogany on an oak frame
(Skokloster Museum, Sweden)

Below right: a 1911 Garrard-Speke two-cylinder, two-seater
(Cheddar Motor Museum, England)

Detroit factory of 82,400 Model Ts . . .

An important factor in the growth of the Ford Motor Company had been their removal, in the New Year of 1910, to a magnificent new factory at Highland Park, to the northwest of Detroit. Four stories high, 865 feet long and 75 feet wide, this 'Crystal Palace' boasted 50,000 sq ft of glass, and was the largest building under one roof in the state of Michigan. The 60-acre site on which it stood was soon filled with subsidiary buildings. The old Picquette Avenue plant, of which Henry Ford remarked proudly 'As good as, perhaps a little better than, any automobile factory in the country', was sold to Studebaker.

Ford was only following a long American tradition in insisting upon complete and absolute standardisation of components; Samuel Colt, for instance, had used interchangeable parts in his gun factory half-a-century earlier. But at Highland Park, Ford was moving towards a new concept of mass production. It didn't come all at once; there were brilliant individual aspects like the machine which dipped wheels six at a time into vats of paint, spun them round to throw off the surplus and put them out to dry, turning out 2000 wheels a

day; or the radiator assembling machine which assembled 50 tubes and plates into a complete matrix in one operation. Then there was the drilling machine which bored 45 holes at four different angles in the cylinder block in one operation; most significant was the sub-division of magneto flywheel manufacture into 29 operations performed by 29 men seated along a moving belt, a step which cut the time taken to assemble a magneto progressively from 20 to 13 minutes, then to 7 minutes and finally to 5 minutes.

A similar process was soon adopted for the assembly of the engine, and in the summer of 1913 experiments began in hauling a line of chassis on a rope, six men following each chassis as it was dragged past piles of parts brought to the line in little trucks. An overhead chain hoist dropped the engine into each chassis at the appropriate point. This improvised experiment cut the time taken to assemble each chassis from $12\frac{1}{2}$ hours to 5 hours 50 minutes. Moving production lines were soon installed on a permanent basis, and work further subdivided, so that by the beginning of 1914 it only took 1 hour 33 minutes to assemble each Ford chassis.

Such moves gave spectacular impetus to Ford output; in 1913, 199,100 chassis were produced at Highland Park, while in 1914 the figure rose to 240,700. In 1915, which saw the production of the millionth Model T, 372,250 Fords were manufactured, an achievement which was eclipsed in 1916, which saw 586,202 Ts leave Highland Park, while the following year witnessed the building of 834,662 Ford cars.

It was a total which more than fulfilled the apparently rash statement made a few years previously by Ford's rival, Billy Durant, that one day the American public would buy 500,000 cars every year. Durant, who had tried – and failed – to buy out Ford, had united the Buick, Cadillac and Oldsmobile marques in an organisation which he called General Motors, and for which he had raised capital of $12,500,000. It was, apparently, a winning line-up, especially as Cadillac was headed by Henry M. Leland, the 'Master of Precision', who worked to limits of 100/000th of an inch, and who had won the British Dewar Trophy in 1908 when three cars had been dismantled, their parts jumbled, and reassembled in the most convincing demonstration of standardisation that had yet been given. However, to its four profitable lines – Buick, Cadillac, Oakland and Oldsmobile – General Motors now added unremunerative dross like the Ewing, Elmore, Cartercar and Rainier, which dragged the group down until, in 1910, the bankers were forced to take over and oust Durant. Under its new president, Charles W. Nash, appointed in 1912, and its works manager, Walter P. Chrysler, General Motors made a spectacular recovery – without the loss-making firms . . .

Durant made a reappearance on the scene as the backer of the new Chevrolet

Below: this 1913 Vauxhall Prince Henry is a 4-litre development of the 3-litre car designed by Laurence Pomeroy Snr for the 1910 Prince Henry Trials. With a four-cylinder, 75 bhp engine it originally sold for £615. It has a top speed of 75–80 mph

The details, *right*, show the distinctive bulbous, fluted, radiator cowl and the intricate horn (National Motor Museum, England)

company, which he changed in character from a producer of quality cars to a builder of medium-priced vehicles, made $6,000,000 in six years and regained control of General Motors.

Against such spectacular growth, the achievements of such mass-producers as Hupmobile, with their annual sales of around 12,000, looked a little wilted, although they were still able to compete in the low-priced car market; in 1913 a survey showed between 23 and 30 car makers active in the 'under $1000' sector.

However, they could not hope to compete on equal terms with the big boys as far as bulk buying of components was concerned; even then, the annual raw material consumption of a major producer like Ford was pretty awe-inspiring. In 1913, the company ordered: 1,000,000 lamps; 800,000 wheels; 800,000 tyres; 90,000 tons of steel; 400,000 leather hides; 2,000,000 sq ft of glass; 12,000,000 hickory billets for wheel-spokes . . .

That America (for so long the backward cousin of the European motor industry) had now taken over as the world's leading car manufacturing nation, was a proven fact. The biggest European companies were no more than dwarfs

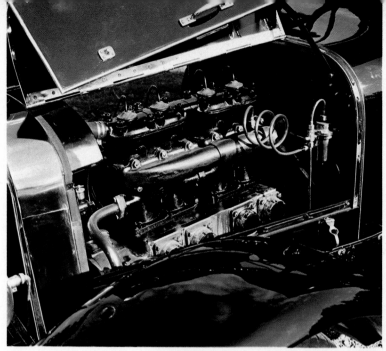

by New World standards; the total output of the entire British motor industry in 1912 was only 23,200 vehicles, and even the major producers like Wolseley only turned out some 3000 vehicles yearly. Of course, in Britain the car was still regarded as a luxury, not a necessity, a fact proven by Lloyd George's introduction in 1910 of a taxation system for cars based on the horsepower of their engines, measured under the somewhat dubious RAC rating formula, which took only the bore of the engine into account, and thus bred generations of cars with long strokes and narrow bores. Under the 1910 taxation formula, cars of up to 6½hp paid £2 2s in tax, and larger vehicles were taxed in a progressively steepening ratio up to a rating of 60hp and over, which attracted an annual impost of £42, a frightening figure when translated into modern terms, but doubtless just about bearable by rich owners accustomed to paying over £500 per annum for replacement tyres.

Above and right: By 1913, Argyll of Glasgow was the fifth-largest manufacturer in the British Isles, turning out quite a large range of cars. This is a 1913 15/30hp (National Motor Museum, England)

The inevitable result was the encouragement of smaller and smaller vehicles and, before long, a new word was enriching the motoring vocabulary: 'Cyclecar'. The name was an amalgam of the two terms 'motor cycle' and 'car', and usually seemed to be applied to a vehicle which combined the worst features of each in the interests of simplicity and cheapness. Perhaps the most revoltingly crude vehicle of this type was the Dewcar of 1913/14, which had a 'chassis/body' unit consisting of two planks butted at their extremities, and with a viciously pointed petrol tank mounted immediately above the single-cylinder motor-cycle engine, in just the right position to cause a merry blaze at the least spillage of fuel. The opportunities for self-destruction with a vehicle of this type were endless; and yet they were bought and driven with enthusiasm, their owners professing disdain for the humble Ford (which at £125 cost little more than the average cyclecar, and offered accommodation for five against the maximum of two small people which could be forced into the cyclecar's cramped cockpit).

Only two British makes of cyclecar exhibited any lasting merits, and these were the four-wheeled GN and the three-wheeled Morgan, which was the better-engineered of the two.

The prototype Morgan was built in the workshops of Malvern College by young H. F. S. Morgan while he was convalescing from a crash on his Peugeot motor cycle, and represented car design reduced to a workman-like minimum. The chassis was based on a tubular-steel backbone down which ran the propellor shaft, at the forward end of which was hung the big V-twin engine from the Peugeot and at the rear of which was a two-speed bevel box (this not only drove the single rear wheel *via* twin chains, but also served as a mounting point for the quarter-elliptic rear suspension). A tubular framework at the front of the chassis carried sliding-pillar independent front suspension with coil springing. The prototype had tiller steering, but when popular demand spurred Morgan to put the little vehicle into production, high-geared wheel steering was adopted. The bottom tubes of the chassis also served as exhaust pipes, thus keeping the number of parts to a minimum.

Its excellent power-to-weight ratio gave the Morgan a particularly sporting performance, a fact which was not lost on H. F. S. Morgan, who began to enter competitions; he found an enthusiastic, if somewhat unorthodox, 'public relations officer' in his clerical father, Prebendary H. G. Morgan of Stoke Lacy, Worcestershire, who wrote enthusiastically to the press about his son's achievements. He even turned up, clad in top hat with side strings, frock coat and dog-collar, to watch H.F.S. cover sixty miles in the hour at Brooklands in 1912 at the wheel of a special single-seater Morgan. Although various makes of V-twin power unit – MAG, Green-Precision, Blumfield – were used, it was the JAP power unit which became identified with the Morgan.

In the 1913 French Cyclecar Grand Prix, a Morgan came first, and was immediately reclassified as a motor cycle and sidecar by the French authorities for having had the temerity to beat Gallic cyclecars like the Bédélia and the Violet-Bogey; it retained the moral victory.

The Bédélia, produced by two extroverts named Bourbeau and Devaux, was a tandem-seated device which also had its origins in components retrieved after a motor-cycle accident. However, its crude centre-pivot steering, controlled by

This is one of the last Lion-Peugeot models made; by this time, 1933, the two Peugeot companies had recombined and were housed under one roof. The C3, of which this is a fine example, was equipped with a V4 engine, as had been tried in some previous models, complete with high-pressure lubrication; the rear wheels were fitted with pedal-operated brakes as well as the two outside handbrake levers shown. (Peugeot collection, France)

steel wires wrapped round the tubular column, and belt drive (with ratio changing controlled by the front-seat passenger on racing versions) were symptoms of a somewhat more casual attitude to design than that of the Morgan's progenitor . . .

Its protagonists called the cyclecar movement 'The New Motoring', although much of it was really a restatement of mistakes that had long been forgotten. Nevertheless, at its peak in 1913/14, it attracted a large number of would-be motor tycoons to chance their arm at entering the market with totally unproven designs, some of which seemed remarkably tenacious of life, like the Carden, a narrow-tracked projectile with centre-pivot steering, which carried its power unit at the rear of the bodywork. It started off meekly enough, with a single-cylinder 4hp engine, but then developed a lethal sting in its tail, like an earthbound *kamikaze* bee, with a V-twin JAP engine of around 1000cc, whose weight and power must have reduced the already minimal directional stability of the machine to almost negative proportions. Yet, this offence against all engineering decencies was revived after World War 1 and continued to be manufactured, under the new alias of 'AV Monocar', until 1926.

To show the depths which cyclecar manufacturers were prepared to plumb, it should be noted that the constructors of the Globe cyclecar of 1913/16 were the well-known firm of sanitary engineers, Tuke & Bell of Tottenham, better known for custom-built sewage-disposal plants . . .

Just before the outbreak of war, there were dozens of different makes of cyclecar on the British market, and there was the inevitable tendency for them to grow into proper little cars. Many lapses of good judgment occurred during this growing-up period, like the unfortunate case of the 1095cc V-twin Buckingham exhibited at the 1913 Motor Cycle and Cyclecar Show. On this belt-driven and somewhat sketchy chassis, the car's designer, J. F. Buckingham, caused a dainty saloonette body, replete with lace curtains and cut-glass flower holders to be erected. He called it, of course, the 'Buckingham Palace'. Mr Buckingham was to achieve greater fame during the ensuing world conflict as the inventor of a particularly anti-social device known as the Buckingham Incendiary Bullet, much favoured by the British and allied forces for shooting Zeppelins down in flames.

Herbert Austin, who had resigned from his job as chief engineer at Wolseley in 1906 to form his own car-manufacturing company, building mainly large, powerful four and six-cylinder models, had gone to the opposite extreme in 1910/11 with an 1100cc single-cylinder (built by Swift) which cost £150; it was not a success, and was soon dropped. Thereafter, the smallest model in Austin's pre-war lineup was an 1145cc 10hp, uprated in 1913 to 1452cc.

In that year, incidentally, Austin increased his factory area to nine acres, an addition of 25 per cent, and modernised the production machinery to meet the demand for his products (although the area was marginally reduced again early in 1914 when suffragettes burned down the employees' library).

Others were more faithful to the small-car concept, partly because it brought a new type of customer onto the market: the woman driver. It is often claimed that it was the introduction of the self-starter by Cadillac which really attracted the lady motorist, but in fact the electric starter was a necessary evil which had to be developed once the old trembler-coil ignition system had been ousted by high-tension-magneto or battery-and-coil installations for, while a car in good tune would start on the tremblers once its cylinders had been primed, the more up-to-date ignitions lacked this useful facility.

The advent of lady drivers was not altogether welcomed by a generation of males somewhat apprehensive of the outcome of the emancipation movement. 'Several prominent gentlemen have been assuring us lately that our comrades of the other sex are something of a terror on the roads. If memory serves rightly, most of these gentlemen are somewhat advanced in years. Possibly,

These photographs show the beauty of the 1913
Daimler Cranmore landaulette; this was made in
Coventry and was fitted with a six-cylinder,
4.9-litre, 30 hp, Knight double-sleeve-valve
engine, which drove the Rudge-Whitworth
wheels via a cone clutch and a four-speed gearbox

As the pictures show, the interior was exquisitely
trimmed, with leather seats and separate
cushions, while the smooth, quiet straight-six
engine is a joy to admire. One particularly
interesting feature of the Daimler is the solid-
nickel oilers fitted to the front hubs (*above*)
(Cheddar Motor Museum, England)

146

when a man has turned the corner of, say, fifty, he objects to piling his new £500 car up the bank in order that a lady piloting her 8hp two-seater may wobble past', commented W. H. Berry in April 1914. 'But, come, sirs! What do we do when any other road obstruction causes delay to our imperial progress? Why, slow down and, if necessary, stop until the danger is past . . . We cannot claim that all women are unsuited to be drivers, forsooth, because some few are inclined to be wobbly on the road. For weal or woe we must make up our minds that the lady driver will be seen on the roads in increasing number . . . Manufacturers are catering specially for the lady driver. They are building cars for her particular benefit, and she is seizing advantage of the opportunity in order to do her shopping and to take out her friends and to run down to town and to the links. What difficulty does the little Swift, or the Humberette, or the Singer, offer a lady driver? Is there any reason why a woman should not handle a Rover, or a Darracq? Assuredly not. Very well then!'

Berry's choice of typical light cars is interesting for, while the Swift and the Humberette were unashamedly cyclecars, albeit of the better-designed sort,

Below: the smallest car in the 1913 Fiat range was the Tipo Zero. This car had a four-cylinder, 1.8-litre, engine and shaft drive. An independent Fiat Motor Company formed in 1910 built and marketed the range in the USA (National Motor Museum, England)

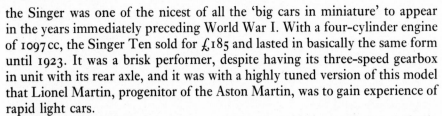

the Singer was one of the nicest of all the 'big cars in miniature' to appear in the years immediately preceding World War I. With a four-cylinder engine of 1097cc, the Singer Ten sold for £185 and lasted in basically the same form until 1923. It was a brisk performer, despite having its three-speed gearbox in unit with its rear axle, and it was with a highly tuned version of this model that Lionel Martin, progenitor of the Aston Martin, was to gain experience of rapid light cars.

However, the Singer was only one of several attractive small four-cylinder cars of around 1–1·5 litres capacity to make their début at this period; Calcott and Calthorpe were honoured names, whose origins went back to bicycling days, while Swift added a Ten to their range in 1913 (although it was not nearly as popular as their cyclecar). In Oxford, a successful cycle and motor agent called William Morris was just beginning to market a diminutive model, mostly assembled from proprietory parts. It had a handsome 'bullnosed' brass radiator, a feature shared with the little AC from Thames Ditton, Surrey, which was built as a handsome sporting model as well as in standard two-seater form.

One of the smallest four-cylinder cars to be produced was the little Bébé Peugeot, designed by Ettoré Bugatti, who had not long set up in business as a maker of very expensive, but inordinately rapid, small cars of 1327cc; his Bébé, a design which he had sold to Peugeot, had a monobloc four-cylinder engine of only 855cc and a curious transmission in which the ratios were provided by concentric propeller-shafts terminating in pinions of differing diameters. Normally, the Bébé was endowed with two-seater bodywork rather reminiscent of the bath in which Marat was assassinated, but the little engine was powerful enough to permit at least one example of this model being fitted with a diminutive two-seater coupé body of undoubted charm, if minimal practicality.

Perhaps the oddest marketing technique employed by any Edwardian light-car maker was that employed by Motor Schools Limited, who built a friction-drive 10hp car with a 1244cc Chapuis-Dornier four-cylinder engine. As their name implied, Motor Schools ran a training institute where drivers and mechanics received instruction at fees ranging up to £25 for 'three-months practical work in garage and works, 72 driving lessons and daily attendance at class lectures'. They had what was claimed to be the largest fleet of dual-control vehicles – fourteen of them, and probably of their own make – and also published a little *aide memoire* booklet entitled *200 Practical Points on Motoring*. With every copy of this was given a coupon entitling the purchaser of the book to enter a competition in which the prize every month was a £150 Car and Course of Instruction FREE'. The car, of course, was their own little friction-drive Pilot 10hp, and the competition was one in which competitors had to fill in the missing words in a story which throws an uncomfortable light on the problems of small-car owners of the day (and the answers to which were to be found – surprise, surprise – on a diligent reading of *200 Points . . .*).

'While travelling between Uxbridge and Ruislip in our car, we heard a sharp metallic click, as if something had been picked up by the wheel and hurled against the front mud-guard', ran the puzzle story. 'On examination, we found that (1) . . . had worked loose, with the result that (2) . . . had come off, and evidently been thrown up by the wheel. Fortunately, we had another with us, and were soon off again. Much to our dismay, after stopping for petrol, we found on turning the starting handle, that we could get no (3) . . . but we soon found the simple cause of the trouble. The next day we found it necessary to use the spare (4) . . . This is one of the spare parts that *200 Practical Points on Motoring* advise all motorists to carry. Everything went all right on the way back until after lunch. Somehow we had lost the (5) . . . but what would have been a problem to us amateurs was solved by the answer to question No. (6) . . . in *200 Practical Points on Motoring*.'

And, indeed, if contemporary instruction books are to be believed, the average journey by light car was fraught with such nameless perils. Spectacular collisions must have been commonplace, for manuals gave graphic, if improbable, instructions on how to get home if a crash carried away the front wheels

('For one wheel smashed, replace it with a skid made from a purloined fence
post, for two wheels smashed, borrow a coster cart, fasten it to the front axle,
and use reins to steer . . .'), while Sankey, makers of pressed-steel artillery
wheels advertised how their products withstood violent impacts, like Lionel
Martin's crash with his Singer in the 1914 London–Gloucester Trial: 'For
no apparent reason, for there was no evidence whatever of a skid, the car left
the road at high speed, dashed into the grass at the roadside, jumped a three-
foot gulley, was hurled sideways and overturned. The front axle was twisted,
the springs torn off, and the nearside chassis member snapped in half – yet in
spite of this wreckage, the Sankey Wheels which took the brunt of the impact
were absolutely unharmed'.

It is hardly surprising that in the same issue which described this crash,
The Motor ran a leading article entitled 'Subtleties of Insurance Policies', just
to help out readers.

In fact, although petty annoyances could still mar an outing by car (the
author's great-uncle, who was one of the first Ford agents in Britain, and often
drove with S. F. Edge, recalled having to spend nights sleeping by a broken-
down car on a heap of roadside gravel at this time), the internal-combustion
engine was becoming increasingly more reliable, its development immeasurably
aided by the opening of Brooklands in 1907 as a venue where endurance, as
well as sheer speed, could be tested.

Quite the most remarkable proof of the growing maturity of the motor car
was given on 15 February 1913, when Percy 'Pearley' Lambert covered 103 miles
1470 yards in an hour at Brooklands driving a 25hp Talbot, basically a production touring model, endowed with wind-cheating single-seater body. The fact
that, without excessive modification, a car which could be bought for only
£515 could put 100 miles into an hour caused a sensation among the motoring
public, especially since the speed limit on British roads was only 20mph (and
would remain so until 1930!).

Sunbeam snatched Lambert's record from him with a purpose-built racing
car, and 'Pearley', attempting to regain his honours before the opening of the
1913 Motor Show at Olympia, crashed, was killed, and was buried in Brompton
Cemetery in a coffin streamlined to match the contours of his car, quite a
fitting epitaph to the man.

It was the achievements of men like Lambert which built up the motor
business in Britain, despite hostile legislation and official apathy, to the status
of a major international industry. In 1905, exports had been only £501,802;
in the year ending 31 March 1914, Britain's motor industry exported cars
worth £4,324,000. But a far sterner test of the industry's abilities was immi-
nent . . . on 4 August 1914, World War I began, and with it came the first
demands for mechanical transport for military purposes. Although the horse
was still favoured by the army at this time, the motor vehicle, in various forms
was becoming rapidly more efficient.

CHAPTER 8

The Motor Car goes to War

Left: this 1914 Hallford 3-ton lorry was typical of the kind of vehicle which was used for military purposes at the beginning of World War I. It was powered by a 5.3-litre engine, had chain drive and ran on solid tyres. Later vehicles became more specialised to suit the appalling conditions in which they were often expected to work
(National Motor Museum, England)

Military vehicles had first appeared – except for steam-traction engines – during the Boer War, when a couple of MMC tricycles and a Locomobile steam car had been tentatively used by officers in the British Army, but they had proved of limited utility. The War Office obviously had some idea of the potential of self-propelled vehicles, for they held trials for lorries as early as 1901, and there had been a number of experiments with motorised troop transport on manoeuvres, notably a London–Hastings run organised by the Automobile Association in conjunction with the Guards.

However, the military hierarchy was still enamoured of the horse and, when war broke out in 1914, the Army was woefully short of fighting vehicles. A subsidy scheme had been in operation for some years, under which lorry owners whose vehicles conformed with certain specifications received payments from the War Office on condition that their vehicles were made instantly available for military use on the outbreak of war. The Army obviously had need of them, for its own motorised strength in August 1914 only amounted to some eighty vehicles. Subsidy lorries brought the strength of the British Expeditionary Force's motorised units up to 1200 vehicles. To supplement this inadequate force, the authorities commandeered some 1300 London buses which were shipped over to France for troop transport. Eventually, when time permitted, they were repainted in olive drab, but at first they ploughed their stolid way across the Flanders fields flaunting the bright red livery and boldly lettered advertisements that they had worn on the streets of London.

London taxis, too, were commandeered for service in France, but it was the French who made the first decisive use of internal combustion for military purposes when the military commander of Paris, General Gallieni, commandeered the city's taxis to rush French reinforcements to help stem Von Kluck's advance on the city. It was a decisive move in the Allied victory in the Battle of the Marne, and one of the Renault taxis was preserved for posterity in Les Invalides. Incidentally, the cab-drivers not only received the full cab fare shown on their meters, but also a 27 per cent tip!

Some of the first British vehicles to reach France were quickly involved in the fighting. One three-ton Leyland truck, still bearing the name of 'John Jackson & Son of Bolton & Manchester' on its headboard, was captured by the Germans and later recaptured in damaged condition by Lancashire troops.

Some of the first buses taken over for military use were stripped of their bodywork by the Royal Naval Flying Corps and fitted with boiler-plate armouring. Noted the *War Illustrated*: 'There are a number of British armoured cars at the front, and their services are invaluable for obliterating small parties of German cavalry. The horsemen stand no chance against these swiftly moving and well protected engines of war, unless they vault hedges and ditches and take to the woods, where, naturally, the motor car cannot follow. In the matter of putting an end to the sneaking services of German spies, they are also useful'.

War Illustrated also commented on the activities of one of these motor heroes: 'Commander Samson, the best known of our naval airmen, has added to his renown by a dashing exploit. On 16 September, near Doullens, seventeen miles north of Amiens, he went out with a small armoured-car force and encountered a patrol of five Uhlans. He killed four of them and the fifth was wounded and captured. The British party suffered no injury. Commander Samson was the airman who, three years before, flew over the German Emperor's yacht when it arrived in the Medway. On that occasion, the Kaiser admired his daring, and Commander Samson is evidently determined to continue to merit his admiration'.

This was the stuff of high adventure and, before long, armoured cars were being featured in the stirring tales of authors like Percy F. Westerman, in which the heroes were inevitably plucky, resourceful, lantern-jawed British lads of around fourteen years of age . . .

Private-car chassis were used as the basis for armoured cars, too: the Belgian Minerva company, whose factory at Antwerp was right in the path of the German advance in 1914, hastily turned its workforce to converting its

7·4-litre 38 hp chassis into armoured cars, some of which could even boast a rotatable domed gun turret at the rear. These were used for forays from Antwerp and against the German cavalry, although one naval airman in command of a Minerva threatened a patrol of German cycles with his machine-gun, whereupon 'those that were not killed left their machines and hid in the woods'.

However, of all the chassis used for armoured cars, the most outstanding were the Rolls-Royce and the Lanchester, both capable of attaining speeds of up to 50 mph against the 16 mph or so of the normal army truck.

Apart from minor modifications to the suspension and running gear, both were based on standard touring-car chassis, yet withstood the extra weight of the armour-plating with complete reliability. Some of the Rolls-Royces used in Arabia which survived World War I, were active in the local skirmishes of

Below left : motor cars also played their part in carrying the War to the air. In this 1911 photograph, a 26 hp eight cylinder De Dion is being used as an aircraft tender

the 1920s and 1930s, and fought in World War II, by which time their original wheels had been changed for a later pattern carrying large-section tyres, as the original beaded-edge high-pressure type had proved incredibly vulnerable in service. In fact, except when in action against the enemy, the Rolls-Royce armoured cars were limited to 20 mph, as they were quite capable of gobbling up a dozen tyres in a day.

The Lanchesters, on the other hand, with their all-round cantilever suspension, were markedly kinder to their footwear, and did sterling service on the Russian Front. Also, their mid-mounted engines were less likely to be damaged by enemy fire. The Lanchesters fought in squadrons of six, supported by three high-speed service vehicles on the same chassis (a general-purpose lorry, a mobile workshop, and a field kitchen). This chassis was also used, incidentally, for searchlight tenders and powered winches for observation balloons.

Nearer home, the raiding of London by Zeppelins, which began in 1915, prompted the authorities to institute a mobile air-raid defence system based on the V8 De Dion Auto-Canons which were being successfully used by the resourceful General Gallieni in the defence of Paris. In charge of the project

Above and above right : two variations of an early AC armoured car, as used in 1914. As can be seen, the most vulnerable parts were the wheels and particularly the tyres, which were very prone to punctures. An attempt has been made to protect the radiator from attack on the car above

was Commander Rawlinson of the Naval Armoured Car service, who duly collected his auto-canon and its attendant *caisson*, or ammunition truck, from Paris in September 1915: 'Although driving an exceptionally fast car and sending it along at its best speed, it was no easy task to catch up the gun, as that most remarkable machine, the Auto-Canon, with well over 100 horsepower, did an easy 50 miles an hour on the level, although its weight of over five tons delayed it somewhat on the hills'.

At first, the De Dion was based in the RNVR Armoured Car Headquarters in the Talbot Works in Ladbroke Grove, and its firing position was on the Artillery Ground in Moorgate, for it was reckoned that this would be the ideal place to defend the Bank of England against airship raids. However, from the way that Rawlinson's detachment went into action, it seems as though the Zeppelins were the lesser menace!

'At that time, there was no system of "air-raid warnings", "raid shelters", or "maroons", such as was organised later on, and the streets on this occasion were crammed with vehicular traffic and pedestrians . . . the *most pressing* and *most vital* thing they had to do was TO GET OUT OF OUR WAY . . . omnibuses in every direction were seeking safety on the pavement . . . people were flattening themselves against shop windows . . . sinking the hill in Holborn . . . my speedometer registered 56 miles an hour.'

At this point, Rawlinson was going so fast that he could not stop when he came upon a section of the road blocked off for repairs, and had to charge through the barriers. The whole journey across London was so rapid that, twenty minutes after leaving the Talbot factory, the Auto-Canon was set up and firing at a Zeppelin that was dropping bombs on Moorgate. The airship was frightened off, but apparently undamaged.

More 'Automobile Anti-Aircraft Guns' were now constructed on Daimler and Lancia chassis, and a 'Mobile Anti-Aircraft Brigade' was formed under Rawlinson's command, and billeted in the stables of the Grand Duke Michael of Russia's palatial house, Kenwood, in Hampstead; total strength was now seven automobile guns, as well as fourteen other vehicles.

Although the Auto-Canons do not seem to have scored any positive successes against the Zeppelins, they did at least exercise a considerable deterrent effect, and scared several marauding airships into releasing their bombs before they could do any damage on their prime targets.

More effective as a weapon was the Tank, developed in great secrecy by the British motor industry, and based on such pre-war experiments as the Ruston & Hornsby caterpillar-tracked vehicles and the Diplock Pedrail attachment for traction-engine wheels.

The prototype tank was nicknamed 'Willie', and was completed in December 1915 at the Lincoln works of William Foster & Company; its top speed was 3½ mph.

By the summer of 1916, the Tank was a fighting proposition, and fifty were sent to France. For security, the units which later became the Tank Corps were then known as the Heavy Branch, Machine Gun Corps. Psychologically, these first 'Land Ships' were a terrifying addition to the machinery of war (although that ingenious author, H. G. Wells, had forecast such a weapon several years earlier in a short story called 'The Land Ironclads'), and they terrified the Germans, whose rival experiments were fruitless.

The British Tanks went into action on the Somme on 15 September 1916, and were soon to play a significant part in the winning of the war, turning the static fighting of the trench lines into a more mobile battle. At Cambrai, for instance, in November 1917, 378 tanks penetrated 10,000 yards behind the Hindenburg Line.

This took just twelve hours, compared with the three months it had taken British troops to advance this far at Ypres, at the cost of 400,000 casualties and millions of pounds in ammunition – the preliminary bombardment alone had represented £22,000,000-worth of shells. At Cambrai there was no preliminary bombardment and only 5000 casualties. Petrol power was proving its worth in warfare.

Even more spectacular was the Allied victory at Amiens, in August 1918, in which the Tanks played a decisive role; the German commander Von Ludendorff called this the 'black day of the German Army', but less than 1000 Allied troops were killed or wounded.

It's instructive to look through photographs of the War to realise how quickly the motor vehicle ousted the horse from the roles which it had played in

Left and on facing page: Ford's mass production techniques were an essential part of the war effort. Although Henry Ford himself was a pacifist, his overseas factories kept the allies supplied with a steady stream of Model Ts. These photographs show the petrol tank and wheel assembly operations and cars on test in the yard at the Highland Park factory in 1914

battle for hundreds of years. In 1914 photographs of the fighting forces, horses predominate, with only the occasional motor vehicle visible; by 1918 the situation is entirely reversed. Some idea of the rapid increase in numbers of military motors is given by the fact that when the British Government took stocks in 1919, it found that it had 165,128 self-propelled vehicles of all kinds on the strength, of which some 100,000 were overseas – and that didn't include all those vehicles which had been damaged beyond repair.

Indeed, so rapidly did the tempo increase that in 1915 the commercial vehicle manufacturer AEC became the first British company to follow the Ford example and install a moving production line to increase output (although in AEC's case production seems to have run at about thirty vehicles a week, so the line must have moved somewhat glacially.

The initial stages of the war in Europe had seen no American-built Fords on active service: Henry Ford was a pacifist, and at first refused to build for the warring nations. His overseas factories, in Manchester, Bordeaux and Canada, took a different view of things, and supplied Model Ts by the thousand to the Allies. British-built Ford light trucks were especially useful in Mesopotamia, where they proved to be one of the only two types of vehicle – the other was the Rolls-Royce Silver Ghost – capable of withstanding the tough desert conditions.

160

Once America had come into the war, however, the American Government set the ball rolling by ordering 2000 ambulances from Ford's Detroit factory; among the diverse orders which followed were those for 820,000 steel helmets, naval patrol boats and V8 and V12 Liberty aero-engines and cylinders. Henry Ford also formed a new company to produce the Fordson tractor, thousands of which were shipped to Britain at the order of the Ministry of Munitions to enable farmers to improve the yield of home-grown produce.

In fact, the War taught many motor-manufacturing companies how to diversify their products; Austin built complete aircraft; the Clyno motor-cycle company and the Guy truck company both built ABC Dragonfly aero-engines; others produced shells, fuses, paravanes for minesweepers and a host of other military requirements which had little in common save that they were made of metal.

Prominent among British aero-engine makers was Rolls-Royce, whose excellent Eagle power unit had six cylinders and an overhead camshaft, and could develop 225 bhp on its first trials in October 1915, a figure which had increased to 360 bhp by the Armistice.

Right: a Scania-Vabis ambulance of 1914, based on the combine's 20 bhp model; the four-cylinder engine was made with a one-piece cylinder block, as opposed to the two-piece version of the 60 hp model of the same period
(Saab-Scania collection)

Right: De Dion Auto-Canons were used successfully to defend Paris against Zeppelin attacks during World War I and, indeed, were brought to England to help protect London against the same threat; this is a 1914 example, based on the De Dion V8 chassis

Strangely enough, after the war, Continental manufacturers generally put the lessons they had learned in aero-engine design into the power units of their motor cars; in Britain, almost without exception, makers stuck stolidly to side valves (admittedly Wolseley, who had built Hispano-Suiza V8 aero-engines, *did* produce a range of overhead-camshaft engines, but these failed to realise their potential to such a degree that their makers might just as well not have bothered . . .).

Standardisation was a wartime lesson that many quickly forgot, too: once the armed forces had built up their requirements by commandeering a wide variety of machinery, they then chose a limited number of makes which would be the standard military issue for staff cars. Roughly, in descending order of rank, the list ran: Rolls-Royce (for the *very* top brass), Vauxhall, Daimler, Sunbeam, Wolseley, Austin and Singer. So strictly was this adhered to that when Sunbeam's output of aero-engines became so great that the company couldn't continue building cars, Rover were contracted to build Sunbeams under licence, even though the Rover car was fully the equal of the Sunbeam for quality.

The Royal Flying Corps (which became the Royal Air Force on 1 April 1918) was an individualistic sort of a service, so it exercised its own choice of motor vehicles, most of its heavy trucks being Leylands, most of its staff cars and tenders Crossleys. So closely did the air service and its transport become linked that the terms 'RAF Leyland' and 'RFC Crossley' were often used as model names.

Individualistic, too, seems to be the only word to describe the attitude of a large part of the French Army to motor transport. Although there was, of course, much standardisation, there were also eccentricities which could not

Right: photographed at Magnicourt in May 1915, these are French naval armoured cars, whose single weapon is a machine gun

Below: another De Dion V8 chassis of 1914, in this case specially modified and put to use as an ambulance; despite the obviously cold weather, this particular example seems to have overheated

have happened elsewhere. Ambulances were a fruitful medium for self-expression: one conversion consisted of a tandem-seated Bedelia cyclecar (which was driven from the back seat) with a stretcher mounted over the front seat, engine and petrol tank, the last of which was apt to leak on to the hot cylinders and set off a merry blaze. One can imagine the hapless *poilu* pleading to be left to die in peace where he was rather than be rushed off to the field hospital on such a crazy device. An even more casual casualty wagon had appeared in the early stages of the war, however; fitted on the back of a 12/15 hp Mors chassis was a sort of three-storey dishrack, in which the injured were stacked in tiers, completely exposed to the open air. 'Science is required in carrying wounded, a lack of which would often have fatal results', added a cryptic caption. 'Our allies' simple but ingenious method of quickly conveying wounded soldiers from one place to another has proved invaluable in practice.'

A more sensible French conception was the conversion of motor buses into mobile operating theatres.

Where the English used motor cycles for carrying despatches, the French used Bébé Peugeot cars; but where there was a need for rapid communications, Gallic ingenuity received free rein. When war broke out, the Mércèdes company, which had just gained a one-two-three victory in the French Grand Prix, was celebrating its win by displaying one of the team cars (under false colours, as they had repainted it with the winning number!) in their showroom

Right: artillery batteries are taken to the front at Verdun by 'heavy' lorries of the period; the wheels and tyres on the trucks are all paired to withstand more load, to increase reliability and to reduce the risk of total tyre failure due to gunfire

Below: an armoured-car prototype of 100–120 hp, designed by Charles Tarrott and submitted to the French Government for appraisal in November 1914

on the Champs-Elysées. Noted *The Autocar*: 'One of the high officials of the French motor transport service, requiring a car with which he could reel off three or four hundred miles between breakfast and dinner, secured possession of it, to find that connecting rods were broken and the bearings had gone. Put into good mechanical condition, fitted with a windscreen and mudguards, the enemy car rendered valuable service, frequently covering the three hundred miles separating Lyon from Paris after morning business had been attended to, and making another run of about a hundred miles to Châlons, or another point behind the lines. This experience showed that a racing car can be used very successfully for long distance travel, for the officer who had charge of the Mércèdes states that his petrol consumption was eighteen miles to the gallon, that tyre trouble was practically nil, and that the car was so easy to handle that after three hundred miles he was not too fatigued to work'.

Another ex-racing car used for high-speed dashes was the Renault which had won the 1906 French Grand Prix; this car was appropriated by the celebrated Escadrille Cigogne ('Stork Squadron') of the French Air Services, who thought that it would be 'a suitable machine for wild dashes from the front to the base, from camp to Paris or from point to point of the line'. Despite its 10mpg petrol consumption, and tyres which refused to last for more than 500 miles, the Renault was used with success by the leading French air aces –

Left: the Germans' answer to the armoured vehicles of the allied forces; ludicrously, great pains were taken to protect the mechanical parts and the occupants, but the wheels were left totally exposed

Guynemer, Fonck, Nungesser and Navarre.

Perhaps the most hilarious conversion was that carried out by the Italians on the 115 hp Itala which Henri Fournier had driven in the 1908 Grand Prix at Dieppe; this was converted into an ambulance to make a nightly climb up a mountainside in search of wounded on the border between Austria and Italy. But the machine was so unsuitable for the task, and ran so badly that the secret police became suspicious of its activities, and arrested the driver and passenger, keeping them under observation for twelve hours until their innocence could be proved . . .

Keeping all these diverse Allied vehicles supplied with petrol was an immense task in itself, and sterling work was carried out by the petrol companies, both in shipping crude oil from the oilfields, despite the constant threat of U-Boat attack, and in refining it and getting it to the Front. Shell, indeed, built a refinery, shipped it across the Channel one weekend, and had it working within 36 hours. Even the humble two-gallon petrol tin played its part: a special factory was set up for the manufacture of this indispensible item, which, when drained of spirit, was used for countless purposes in the trenches –

Above: a Büssing armoured car, based on an 80 hp Daimler truck chassis and made for the German army during World War I; this machine was equipped with four-wheel drive and steering, together with a driving position at each end so that the machine was truly reversible; it had a top speed of about 30 mph

Above, far left: an Ehrhardt armoured car, built, again, for the German forces and known as a street wagon

Above left: German troops on their way to the front line, during World War I, in a chain-driven, twin-rear-wheeled truck; the newness of motorised military transport at this time can be judged by the fact that the lorry is following closely behind a team of horses

even as building blocks for shelters and, beaten flat, as flooring for the trench.

The Germans, who had entered the war somewhat better equipped with military motors than the Allies – as early as 1900 the Kaiser had offered a prize equivalent to £4000 for the 'best automobile war carriage which will combine all the requisites for service in the field' – suffered badly from the British naval blockade. As their supplies of rubber dwindled, the Germans were forced to resort to all kinds of substitute spring metal tyres, which proved a great hindrance to their mobility. Their choice of staff cars fully reflected their highly class-structured society, ranging down from Field Marshal Von Hindenburg's 21-litre Benz tourer (which still exists in England . . .) to the sub-utility 10 hp Phanomobil, which had its single-cylinder engine mounted above the front wheel. This eccentric tricycle was more often seen in the guise of a delivery van. Komnick, Opel and Stoewer were other makes favoured by the Kaiser's armies.

The unparalleled use of mechanical traction during World War I was to prove of major significance in the future growth of the motor industry. Thousands of men, whose peacetime experience of motor vehicles was no more than a rare ride on an omnibus – if that! – had been trained as drivers and mechanics, and tasted the rare mobility that only the rich motor owner had known pre-war.

CHAPTER 9

The Industry returns to work

For a time after the Armistice it was only too easy to make money out of motor vehicles. There was a wider market than ever before, ranging from the war profiteer with a fortune to spend to the demobilised soldier with a hundred pounds or so for a motor vehicle of some kind. Between these two extremes, cars of all types were available, although in insufficient numbers, as it turned out, to satisfy demand. For many manufacturers who had spent the last four years engaged solely on war work, the buoyant car market proved propitious. Now that all the military contracts had faded away in the euphoria of peace, the aircraft manufacturers and munitions engineers needed to find something that would tide them over until the next bout of international unpleasantness brought the orders in again. So the Grahame-White Aircraft Company built bodies for luxury cars, wardrobes and even a crude cyclecar, while in France the two most famous native aircraft manufacturers, Voisin and Farman, metamorphosed into makers of quality cars. Of course, it was in many ways an artificial situation, for an aircraft industry can hardly have been said to have existed at all before the outbreak of war.

In one respect, the car buyers of 1919 were disappointed, for very few car manufacturers had incorporated the engineering lessons learned in the war – especially the war in the air – in their post-Armistice offerings. Most 1919 models, indeed, were almost indistinguishable from their 1914 counterparts except for a few details like the replacement of acetylene and oil lighting with electric light . . . and in respect of the price tag, for inflation had sent prices soaring. A car which had cost £400 before the war was now nearly twice as much; and it was impossible for a manufacturer to hold prices steady between the announcement of a new model and its appearance on public sale.

It was in this climate that the American manufacturers, many of whom who had stuck a cautious toe in the European water in 1914–15, before a total ban was placed on the import of cars for private use, flourished. Less affected by the hostilities than European companies, they had continued with the development of new manufacturing processes, so that, despite the $33\frac{1}{3}$ per cent import duty placed on their products by the British Chancellor of the Exchequer, Reginald McKenna, they could still undercut the home products – except in one important respect: economy of use.

American cars were designed for the wide-open spaces of their homeland, where a nationwide road-building programme was at last making possible long cross-country journeys. In America, fuel was cheap, and drivers disliked gear-changing, so engines were big – and thirsty, so thirsty in fact that one pundit suggested that the nation's oil reserves would all be exhausted by 1932. And in Britain, where petrol had been strictly rationed until January 1919, such prodigality was received with suspicion; indeed, running costs were a great source of worry to the motoring public, who in 1920 sent a nationwide petition to Lloyd George demanding a reduction in the price of fuel, which was then 3s $8\frac{1}{2}$d a gallon (and was even more on the Continent, where in 1921 Frenchmen were paying Fr10·50 for a gallon of petrol, equivalent to 5s 4d at the prevailing rate of exchange, while Italians, who bought their petrol by weight in *lattes* of 3·9 gallons, paid 62 lire for this quantity, which at 80 lire to the pound meant a price of 4s a gallon).

Despite the duties, which in total added over fifty per cent to the price, American cars could compete in price with the home product to such an extent that in 1920 over 33,000 of them were imported into Britain. Ford, with its factory in Manchester and its Irish plant opened at Cork in 1917 to build tractors and provide castings and other components for the assembly lines at Trafford Park, did even better, for the Model T was becoming increasingly British in content (if not in design, for a Ford edict of 1919 specified that all Ford cars worldwide should be built left-hand-drive, a state of affairs which prevailed until 1921); in 1919 two-fifths of all the cars on British roads were Model T Fords.

But at the end of 1920 the axe fell. The British Government completely changed the basis of car taxation, which had hitherto been based on a fairly nominal carriage tax according to the rated horsepower of the engine, allied to

Right : one of the original Thulin models of 1920,
built in Sweden and based on the German Aga;
it is fitted with a four-cylinder engine and
characterised by its pointed radiator grille and
concave body sides. Only three hundred examples
of this model were made before the company
went bankrupt in 1924 and when the concern,
which had previously made aircraft, was
reconstituted a new model was produced
(Skokloster Museum, Sweden)

Left and below : one of the last steam cars to be
made and sold in commercial quantities was this
American Stanley 735-A of 1920; this particular
example was used as the British importer's
demonstration model. The 735 had its boiler
under the bonnet and its double-acting twin-
cylinder engine on the rear axle
(National Motor Museum, England)

a high petrol tax. In August 1920 petrol had reached its highest price level since the war – 4s 3½d a gallon – and the Taxation Committee set up by the first Minister of Transport, Sir Eric Geddes, decided that a horsepower tax should be substituted for the petrol duty. (Of course, by the end of the decade the hapless motorist was paying *both* taxes. . . .)

To cushion owners of high-powered pre-war models against the effects of £1 per horsepower, a reduction was given where a car was over ten years old, although this concession, too, was soon forgotten by the rapacious Ministry.

The effect of the new taxation was immediate: by 1922 imports of American cars had tumbled to only 14,000 annually, and, in order to minimise the effects of their own products by an outmoded rating system which only took the cylinder bore into account, British manufacturers began developing the classic long-stroke engines which were to characterise their products for the next twenty or thirty years.

If the introduction of the horsepower tax in 1921 was, unintentionally, a watershed in engine design, the proof of the value of the car as a means of private transport had come less than two years earlier, in the autumn of 1919, when Britain's railway workers went on strike. The weapon used to break the strike was the motor car. The Government took powers to commandeer motor vehicles, and Hyde Park became a vast clearing house for London's food supplies. Petrol rationing came into force for the duration of the strike, which collapsed on 15 October, largely due to the role played by the motor vehicle, which had now proved itself an alternative, not an auxiliary, to the railways.

But such labour troubles also proved the undoing of many of the optimistic firms which had so bravely plunged into the market in 1919, assembling cars in penny numbers from bought-in components. Now, in 1920, foundry workers went on strike for four months, and the supply of iron castings ran short; other strikes, hold-ups and shortages combined to cause a major slump in the motor industry in 1920–21: similar conditions hit the American industry, even more vulnerable because of its great size and reliance on volume production for adequate profits, even harder.

In April, 1920, there was a collapse of automotive shares on the New York Stock Exchange, precipitated by higher interest rates and other restrictions which had limited hire-purchase sales of cars. However, although sales were falling, raw material costs continued high; in order to move ahead again, manufacturers would have to take drastic action, but they were quite unprepared for what the ever-surprising Henry Ford did . . .

Slashing prices by figures ranging from $165 on a $525 chassis to $105 on a $745 coupe and $180 on a $975 sedan, Ford announced: 'The war is over, and it is time war prices were over . . . Inflated prices always retard progress. We had to stand it during the war, although it wasn't right, so the Ford Motor Company will make the prices of its products the same as they were before the war. We must, of course, take a temporary loss because of the stock of material

Far left: the boat-backed Opel 8/25ps of 1920; this machine had a 2.2-litre, side-valve engine, with a four-speed gearbox, a transmission brake and shaft-drive
(National Motor Museum, England)

Left: the 11.9 hp AC of 1921, with a four-cylinder, side-valve Anzani engine with a three-speed gearbox, mounted on the rear axle; the car relied for its stopping power on a single transmission brake
(National Motor Museum, England)

Below: a beautiful example of 'The Best Car in the World', in this case a 1921 Silver Ghost; interestingly, the bodywork of this car was not fitted until 1925, having been built by Gustaf Nordberg's Vagnfabrik, and it was restored by the same company thirty-five years later

Left and above: two versions of Peugeot's 'sensation' of 1919, the Quadrilette; this model started life with a 628 cc four-cylinder engine, but this had grown, by the time the car was withdrawn in 1929, to 694 cc; the three-speed gearbox was mounted in unit with the worm-driven rear axle. The 1921 car, *above*, has tandem two-seat bodywork, while the other version, made a year later, has offset, side-by-side seats (Peter Hampton and Peugeot, France)

Right: a strange vehicle, made in Germany and called the Phanomobile 6/12ps; this particular example, with a transverse, air-cooled, four-cylinder engine mounted over and chain-driving the tiller-steered front wheel, was manufactured in 1922, but earlier examples of the model had been used by the German army as ambulances during World War I. Primary drive was by friction to a two-speed epicyclic gearbox, while, as one photograph shows, cooling was aided by twin fans (National Motor Museum, England)

on hand, bought at inflated prices . . . but we take it willingly in order to bring
about a going state of business throughout the country'.

What he didn't say was that with each car sold at a loss of $20 went $40-worth
of spare parts on which there had been no price reduction, thus cancelling
most of the loss. Other manufacturers were incensed by Ford's boldness, but
the majority of them soon followed suit, and there was a brief Indian summer
of reviving sales; then the sales graphs began to slide at a dizzying rate.

William Durant tried to save his General Motors combine by buying huge
blocks of shares, but it was a futile operation, and the DuPonts and J. P.
Morgan & Company bought him out for $27,000,000.

Ford owned most of the shares in his own company, and was soon to acquire
the few that remained in outside hands, thus freeing himself from what he
regarded as the menace of the bankers (save that he had a $25,000,000 loan to
be repaid in the spring of 1921, a figure which, taken with outstanding tax bills

and employee bonuses, added up to over $50,000,000 – or $30,000,000 more than the company's cash reserves). A crash programme of waste elimination was carried out, and the company stopped buying raw materials, and stock-piled cars using the materials on hand, thus saving costs.

Throughout November and December 1921, the leading motor manufacturing companies began to close down their factories 'for stocktaking', and thousands of men were laid off. On Christmas Eve, Ford closed down 'for inventory' too. Within three months, the number of men employed in the motor industry in Detroit had fallen from 176,000 to 24,000.

Managers laid a machine-shop floor in the Ford factory, and when that was done, acted as watchmen, patrolling the empty buildings on bicycles and roller skates. Office staff were dismissed in their hundreds, and all the spare office and catering equipment was sold, raising an estimated $7,000,000. But these dark days were the nadir of the depression; in January there were signs that car sales were picking up again in New York, and some manufacturers began production again. The Ford plant remained shut, however, with demand met by dealers' stocks, built-up cars which Ford had stockpiled and vehicles assembled from spare parts at the Ford branch factories. At the end of January, Highland Park opened up again, and Ford began shipping cars out to dealers, to be paid for on delivery. Thus, instead of having to borrow the money needed to pay off his $50,000,000 debts, Ford compelled his dealers to borrow to pay for the cars. Most of them found little difficulty in disposing of the extra vehicles as sales continued to recover through the spring of 1921. Once again, Henry Ford had proved his ability to survive in adverse conditions.

The slump was slower in reaching Britain: the postwar boom began to collapse at the end of 1920, and it was not until the spring of 1921 that the full effects were felt. William Morris, now entering the mass-production market with his Morris-Cowley, saw sales plunge from 288 in October 1920 to 68 in January 1921. He reacted by following the Ford lead and slashing prices, knocking £100 off a £525 Cowley four-seater, and reducing other models by figures ranging from £25 to £90. Other makers, notably Bean, had earlier cut prices, but Morris had chosen the right psychological moment, and succeeded where the others had failed. Not only did his sales increase – his profits rose, too.

The collapse of the post-Armistice boom was also to provide Morris with his keenest competitor, although in a somewhat circuitous fashion. The Clyno Manufacturing Company of Wolverhampton were one of the country's most respected makers of motor cycles, whose machines had been widely used during the war (one of their motor-cycle machine-gun outfits can still be seen in London's Imperial War Museum), in which they had developed an ohv four-cylinder power unit originally intended as the motive power for a sidecar combination. However, Frank Smith, the company's managing director, was an enthusiast for sporting light cars, and decided to enter the car market after the war with a 10hp ohv four-cylinder model using the motor-cycle engine, which could almost have been the British equivalent of the Brescia Bugatti; three prototypes were built before the company's backers, De La Rue, withdrew their finances and Clyno went into receivership. Reformed in 1922, Clyno abandoned both motor cycles and sporting light cars and instead moved into the mass-production market, building a 10·8hp model, largely from bought-in components, powered by a side-valve Coventry-Climax engine. Right from the start, Frank Smith followed the Morris star, continually trimming the prices of Clyno models so that they were identical to those of the equivalent Morrises. It was a policy which worked spectacularly well – at first – raising Clyno eventually to third place in the British production league behind Morris and Austin, at which stage they were producing 300 cars a week in a tiny factory in the heart of Wolverhampton, its inadequate floor space augmented by an asbestos roof over the dirt yard outside.

One of the reasons for the popularity of the Clyno was its excellent handling, which was apparent right from the earliest. In April 1923, *The Autocar* took one of the first few hundred Clynos on the road, and was highly impressed . . . 'It is curious how obvious in the running of a new car is the handiwork of the designer who is also an artistic driver. For example, the family model Clyno

A 1923 11.9 hp Calcott, built by one of Britain's smaller manufacturers who were to succumb to William Morris's price war of 1921 and never recover. This car is powered by a four-cylinder side-valve engine of 1645 cc, and is of the type in production from 1920 to 1924. Calcott was taken over by the Singer concern in 1926 (National Motor Museum, England)

handles in such a way which suggests that those who are responsible for it understand very fully the finer points of roadworthiness and have attended to each with exceeding care. As a result, there is, indeed, very little to criticise and much to commend'.

One reason for the good handling of the car was the fact that one of the firm's backers apparently owned a Grand Prix Peugeot, and specified that the Clyno should have steering that was equally light and positive. In this, the Clyno's designer, George Stanley, who had previously worked for the Triumph motor-cycle company, was entirely successful: 'It must be admitted that the Clyno steering gear is one of the best . . . the necessity of effort is so small that the car is steered as unconsciously as a bicycle'.

Although the Clyno company built some components (like the gearbox) themselves, the Clyno was still largely an assembled car, albeit a very successful one. One reason for its steadily rising sales graph was probably that it bore an established and respected name with a good war record, which would have overcome the sales resistance felt by an entirely new marque. In this respect, it is interesting to observe the fate of the Cooper, a handsome light car also

Below: Peugeot's Type 163 of 1923, which is powered by a 1437 cc, 10 hp, four-cylinder engine. This is the Torpedo version, but the model was also available with de luxe Torpedo or boat-tailed, sporting four-seater bodywork (Peugeot Collection, France)

Right: the first of the mass-produced Fiats was the 501, which appeared in 1919 with a 1½-litre, side-valve engine. This is the 1924 Torpedo, one of the second series of 501s on which were introduced front brakes and, low pressure pneumatic tyres
(Centro Storico, Italy)

Bottom: this fine example of the very rare 1923 Humber Chummy was restored by Humber apprentices. It is powered by a four-cylinder 8 hp engine
(Coventry Motor Museum, England)

introduced in 1922, which used almost exactly the same mechanical mix as the Clyno. This marque lasted one year, and produced perhaps forty cars; Clyno lasted nine years and sold nearly 40,000.

Another factor which sorted, in the public's eye at least, the sheep from the goats as far as light cars were concerned was the burgeoning number of trials.

These trials were not just Sunday afternoon map-reading exercises, either; take the 1921 Scottish Six Days' Trial, which covered 900 miles 'deliberately designed to smash up every frangible part of the machines'. It included such

fearsome ascents as Tornapress and Applecross, where the road rose steadily for five miles on end, 'stony cart tracks in regions chiefly inhabited by sheep, eagles and deer . . . they have a knack of topping off a frightful bottom gear grind with two or three C corners on a grade of one in five, with a road width so restricted that a car must be reversed to get round. Or take Inverfarigaig Corkscrew, a 6 ft track, paved with dust or mud (according to the weather, and doubling back in itself six times within 800 yards; at each hairpin, the inside wheel must clamber up one in five or six, while the outer wheel races up a comparatively mild pitch of one in eight . . . The trial is run on a basis of 20 mph, plus or minus five minutes per hour. Twenty miles in sixty-five minutes on the Portsmouth Road is, of course, child's play, even for a tiny car, but Scotland has no equivalent for the Portsmouth Road. In the loch districts, a so-called main road swirls along in a precarious serpentine switchback, full of humps, dips, blind angles, and the most poisonous little skew bridges, too narrow for a pair of vehicles and generally quite invisible till the last second. Such a road spells violent acceleration and violent brake work . . . it makes for chassis testing'.

Below: one of the most popular cars on British roads during the early 1920s was the Morris Cowley, with its bull-nose radiator. Power for this car was provided by a 11.9 hp four-cylinder engine 1548 cc which utilised side valves (Coventry Motor Museum, England)

Such conditions would prove a stiff test for modern small cars, yet of the fifteen light cars taking part in the trial, fourteen finished, ten won gold medals, one a silver and three were awarded bronzes. The car which retired was an 8 hp air-cooled, two-cylinder Rover, which ran off the road into a ditch and broke a spring. 'The other four Rover Eights all won gold medals, losing no time and climbing all the hills', reported *The Autocar*. 'This is simply a stupendous performance . . . They did not smoke, they did not smell hot and oily, and they very rarely gave an audible pink even when they had to pick up on a fierce grade after a terrible hairpin at the top of a long climb. They have scored a great triumph for air cooling, and their success possibly sounds the tocsin for the big sidecar'.

In fact, the car which was to prove the doom of the sidecar outfit as a common means of family transport was probably no more than a doodle on the back of an envelope when those words were written, for it was in 1922 that Sir Herbert Austin announced his new 7 hp baby car, which he had designed on the billiard table at his home to avoid the criticism of colleagues opposed to the project. The Austin Seven was designed to occupy the same ground area as a motor

cycle and sidecar, and it *did* look ridiculously small and pramlike to British eyes (although the Continentals were well used to tiny cars); but, like the Model T Ford, it was designed for that section of the market that hitherto could not afford a car. The initial scorn and derision which greeted its announcement turned to admiration when the aviation pioneer E. C. Gordon England decided to prove the new car's mettle. Nearly fifty years later, the author interviewed him about the competition début of the Austin Seven, and his recollections of the events of 1922 were still crystal-clear.

'I'd crashed in the *Daily Mail* gliding contest at Itford, in Sussex, and I was laid up in hospital at Eastbourne for some weeks with my leg in plaster right up to the knee. It was this that started me off, because I was lying in bed recovering and I read all about this new Austin Seven. One thing that became rooted in my mind was: "He'll never sell this thing, because it's being described in the motor press as a toy – and the public won't buy toys, they want cars".

'I went into it very thoroughly, and came to the conclusion that the Austin Seven would make a very good show as a racing car. So I wrote to Sir Herbert Austin, as he was in those days, and said: "I am intrigued by this car, but I don't see how you are going to get it over to the public unless you can hit them squarely between the eyes from the word go – and the only way to do that is to race it. I've taken the trouble to go into the whole position very carefully, and I find that Brooklands has a whole series of 750 cc class records. Not one of them has ever been touched.

'"Therefore, if you do what I suggest, you can go out and get all these records – I'm certain you can set them at over 70 mph – you can go before the public announcing the availability of 'the Austin Seven, which has already taken all these records at Brooklands'.

'"At present, I am in hospital recovering from a damaged leg, but as soon as I'm mobile, may I come up and have a chat with you about the whole idea"?

'I got a very nice letter back, saying that he'd be glad to see me and perhaps I'd let him know when I was fit to travel. In due course, I was released from hospital, and the first thing I did was to go up to Longbridge. "Before I go and

see Sir Herbert", I thought, "I'd better find out just what the climate is like here". Well, the climate was what I'd expected – I might almost say hoped! – the whole staff thought the old man was going soft in the head. I had a long chat with the sales manager, a very brusque fellow, who said "The whole thing's nonsense . . . they'll never sell!".

'"Isn't that marvellous", I thought. "This is the chap who's going to put this car on the market!".

'Having got this view, and one or two others quite similar, I marched in to see Sir Herbert Austin. Now he had a secretary called Howitt, who had a most peculiar squeaky voice. "He's in there", he said, nodding towards Austin's door, "but I don't think you'll do anything with him".

'However, I walked in, and Austin was perfectly polite, really . . . for him! He said, very gruffly: "Well, what do you want?".

'Then we had a two-hour battle straight off. He opposed every mortal thing

I said – and I told him he didn't know what he was talking about. We really got down to a slogging match, which was inevitable with him – it was his nature – and I said: "Look here, I've been round your organisation, and you haven't got a friend in the place. They don't believe the Austin Seven's got any future at all. The only way you can get round it is by doing what I suggest".

'Towards the end of the two hours, I think I'd beaten him down on every point. He didn't like that very much, so his final gambit was, I think, a lovely one. Pointing at my leg in plaster, he said: "You'd make a bloody fine racing driver!".

'"You damned fool", I replied – we'd got to that stage then – "You couldn't build a racing car by the time that leg's all perfectly sound!".

'"Can't I?", he said. "All right, that's a bet!".

'And that's how we ended the conversation – he muttered something about "he'd bloody well show me". So I went home and carried on with my business, getting fit among other things. One day I received a telegram: "RACING CAR ON TRAIN NO . . . ARRIVING PADDINGTON . . . O'CLOCK. PLEASE MEET AND COLLECT. HERBERT AUSTIN".

An Austro-Daimler of 1926, which is powered by a straight-six overhead-camshaft engine of 3 litres, whose 100 bhp can push the car along at a speed of 100 mph. This example is believed to be the 1926 Ulster TT machine

'He'd won . . . I still had my leg in plaster. He must have gone at it like a bull at a gate to get the thing done. I went up to collect it, and there it was – shockingly badly interpreted from what I'd asked for, I thought, but the essentials were there. That was all I cared about. I knew I could do the rest. So I took the car straightaway to my little works at Walton-on-Thames, full of joy because I hadn't expected to get it so soon, and we set about making it run.

'In those days, I saw a lot of Sammy Davis. "I'm going for records at Brooklands", I said. "Can I count on you to come and help me?"

'"Of course you can", he said. Then I knew I had *The Autocar* behind me.

'Dear old Lindsay Lloyd, the Clerk of the Course at Brooklands, was himself all over . . . "You can't do anything in *that* car!", he said.

'"Never mind", I replied. "Will you be there, because we want all the tapes down for the mile and half-mile and so on".

'Well, as luck would have it, the little car behaved awfully well, and Lindsay Lloyd reported back that we'd done the half-mile at 75·8 mph, I think it was, and the mile at 72 mph. We'd lost some speed because we'd gone round on to the banking. Anyway, it was very good.

'I was able to telegraph back to Sir Herbert Austin that we had set up the records. And that was the beginning of the Austin Seven!'.

And that, too, was the end of the cyclecar, which had reared its unlovely head again in the post-armistice boom, due partly to the tremendous amount of Government surplus material which was dumped on the market at knockdown prices. Timber and ply featured large in the make-up of many of the nastier cyclecars – I once saw the remnants of a Gibbons, manufactured in suburban Essex by two incurable optimists named Gibbons and Moore: it resembled nothing more than a tea-chest mounted, somewhat haphazardly, on four old pram wheels, with a motor bike engine bolted on the offside. In 1921 this unlovely machine sold for £115 – which must have represented a profit of around 900 per cent on the material costs – and a 'set of fittings' (presumably luxuries like hood, windscreen and lights) was another £18.

The advent of the Austin Seven, a proper four-cylinder, four-seater car for £165 fully equipped, consigned such aberrations to the everlasting bonfire they so richly deserved; it also proved the salvation of the Austin company, whose other post-war products could be summed up as 'worthy'; well engineered,

they were ponderous machines which had lost all the excitement of the pre-1914 Austins, which rejoiced in model names like 'Vitesse' and 'Defiance'. Herbert Austin's post-war policy had initially been to produce a 20 hp model which adapted American design philosophies to British taste, and, insofar as the Austin Twenty was really rather a dull machine, he succeeded admirably; its younger sister, the Austin Heavy Twelve, which followed soon after as a sop to the horsepower tax, was another well engineered car which was totally lacking in 'sparkle', and was said to be much favoured by maiden aunts (as a digression, uncles seemed to go for Morris-Oxfords, but one's father tended to favour the Clyno; thus early did popular cars acquire a 'market image').

More attractive light cars appeared in 1922: there was the pretty little 8/18 Talbot designed by Louis Coatalen, and sold in France with a different radiator as the Darracq by another component of the Sunbeam-Talbot-Darracq combine in one of the earliest successful examples of corporate badge engineering; there was the 8/18 Humber, with its close-coupled 'chummy' bodywork; there was the attractive Gwynne Eight, unique among British cars in being taken originally from a Spanish design, the Madrid-built Victoria, whose progenitor,

Arturo Elizalde, was normally associated with the production of large, luxurious, sporting cars. And there was the Trojan . . .

The Trojan was designed by Leslie Hounsfield, who had made his name as a designer of steam-propelled military transport at the time of the Boer War, which may explain some of the more curious features of the car's eccentric make-up. Hounsfield had built a prototype of his 'people's car' as early as 1910, but it wasn't until he had attracted Leyland Motors, who had prospered greatly during the war, building trucks for the Government, to back the venture that production began. Surprisingly, Leyland chose the Trojan to supplant its super-luxury Leyland Eight car, killed by the slump after some fourteen examples had been built. You couldn't have found two more disparate designs – Leslie Hounsfield summed up his brainchild in the succinct phrase: 'It's weird . . . but it goes!'.

In many ways, the Trojan was the British equivalent of the Model T Ford: it was designed to be a go-anywhere car – simple to drive and cheap to maintain. Its two-speed epicyclic gearbox gave crashless gear changing and, by pulling up a hefty lever, the engine could be started from the seat, a notable advantage when few light cars had the luxury of a self-starter. Mechanically, it was like nothing else on the road: its 'chassis' was a sort of metal punt in which lay the odd four-cylinder two-stroke engine. This engine was said to have only seven moving parts, its cylinders being arranged in a square, each pair sharing a common combustion chamber. This arrangement was possible because the engine was a two-stroke and it gave maximum control over the timing of the induction and exhaust strokes. Each pair of cylinders also shared one long, V-shaped con-rod, which, instead of articulating as the pistons moved up and down the bores, simply flexed itself. Maximum power output of this strange 1529cc engine was a puny 11 bhp, although, to compensate for this, bottom end torque was remarkable, enabling the Trojan to grind slowly up the steepest gradients with the inexorability of the mills of God (which is probably an appropriate place to remark that the Trojan was the only marque of the day to advertise in the *Church Times*, as its low price and commodious – and ugly – bodywork made it the ideal transport for impecunious clergymen with large families). Other idiosyncracies were chain final drive and long, supple cantilever springs fore and aft, which were intended to take the jolts out of the narrow solid tyres which were the model's standard wear ('Wondersprings', the Trojan's promoters called them with pride). Because of the underfloor location of the engine, the bonnet held only the petrol tank, hooter, steering box, carburettor and lots of emptiness . . .

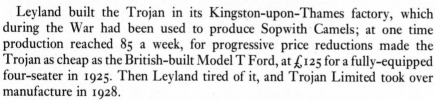

Leyland built the Trojan in its Kingston-upon-Thames factory, which during the War had been used to produce Sopwith Camels; at one time production reached 85 a week, for progressive price reductions made the Trojan as cheap as the British-built Model T Ford, at £125 for a fully-equipped four-seater in 1925. Then Leyland tired of it, and Trojan Limited took over manufacture in 1928.

One wonders how such a strange vehicle would have succeeded on the export markets, had anyone been particularly interested in selling abroad, for, having put up a high tariff wall, British manufacturers sat tight behind it and rarely bothered to sell their products overseas. One of the few manufacturers to establish an export department and to build a special 'Colonial Model' was Clyno, who, after the 1924 Empire Exhibition, received the following letter: 'I have corresponded with over sixty English manufacturers on the subject of trying to get into the Colonial trade during the last six months, and as far as I can see, you are the only people in Britain who have any ambition to do so. I must honestly say that, with the exception of yourself and one other firm, the correspondence I have had has made me feel ashamed to be an Englishman, and if your manufacturers persist in their attitude, England is doomed from a manufacturing point of view'.

Certainly no British manufacturer showed the enterprise of General Motors or Willys-Overland, who established factories in England, supplied with

Above left: Peugeot produced this type 177 car in 1927. The bodywork is of the popular Weymann fabric type
(Peugeot collection, France)

Above: Humber's 14/40 Doctor's Coupé of 1927; it featured a four-cylinder engine of 2050cc and had a top speed of just on 60mph
(Coventry Motor Museum, England)

components, in General Motors' case, from their Canadian subsidiaries to minimise the rate of duty paid. Also, Britain was almost unique in the number of little 'localised' firms whose products rarely sold outside their own area; there was the Clyde from Leicester, the Jewel from Bradford and the Airedale from Esholt, Yorkshire. Only France could rival Britain in the production of such esoterica, and many French light cars were of a flimsiness of construction that beggared belief.

But the French mass-producers built solid cars of almost indestructible reliability; and of those mass-producers the most spectacular was André Citroën, who had worked for Mors before the war, and had emerged in 1919 as the first European manufacturer truly to assimilate the Ford system of mass-production of a single model. In his new factory on the Quai de Javel, Citroën proposed to build one hundred cars a day, which would be sold, fully equipped, at a moderate price . . . and received 30,000 orders before production began. Citroën's first car was the 10 cv Type A four-cylinder tourer.

He was even inspired to announce grandiose plans for a factory in America, but this scheme was soon abandoned. However, Citroën did establish an assembly plant in England as well as subsidiaries in other European countries. The English works, at Brook Green, Hammersmith, was opened in 1923, by which time Citroën had announced the Type B, an improved version of the Type A, and the little 5 cv which, since it was normally seen in bright yellow

189

paintwork, was punningly known as the 'Citroën pressée', which phonetically could be rendered either as 'Citroën in a hurry' or 'lemon squash!'.

For the English market, Citroën imported the Type B in chassis form, coachwork, in the British idiom being fitted by Short Brothers of Rochester, Kent, another firm of aircraft builders who had turned to car-body manufacture in the post-war slump. But the little 5 cv was imported complete from Paris. Then, in 1925, Citroën pioneered the all-steel body built under the American Budd patents, and proved the strength of this form of construction by standing an elephant on the roof. There were only three main pressings to this type of saloon body – the two sides and the roof. To the consternation of the panel-beaters of the day, these pressings couldn't easily be repaired if the car was involved in an accident; they had to be replaced complete. To a generation unaccustomed to the philosophy of repair by replacement, such a concept came as a shock.

Citroën always thought big: when the British Government announced that import duties were about to be reimposed, he ordered cars to be shipped to England in large numbers. Nearly 100 5 cvs were parked on the flat roof of the

Right: André Citroën hired the Eiffel Tower between 1925 and 1934 just to advertise his company. There are a quarter of a million lightbulbs in the display

Below left and below: commissioned by H.E. Nawab Wali-ud Dowla Bahadur, the President of Hyderabad State, India, this 1926 Phantom 40/50 hp Rolls-Royce saw service right up until 1948. The immaculate aluminium body was built by the Barker company
(Stratford Motor Museum, England)

Hammersmith works, the yard was crammed with Citroën taxi chassis, and storage space was hired for the 10 cv models. And André Citroën – his rival, Louis Renault, called him sneeringly 'Le Petit Juif' ('The Little Jew') – was also an astute publicist, who from 1925 to 1934 hired the Eiffel Tower and turned it into France's biggest billboard, with his name written 100 feet high in a quarter of a million electric light bulbs.

Mass-production was spreading all over Europe: though Fiat was Italy's biggest car maker, it had hitherto built nothing in large volumes; or perhaps even that statement isn't strictly true, for Fiat's most popular pre-war model had been the 1847 cc 'Zero', of which only some 2000 had been produced in a little over three years. But 1919 saw the Torinese company with a brand new model designed for mass-production in a brand-new factory (five storeys and a test-track on the roof), even if Communist-inspired strikes prevented either

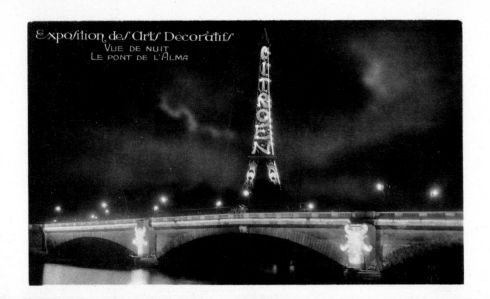

Exposition des Arts Décoratifs
Vue de nuit
Le pont de l'Alma

Left: another example of a Barker-bodied Rolls-Royce Phantom I. This Torpedo-style car was once owned by the legendary Greta Garbo (Château de Grandson, Switzerland)

Above: one of the rivals to the Morris company in the 1920s was Clyno; this is their famous 10.8 hp model

from getting under way for a while, and forced Fiat, in order to remain active, to stick touring bodies on war-surplus 9-litre armoured car chassis (these were a Russian order frustrated by the Bolshevik revolution, so perhaps there was an ironic justice in this method of raising revenue).

The new model was the 1460 cc Tipo 501, a slightly rotund vehicle of conventional design and refined construction, of which some 46,000 were sold between 1919 and 1926. The standard Italian coachwork wasn't too much liked in England, so once again Short brothers had to be called in, while bodies were also bought from the moribund Harper Bean concern, in receivership after an ambitious trade consortium called the British Motor Trading Corporation, had collapsed about their ears.

As motoring became more popular, so the number of accessories available burgeoned. Suddenly, there was sufficient traffic on the roads to warrant the sale of direction indicator devices and 'traffic warners' which gave illuminated advice of the drivers' attentions. Driving mirrors, which had first appeared on cars around 1905, became commonplace, while the increased price of petrol promoted an interest in fuel economy devices. There were, of course, plenty of fitments of dubious virtue available for those who made a fetish of adding to the equipment of their vehicle, fitments such as the 'More-Room' steering wheel, which was designed so that it could be slid forward to make it easier for portly drivers to get in to their seat, or the 'Kwiksail' car mascot, a small biplane fitted to the radiator cap in such a way that at speeds of over 15 mph it began to rise up its mounting pole to a height of around 8 inches, with its propeller revolving merrily. In France in 1921 there was understandable anxiety about the growing number of car thefts, so anxious owners could equip their vehicles with devices such as the Flic steering lock or, if they owned a Ford, the Rapid steering wheel. This could be unscrewed and removed from the car to prevent its being driven away, although what one was supposed to do with the detached steering wheel as one went about one's daily round on foot was not recorded. Nor was it mentioned how one guarded against astute car thieves who had troubled to equip themselves with their own Rapid wheel . . .

Tyres were still a perennial source of worry, as roads which had been neglected during wartime were, if anything, in even worse condition than the pre-1914 highways that had taken such expensive toll of pneumatics. To guard against unnecessary tyre damage, the Michelin Tyre Company introduced an 'ingenious device' at the 1921 Paris Salon. It was 'an invention for warning the driver that this tyre is becoming deflated', and, the reader was informed, 'consists of a tiny gun complete with lock and cartridges. The trigger is rubber-covered, and rests on the base of the rim. It cannot be released so long as there is adequate air pressure in the tube. To cock the gun it is only necessary to press a plunger, and, if a cartridge has been inserted, the device is ready for use. If the tyre becomes deflated, the lack of pressure on the beading releases the trigger, and a loud report gives the warning'.

Slightly less wearing on the nerves was the Jeff Patent Tube, an inner tube of curious construction – its inner surface was made up of overlapping flaps which were claimed to seal punctures as soon as the wounding instrument was withdrawn. *The Autocar* noted: 'At Christmas 1921 we fitted a set of Jeff Tubes to one of the staff cars and started by driving four large nails through the tread of one of the tyres so equipped. We have run the car for about five thousand miles, and have had no trouble at all in the way of air leakage'.

Like all parts of the motor car, however, tyres were becoming more reliable: now owners were claiming mileages of up to 20,000 miles a cover, and manufacturers could actually guarantee their tyres against premature failure for up to 5000 miles.

In 1921, the Royal Automobile Club issued a report on the causes of breakdowns dealt with under their 'get you home' scheme, and found that the most common source of trouble was half-shaft failure, which accounted for no less than 13·9 per cent of all breakdowns. Running it a close second was ignition failure; both these factors, it was stated, were the result of poor maintenance and bad driving rather than any inherent defects, 'and pointed to the necessity

Below : yet another Peugeot saloon to feature the Weymann-type fabric body is this 1928 190S saloon
(Peugeot collection, France)

Right and below right : the Bean Company of Dudley, Staffordshire, produced cars between 1919 and 1929. However, this was just another firm which had to survive the Morris price war. This is a 1928 Light 14, which used the 14/40 hp engine in the smaller 12 chassis to cut costs
(National Motor Museum, England)

for improved accessibility in view of the general disinclination of many owner-drivers to undertake any work on the car which is not rendered absolutely simple'.

'The owner-driver' – that is a phrase that sums up the essential difference between pre-war and post-war motoring in Britain, for the war had reduced both the number of people able to keep a 'motor-servant' and the number of those willing to undertake such an employment . . . and, of course, increased the total of those who regarded the possession of a car as a necessity, but one that they could only just afford. For such people, home maintenance was the only solution – and a dirty and depressing business it could be, especially when the majority of cars on the road had varnished coachwork and plenty of bright metal requiring frequent polishing to prevent tarnishing. For this reason, motoring still tended to be a seasonal business.

'In these days', grumbled a 1921 motorist, 'when to have a car washed by somebody else is a costly and slow process, even the most enthusiastic motorist, who is also his own cleaner, becomes a little tired of using his car during the exceptionally wet days of an English winter, for the simple reason that even an

hour or two's run may entail a similar period splashing about in a cold and draughty yard endeavouring to remove the mud from the chassis and coach-work. Accordingly, the mileage of the car during the winter is liable to be limited; some people – the chicken-hearted, they say – even going to the extent of care-fully greasing and covering their machines so that they may be laid up for a month or two at a time'.

Added to which, of course, was the important factor that the British railway network was still run by private enterprise, and therefore offered a reliable, and often more comfortable, alternative means of transport, especially over long distances, with branch-line communication to the most obscure corners of the country at reasonable cost. Just how attractive railway travel then was can be seen from Great Western Railway Statistics for the year 1921 (and remember that the Great Western had been astute enough to use motor transport as a feeder to the railheads as early as 1903). During the period April to October, some 64 million people travelled by Great Western, and the company was taking a million pounds a month from passenger traffic alone (and at least as much again from goods train receipts). And in the month of November 1922

a total of 115,563 trains was run, the average number of minutes late amounting to just 2.3; no wonder people used to set their watches by the passing trains!

Against this, the motor car did offer the freedom to wander, to change one's plans on impulse, and the romance of the open – if ill-maintained – road inspired hundreds of touring articles in the motoring press of the period. It is interesting to note that motoring novels, which had enjoyed a vogue in the early 1900s and then faded away, were now back in fashion, usually featuring the sort of high-powered luxury car that the average motorist yearned for but knew he could never afford. Because of the romance and glamour attached to such exotic machinery, it is easy to fall into the trap of thinking that they were a common-place sight on the roads of the early 1920s, just as one could be gulled, from reading certain motoring magazines of the 1970s, that there are nearly as many Lamborghinis on the road as Ford Escorts.

Of all the exotic cars of the 1920s, unquestionably the most glamorous was the Hispano-Suiza, known before the war as a well built, if conventional, car emanating from Barcelona, and designed by the Swiss Marc Birkigt, which had attracted attention chiefly because that most enthusiastic of motoring monarchs, the King of Spain, a patron of the marque, had been given one of their 15.9 hp

Top right: Clyno's 12/35 hp of 1928 used a 1593 cc side-valve engine

Above and right: the last Mercedes-Benz car to be built at Mannheim and the last one designed by Dr Porsche is this Nürburg 460 of 1928. Power is from a straight-eight, overhead-camshaft engine of 4.6 litres. This car features the classic Mercedes U-section frame, rigid axles and semi-elliptic springs

196

sporting models as a present by his English Queen. They had even opened a French factory at Levallois-Perret to assemble their cars, of which this Alfonso XIII model was undoubtedly the favourite with the French. Among its high-society owners, one notes that the 15.9 hp Hispano was the chosen vehicle of that notorious society adventuress 'La Baronne De La Roche' (actually one Elise Delaroche); it was in this car that her lover Charles Voisin, the aviation pioneer, and brother of the more famous Gabriel Voisin, was killed in 1912.

However, the firm's post-war glamour model had nothing in common with the Alfonso; instead, it drew heavily on Hispano-Suiza's contribution to the war, during which over fifty per cent of all allied aircraft were powered by Hispano-Suiza aero engines, either 'genuine' or built under licence. Until his mysterious disappearance in 1917, the French air ace Georges Guynemer was associated with Hispano-Suiza-powered aircraft, scoring his most famous victories on a SPAD biplane. Guynemer, with 53 victories to his credit, and France's other top ace, Rene Fonck, both flew with the famous Escadrille N3, the Hispano-powered French 'ace of aces' squadron, whose good luck emblem was a stork. Guynemer was a personal friend of Birkigt, and indeed designed his own deadly modification for the Hispano power unit, with results recalled by Captain W. E. Johns: 'In July, he took the air in a 200 hp Hispano-Suiza SPAD fitted with a gun of his own design. This was a light one-pounder which fired a shell through a hollow crankshaft; the shell came out of the propeller boss. He met an Albatros and fired his new gun at it from a distance of two hundred yards, and the black-crossed machine blew up in flames'.

Guynemer became part of French wartime mythology, and when the time came to choose a suitable radiator mascot for the new car, Birkigt commissioned a sculpture of the stork that had adorned the fuselage of his friend's SPAD. Launched at the 1919 Paris Salon, and intended for production at the Paris Bois-Colombes factory, opened in 1914, the new 32 cv Hispano H6 had a six-cylinder power unit which incorporated many of the features developed on the war-time V8 aero engine, like an alloy block with screwed-in steel liners and a single overhead camshaft. Designed for the elite few who could still afford the ultimate, the H6 was unequivocally the most advanced car of its day, with powerful servo-assisted brakes on all four wheels; when, five years later, Rolls Royce grudgingly decided to fit four-wheel-braking to their cars, they took out a licence to copy Birkigt's design.

Only one thing marred the Hispano-Suiza, and that was its gearbox, a three-speed affair in unit with the engine; some years ago, the author drove a T49 Hispano, a 3750cc version of the H6 designed for the less well heeled Spanish market, in all respects save the smaller engine identical to its 6597cc French cousin, and noted that second gear had a scream like a sawmill – and that was on a low-mileage car! For the record, the author also recorded that the distance from the driver to the radiator mascot was exactly eight feet!

Although the H6 was a glamour car, it seems to have been pretty sparing in

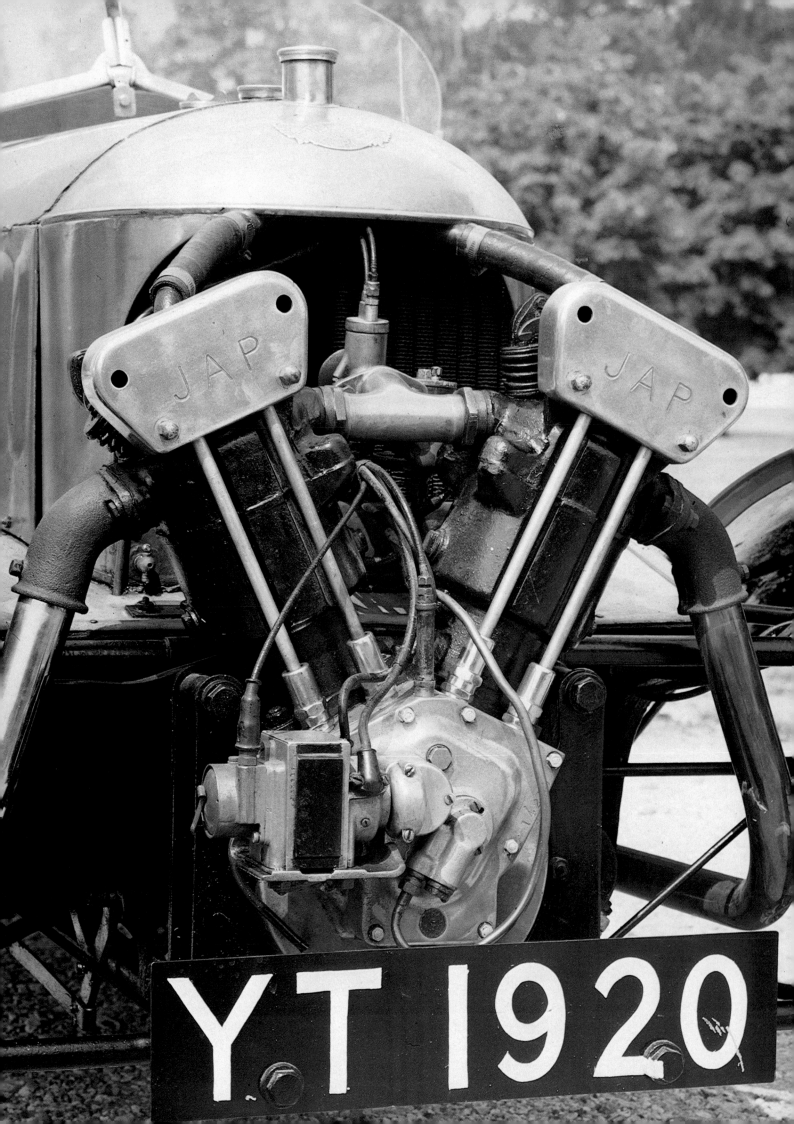

its public appearances in the early part of its life; reporting on the 1921 Glasgow Show, *The Autocar* remarked petulantly: 'At the opening of the Show, by the way, the Hispano-Suiza was conspicuously absent'.

What gave the Hispano-Suiza its especial cachet was the fact that, although it was a super-luxury car, it offered sports-car performance; André Dubonnet, the *aperitif* king, even entered his tulip-wood bodied Hispano for the Targa Florio – this was the 46 cv, eight-litre 'Boulogne' model. A sister car, owned by Captain Woolf Barnato, covered 300 miles at Brooklands at an average speed of over 92 mph.

Such feats by the *richesse dorée* gave the Hispano-Suiza a romantic aura that was enhanced by its 'starring role' in that archetypal novel of the 1920s, Michael Arlen's *The Green Hat* . . . 'Like a huge yellow insect that had dropped to earth from a butterfly civilisation, this car, gallant and suave, rested in the lowly silence of the Shepherd's Market night'.

The French had their Hispano novel, too, in the pages of Pierre Frondaie's *l'Homme a l'Hispano*, written in 1924, but the car does not really feature as more than a passing shadow in this rather turgid romance about the tragic M.

Morgan were responsible for bringing sporting motoring to those who could not afford large cars, their machines being light enough to be motorcycle engined. This is a 1927 Morgan Aero which features a JAP V-twin power unit (National Motor Museum, England)

Dewalter's unrequited love . . . it is just there as a hint of his super-richness . . .

Unquestionably, such adulation gave the Hispano the edge in *chic* over its main rival in the Continental carriage trade, the straight-eight Isotta-Fraschini from Milan, but in any case the author has been informed by those who have driven both cars that the Hispano was without a doubt the better-handling vehicle. 'In comparison', they said, 'the Isotta drove like a truck'. Perhaps it is because the Hispano was designed for the man who drove himself, while the Isotta was meant to be driven by a chauffeur, who would not complain.

There was no direct equivalent for such vehicles in England, although the ingenious ohc Straker-Squire 3.9-litre six-cylinder car was a beautifully engineered high-speed tourer that promised great things, but failed to get into serious production. Interestingly enough, the engine design of the Straker-Squire was based on that of the war-time Rolls-Royce Eagle aero engine; Rolls-Royce seemed to have benefited not at all by their aviation experience and resumed post-war production virtually where they had left off, with the basically 1906-designed Silver Ghost, a very fine car, but not, as the company's advertising arrogantly claimed, 'The Best Car in the World'. In sympathetic hands, though, and fitted with appropriate lightweight coachwork, the Rolls could acquit itself creditably against its more technically sophisticated rivals, as

G. R. N. Minchin noted in a letter written in 1922: 'The Alpine Eagle Rolls Royce . . . is a most wonderful car . . . One can run at 50 to 60 mph for mile after mile with absolutely not a sound but the wind and the noise of the tyres, with the springs gently absorbing the bumps in the road. It is such a fascinating motion, it tends almost to lull one to sleep, and one cannot believe one is travelling so fast. No other car approaches the Rolls-Royce in this particular respect, and it is a sensation difficult to describe. One can drive all day at an average of over 40 mph and not feel tired or have a headache at the end. Coupled with this speed is such silence that with the car at rest passengers cannot tell whether the engine is running or not . . . The Rolls can be driven all out all the time, and it will never wear, nor flag, nor cause any trouble. It is one of the cheapest cars in the world to run and, should one want to sell it for any reason, its secondhand value is remarkable'.

The car which caused the greatest sensation among the British motoring public was the 3-litre Bentley, originally announced in 1919, and tested that year by S. C. H. Davis of *The Autocar*, but which did not get into production until 1921, mainly for reasons of finance. Its designer, W. O. Bentley, had been responsible for one of the better war-time aero engines, the Bentley Rotary, which was the most-sought-after power unit for the Sopwith Camel fighter; he had also pioneered the use of light-alloy pistons before the war. And the Bentley car used design features based on racing and aircraft-engine practise – although not on Bentley's aircraft engine, for its power unit was an in-line four-cylinder with an overhead camshaft. Perhaps the prettiest Bentleys were the few built without front-wheel brakes in the very earliest days of production, for these had, unmodified, the elegant radiator shell designed by that greatest of all motoring artists, F. Gordon Crosby (who also created the marque's winged badge). And the first of these was sold, in September 1921, to a wealthy young socialite named Noel Van Raalte, who had financed KLG sparking plugs and who owned Brownsea Island in Poole Harbour; while an undergraduate, he had raced round Cambridge, in reverse, in a Grand Prix Mercédès!

After a year of ownership of Bentley Number One, Van Raalte analysed his feelings about the car which, coincidentally, had a similar ring to Minchin's experiences with his Rolls: 'This chassis has a four-seated saloon body, and I employ no chauffeur. I can truthfully affirm that this is quite the most pleasing and satisfactory car of the many I have had. I find I can drive any distance up to 400 miles straight off in a day without feeling tired, which is an accomplishment I cannot achieve on anything else. The car is extremely fast, flexible and sweet-running. In traffic, it can be driven all day on top speed, except for an actual dead stop. It is not by any means cruelty to the car to do so, as it does it with great ease. Its petrol consumption in Scotland, where I live, and where the hills and roads are not, perhaps, of the most desirable, is over 20 mpg. The brakes and steering are better than any others I know of, and are all that could be desired. The suspension is excellent, and the way the car holds the road at high speeds is most remarkable. *The Autocar* recently stated that this car was a paradox in combining the qualities of the ultra-fast sporting car with those of the sweet running touring car. It can be used as either with great ease'.

The Bentley was also the most expensive car in its capacity class, costing £1395 in September 1922, equipped with a four-seater touring body; a comparable French car of similar conception, the six-cylinder Lorraine-Dietrich, cost £750 in London at the same date.

However, the Bentley's greatest rival among high-class fast touring cars was the 30/98 Vauxhall – 'The Car Superexcellent' – an inspired design by L. H. Pomeroy, which represented the high peak of the Luton company's achievements since their début in car manufacture in 1903. A few examples of this model had appeared just before the war, but it did not get into full production until after the Armistice. Compared with the Bentley, it was old-fashioned in concept, but sound engineering gave it a surpassing performance. It was the sheer joy of owning such a car that led one John Grange to write, in the spring of 1922, a tribute to his car which also encapsulates the heady pleasure of motoring in the golden days of the 1920s: 'I have covered about 3000 miles in my 1922 30/98 Vauxhall without the slightest trouble.

'The tyres are certainly not half worn, and 20 mpg can easily be attained with care. But what do a few drops of petrol, more or less, matter to the proud owner of a car like this? I am old in motordom. For eighteen years I have never been without a car. Yet each model I have possessed had its shortcomings, which became more and more flagrant as experience developed an exacting criterion. Hence my praise of any of my former possessions has always been meagre, restrained and qualified, because none captured the sanctions of my soul like my present machine has done. My pen seeks to portray the truth; and it is a verity that I have never seen a car so accurately described by its makers as the 30/98 Vauxhall. It is endowed with every virtue they claim for it. There is embodied in its vitals ample potency of incredible performance. It is a veritable miracle of mechanism. If one desires speed, it moves with might and majesty along the King's highway at the slightest touch of the accelerator pedal. It gulps giant gradients with greed and gusto. Yet withal the engine shows no symptom of punishment. So far no adjustment has been necessary. Oil consumption is alarmingly small, being more than 1000 mpg. The chassis is very strong indeed, for so light a body as the Velox. Its brakes are silent, sweet, efficient'.

The Mercedes 38-250 SS of 1929, with four-seater, sports-tourer bodywork by the same company. The impressive straight-six engine is supercharged and has a capacity of 7.1 litres. This actual vehicle was specially built for Lord Cholmondeley, who sold it to an Indian Maharajah in 1939; it was rediscovered in a shed in Bombay many years later and remarkably it has needed no restoration
(Stratford Motor Museum, England)

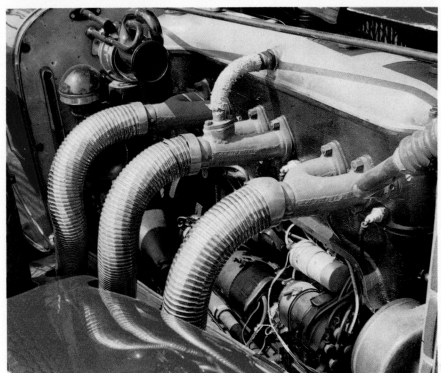

Left: there were no breathalyser laws in the 1930s, when this 1932 Austin 16 was photographed outside the Church House Inn. The fabric-bodied saloon had a 2.2-litre, six-cylinder engine

Below: a 1929 Lea-Francis Hyper, with a Cozette-supercharged Meadows engine of $1\frac{1}{2}$ litres capacity. This is a replica of the car with which Kaye Don won the 1928 Isle of Man TT (Stratford Motor Museum, England)

CHAPTER 10

The Death of the Cyclecar

If proof was needed that the motor vehicle was an essential part of everyday life, then it came in May 1926, when the Trades Union Council called upon Union members throughout Britain to support the miners, whose industry had been badly hit by lower-priced German and Polish coal, as well as by newer sources of energy – oil and electricity. At midnight on Monday 3 May, in defiance of emergency regulations which made it an offence to 'prevent the proper use or working of any . . . railway, canal, bridge, road, tramway, vehicle . . .', railwaymen and transport workers joined the ranks of the strikers.

For a few hours, the nation ground to a halt, and then volunteers came in to keep the roads and railways moving; the 'unprecedented interference with routine' lasted until 15 May (although the miners stayed out until August). During that period, those who could drive took over trucks and buses – buses were festooned with barbed wire and carried a policeman to keep the strikers at bay, although the only serious incident occurred when strikers overturned a Tilling-Stevens petrol-electric of Thomas Tilling's fleet at the Elephant and Castle. There were, indeed, some curious sights; well-known racing drivers at the controls of lorries and buses, a 10½-litre Fiat racing car delivering copies of the Government newspaper, *The British Gazette* . . .

The private car came into its own, carrying people to and from work, and London had a foretaste of things to come, with traffic jams and parking problems; Hyde Park was closed off, and became a distribution centre for milk and fish, while Regent's Park was used as a bus depot at night. Vans and trucks were converted into impromptu buses, too, carrying commuters in from the suburbs in extreme discomfort for 3d to 6d. There was, it seems, no problem in getting hold of petrol, and the brand-new miracle of wireless kept the nation informed of the progress of the strike.

It would be foolish to assume that things went on as normal, but thanks to motor vehicles, abnormality was kept to a minimum. And when it was all over, *The Autocar* commented: 'During the troublous times through which we have all passed one outstanding point emerges, and this is the paramount importance of road transport to the whole community. In the days before the motor vehicle had become a part of our national life the discontinuance of work on so gigantic a scale as that which took place when the general strike was declared would almost certainly have resulted in a paralysis of activity utterly disastrous to every branch and section of the people. In our opinion, the escape of the country with wounds which, deep though they may be, will heal in time, is attributable to the fact that road transport of essential commodities was available to save the nation from irreparable disaster'.

Certainly, the Strike started the habit of commuting by car, and only a few days after one enthusiastic motorist was writing to the Minister of Transport suggesting that 'motorists who drive into London daily to business should be given special facilities in the parking places nearest their offices, and by being allowed a four hours stay instead of the two hours at present available'.

A beautiful example of a Hispano-Suiza H6B, 37.2hp model; this particular machine was specially commissioned by the Maharajah of Alwar in 1929 as a wedding present for his son and it has cabriolet-roadster bodywork by the French coachbuilders Kellner. The Hispano was intended primarily for panther hunting and the spotlights mounted either side of the windscreen were intended specifically for this purpose, having extendable arms which allowed them to be focussed on the prey. The bell, which can be seen in front of the radiator grille, could be rung from the cockpit and was used for frightening natives (Stratford Motor Museum, England)

So, the density of traffic had already risen to such an extent that parking restrictions were becoming necessary in London, although it is obvious that, outside the big conurbations, motorists still parked pretty much where they pleased. In villages and small towns, it was still the custom, a legacy of a more leisurely era, for the local *grande dame* to instruct the chauffeur to halt the limousine in the middle of the road outside a shop and sound the imperious hooter to summon the shopkeeper. He would then stand humbly by the foot-board of the big car, noting down my lady's shopping list for subsequent delivery (probably by pony and trap).

Anticipating the coming increase in motor traffic, various road-improvement schemes of more or less a practicable nature had been suggested. Proposals for special motorways restricted to cars alone dated back to the end of the 19th Century, while a circular road round London had first been suggested in Edwardian times. In the 1920s, the first scheme for a London to Birmingham motorway was published, but it got no further than some of the more fantastical proposals, such as a suggestion that main roads should be put into tunnels to preserve the rural beauty of England, or that in London, where the length of the average traffic jam had doubled since 1914, wide, straight roads should be constructed above the existing buildings to carry through traffic.

Slightly less impracticable was the 1924 proposal that elevated roads should be built above existing carriageways to carry cars along the main east-west

Left: a 1931 replica of one of the 4½-litre, supercharged, short-chassis Bentley's raced by the Birkin-Paget team; this car was based on a production 4½-litre 'blower' – originally a drop-head coupé. The big Bentley, in supercharged and unsupercharged form, is one of the greatest and most famous British sports cars; the Birkin-Paget versions had a top speed of 125mph
(National Motor Museum, England)

Below and right: the 1932 Alvis 12/60, with two-seat-and-single-dicky bodywork by Cross and Ellis, and its 1645cc, straight-four, pushrod engine, with twin SU carburettors, producing 52bhp
(Coventry Motor Museum, England)

through routes in the City of London. The motor age was certainly prompting the construction of new roads, like the Purley Way, constructed to relieve post-war unemployment, and the Kingston by-pass, but these were hardly purpose-built motor roads, just wider versions of the old roads and, although they may have passed through open country for a good deal of their length, indiscriminate speculative building soon made them little better than the thoroughfares they were intended to replace.

It was around this time that the motoring author Filson Young took advantage of the new vision accorded by the aeroplane, and flew over London to see what was being made of the new roads. . . .

'To realise the muddling and blundering that is going on . . . you must get up into the air and see what combined greed and lack of design may do to make the world ugly', he wrote. 'A glance at the Barnet by-pass on its way from Finchley to Hatfield told a tale that is to be seen repeated on the outskirts of nearly all the big towns in England. As soon as this road leaves the dense suburban belt that extends to Mill Hill, this dreary trimming of its edges by little houses begins and continues for miles; one comes to realise the extent of this new method of planning homes in mile-long ribbons along the arterial roads . . . Behind the noisy roads lie patches and spaces apparently unused by man; for the people who inhabit these ribboned roads have no contact with the land, and agriculture means nothing to them.

'Turning south-east from Hatfield, we crossed the end of Epping Forest and the North Circular Road and what I think is called the Eastern Avenue. We looked down upon a world that crowded along even these great arteries; they had been established so that men could escape from crowded populations, but the arteries were themselves becoming choked . . .'

So, for most people the romance was going out of motoring, that fact was reflected in the rise of the saloon car, which was rapidly overtaking the open tourer as the most popular type of coachwork. Not only that, but motorists obviously were not what they were, if an indignant correspondent to *The Motor* in 1926 is to be believed: 'Whilst travelling in my car on Sunday afternoon, 29 August, at 2.30 pm on the Great North Road, just beyond Bromham cross-roads, I was passed by a large touring car, travelling fast and driven by a lady. Seated at her side was a gentleman. A little farther ahead the large touring car ran into the rear of a stationary car, which was on the extreme left-hand side of the road in question. The "colliders" got out casually to view the damage, and obviously observing the stationary car was conveniently unattended, jumped, with guilty haste, into their own car. The gentleman, who now took the wheel, reversed the car, made the gears hum, and burst off at a great speed in the direction of Bromham. For the full benefit of those closely interested, I may say the damaged car happened to be a new Standard blue four-seater, bearing a trade number, the rear number plate and mudguard of which appeared quite "unhealthy" after the unwanted incident on what was to all events her "maiden voyage".

'I can honestly assure you that during my many years of motoring, I have never witnessed such a mean action performed upon a fellow motorist by another supposed loyal member of our colossal motoring fraternity. It complately filled me with utter disgust, and it is evidently some small sample of treatment that one may possibly expect to receive from some of the so-called "Ladies" encountered on the road.'

As a postscript, one may add that at this period – and, indeed, right up to 1930, there was no compulsion on motorists to take out insurance against accidents. Nor was there any form of driving test, two factors which add extra point to this account of a mid 1920s escapade which reads like the scenario of a Mack Sennett comedy: 'On coming to the crossing from the direction of Rugeley, it was apparently deserted, but, my attention being on the signpost ahead to find the road for London, I unfortunately failed to notice the turning coming out at an angle on my left, from which a number of cars and motor cycles were coming and evidently wishing to go to Warwick.

'Failing to locate the London road from the signpost, I decided to drive up to the policeman on the point to inquire. Shouts on my left caused me to

One of the early Volvo six-cylinder models, the first of which had appeared two years earlier, in 1929; this particular example has a 65 bhp engine and all-round hydraulic brakes. Earlier products of this Swedish concern, which did not start making cars until 1927, had been fitted with four-cylinder power units

realise that I had brought my car almost broadside on to the traffic emerging on that side.

'Seeing they had all managed to slow sufficiently to clear me, I again started to make for the policeman, when a car seemed to appear from nowhere, coming head on. Seeing a turning on my left I accelerated and swung into it, as my only hope of preventing a nasty collision, my action again throwing those unfortunate people on my left into confusion.

'At this moment, the policeman, who had evidently been taking a little relaxation from his undoubted strenuous job of regulating the traffic, woke up and in a loud voice inquired what game I thought I was playing. I did not stop to tell him, as I had done no damage, and shuddered to think of the names I might be called if I returned among my victims.'

Mind you, the motoring laws in Britain were so antiquated that it would have been difficult, even for the most law-abiding citizen, to have remained within them. George Bernard Shaw, always ready for a good controversy, claimed that between 1909 and 1929 he had covered well over 100,000 miles, and had never completed a car journey without breaking the law . . . at the time, he was addressing the Chief Constables' Conference! Shaw was quite proud of the fact that he had been summoned for speeding: 'I was informed that I had passed through a police control at a speed of twenty-seven miles an hour. There was no question. There was no room for argument. The constable and I were perfectly civil to one another. He was pleased when he got my name, because he knew he would be in the paper next day. And I was pleased, because what came into my head was that it was a mercy he did not catch me half an hour before, when I was driving at fifty!'.

So, motoring was becoming more commonplace. But what were the makes which made it so? Whose cars were the most popular? We can gain some idea, at least, from the various impromptu censuses which enthusiasts compiled for publication in the correspondence columns of the motoring press. On a Sunday afternoon in Sussex in the summer of 1925, a motorist counted the number of cars using the Bognor-Littlehampton road during the space of an hour: 'Morris 29, Austin 15, Rover 15, Singer 13, Ford 11, Standard 8, Bean and Citroën 5, Wolseley 6, Dodge Brothers 4, Talbot 4, Daimler and Clyno 2, AC 4, Overland 4, Essex 4, Sunbeam 4, Buick 3, Napier 3, Hillman 3, Renault 3, Armstrong-Siddeley 4, Fiat 5, Morgan and Chevrolet 2, Crossley and Humber 3, Unic 2 and one each of the following: Studebaker, Swift, Delage, Charron-Laycock, Lancia, Riley, ABC, Cubitt, GWK, Star, Darracq and Jowett.'.

On the Continent, obviously, things were a little different. Four years later, an inhabitant of that cosmopolitan and somewhat anti-motorist country, Switzerland, made a similar survey of the cars passing his house in Geneva between 5.50pm and 6.20pm one Sunday – and a curiously mixed bag they were: Citroën 43; Fiat 43; Peugeot 22; Renault 21; Chrysler 20; Buick 10; Ford 9; Whippet 7; Talbot, Donnet, De Dion, Nash, 6 each; Delage, Studebaker, 5 each; Ansaldo, Auburn, Erskine, Essex, 4 each; Amilcar, Cadillac, Chenard-Walcker, Pic-Pic, Voisin, 3 each; Martini, Benz, Imperia, Panhard, Packard, Willys-Knight, Wolseley, Victory, Austin, Bugatti, Minerva, Frazer-Nash, Aries, 2 each; Lancia, Sizaire, DeSoto, Opel, Falcon-Knight, Ballot, Berliet, LaSalle, Chevrolet, Maximag, Rally, Mathis, Hudson, 1 each. British cars, our observer added, were almost unknown on the roads of his country, only the odd Morris, Austin or Rolls-Royce serving to remind the Swiss that Britain did indeed have a motor industry.

The sad thing about Britain's apparent indifference to export sales was that the average British-built car was demonstrably equal to the most extreme overseas conditions – a standard 10.8hp Clyno, with no pump or fan to aid its cooling, was reported to be in everyday use in Aden without any overheating troubles. In 1926, Frank Grey, the former MP for Oxford, challenged the British motor industry to build him a car suitable for making the West-East crossing of Africa; the only response came from Jowett of Bradford. On 16 May 1926, Grey and his companion, Jack Sawyer, left Lagos in two two-seater Jowett 7hp flat-twin cars. Sixty days and 3800 miles later, they arrived at

Massawa, on the Red Sea, after an adventurous trip, during which they had freed a young native girl from slave traders. Jowett, who specialised in coining advertising slogans – typical samples included 'The little engine with the big pull' and 'The seven that passes a seventeen like a seventy' – now added 'The car that put the camel on the dole' to the list.

British cars, too, had made the first motor journey from Cape to Cairo a few months earlier; Major and Mrs Chaplin Court Treatt had started the epic 13,000-mile journey on 24 September 1924, driving a pair of 25 hp Crossleys, which reached their destination on 24 January 1926, having survived the muddiest rainy season on record. And in 1927 Mrs Diana Strickland had crossed Africa in a Wolverhampton-built 14/40 hp Star named (in English and Arabic) 'The Star of the Desert'.

On other continents, too, British cars blazed the trails: in 1924 Major Forbes-Leith's Wolseley 14 had been the first car to make the journey by road from England to India.

The British did not, however, have a monopoly of long-distance motoring, for Citroëns fitted with the half-track conversion devised by M. Kégresse,

Three views of the 1½-litre Aston Martin 'Le Mans' of 1933, one of the first Astons to be produced after the company had been reorganised by A.C. Bertelli and W.S. Renwick. This car was fitted with the new single-overhead-camshaft engine, which featured dry-sump lubrication and gave the heavy car a top speed of 85mph. This was one of the most expensive 1½-litre sports cars made at that time, being offered at the same price as three MG Midgets or two Rileys
(National Motor Museum, England)

formerly in charge of the garages of His Imperial Majesty the Tsar of all the Russias, were renowned for opening roads across Africa, where the French had long been trying to establish closer links with their colonies; French West Africa was separated from Algeria by several thousand miles of desert. The equipment carried by the Citroëns, which made the first successful Sahara crossing in 1922–23 is worthy of note, for it shows the inhospitable nature of the country which the cars had to traverse. Wrote André Citroën: 'The body was designed to give the maximum of comfort to the travellers. It had three seats, one of them reserved for a possible guide, boxes of provisions, camp requisites, maps and munitions – for, in the desert, one must think of defence, and the mission carried a rifle per man and three aeroplane machine-guns. Each car carried, rolled up on its side, a tent which could be built up in a few minutes. Two of them, called provision cars, carried from 60 to 120 gallons of petrol. The others had two tanks of 15 gallons each, making 50 gallons with the front tank. They also had two water tanks, holding four gallons'.

In 1924–25, came the famous *Croisière Noire* (Black Journey) in which eight cars were despatched from Algeria, to cross Africa, splitting into four groups which would reach the coast at Mombasa, Dar-es-Salaam, Mozambique and Cape Town, finally to rendezvous again on the island of Madagascar, having carried out 'a feat of transport unsurpassed in the history of the motor car'.

Then, in 1931, Georges Haardt, organiser of these two journeys, achieved the crossing of Asia from Turkestan to Peking at the head of an expedition of Citroën *auto-chenilles* christened *La Croisiere Jaune* (Yellow Journey), only to die from pneumonia in Hong Kong while planning the return trip.

Turning from the well planned to the near-farcical; in 1926 three Chinese men made the overland trip from Shanghai in a beaten-up Trojan, arriving in London to tumultuous apathy (although, along with Parry Thomas, who had just taken the Land Speed Record at 171.09mph in his 27-litre *Babs*, they were honoured at a supper and concert party organised by Leyland Motors.

Above: the strange rear-engined Crossley RE of 1932, based very closely on the earlier Burney Streamline, designed by Sir Dennistoun Burney. Various engines were tried by Burney, but Crossley used their own 2-litre straight six, with a power output of 61bhp (*left*). The model was notable only because of its unusual design and was not a success, soon being dropped from the range
(National Motor Museum, England)

Above right: a 1929 Morris Oxford 14/28 coupé on an inter-club trial during that year

Right: the Czechoslovakian Aero type 500 of 1933, fitted with a single-cylinder two-stroke engine of 499cc, developing 10bhp at 2500rpm
(Château de Grandson, Switzerland)

Then there was Michael Terry who, with £8 2s 3d in his pocket, set out in February 1923 at the wheel of a rickety Ford, accompanied by one Richard Yockney, to make the first-ever crossing of the desolate 'Never Never Land' of Northern Australia, covering 800 miles of trackless desert where, on occasion, the car could only cover ten yards at a time before becoming bogged down, and where four miles could represent a day's journey. And when they reached their destination in October (after running out of both petrol and water in the desert and almost dying before a search party found them), the explorers felt so uncomfortable in the soft beds of the hotel that they rolled themselves in blankets and slept on the bare boards of the verandah!

However, although the Model T Ford was still capable of conquering the desert, during the mid 1920s, its star, which had seemed permanently in the ascendant, began to wane with alarming rapidity as old age caught up with the 'Universal Car'. Sales, which had reached a peak of 2,055,309 during the company's fiscal year (August to July) of 1923, fell off, slowly at first, then, with increasing rapidity as Ford's rivals introduced .more attractive models that were not just a 1908 design gently warmed over like the Model T, Henry Ford, who had envisaged the car going on for ever, was nonplussed as customers turned to the more stylish Overland, Essex, Chevrolet and Dodge models. As

212

speculation that the Model T was approaching the end of production, with some 14 million of the type already built, Ford remained adamant, denying all rumours. 'We have no intention of introducing a "six"', he stated in December 1926. 'The Ford car is a tried and proved car that requires no tinkering. It has met all the conditions of transportation the world over . . . Changes in style from time to time are merely evolution . . . We do not intend to make a "six", and "eight" or anything else outside of our regular products. It is true that we have experiments with such cars, as we have experiments with many things. They keep our engineers busy – prevent them from tinkering too much with the Ford car.'

Ford had, indeed, planned a successor to the Model T, the unorthodox eight-cylinder X-Car, so-called because its cylinders were laid out in the form of two St Andrew's Crosses in tandem. But the engine proved too heavy, and the sparking plugs on the lower cylinders so susceptible to water and mud thrown up from the road, that the design was shelved in 1926, after six years of experimentation.

Rumours that the Model T was to be discontinued after nineteen years' production began to spread. On 26 May 1927, the fifteen-millionth Model T came off the production line, the event marked by a simple ceremony . . . and then Henry Ford passed the death sentence on the 'Tin Lizzy'. When the production lines finally stopped moving, some 15,500,000 Model Ts had been built, of which around three-quarters of this total, amassed since 1908, were still in regular use.

Reaction to the demise of the old model varied from one Ford executive's cynical 'The Model T lasted two years longer than it should have' to that of the old lady who bought and stored away seven new Model Ts so that she should never have to change her allegiance for the rest of her life.

And only when Model T had passed into history did Henry Ford command his company, which had neither advanced design engineering department nor proving ground, to develop its successor.

The first blueprints for the new car had been drawn up in January 1927; such was the speed at which new models were put on the market in those days that a prototype chassis was running inside three months. But it needed plenty more of the 'seat-of-the-pants' testing that was typical of Ford methods in those days. There was not even a full-time test driver; the man appointed to the task normally managed the Ford farms. Once again, Ford returned to his favourite development method of watching engineers draw his concepts in chalk on a blackboard, and only when he was satisfied with the drawing was it translated into metal. Even when the first prototype was complete, Ford insisted on testing it, to 'represent the public' and, having hurtled it across a rough, obstacle-strewn field, insisted that hydraulic dampers were fitted to improve the ride.

By 10 August, development was complete, and the new car was ready for

production. Meanwhile, of course, Ford sales were just coasting on the residue of Model T output and the manufacture of spare parts, so the company's rivals, especially Chevrolet, were able to make damaging inroads on Ford's section of the market. Public interest in the 'New Ford' was intense – probably no car before or since had attracted so much attention and speculation. The purchasers waited with increasing impatience as the weeks dragged into months, while the Ford factories throughout the world were totally reorganised for the manufacture of the new model; the measure of the confidence that the car-buying public had in Henry Ford was shown by the 400,000 orders that were received before anyone had even seen the car.

Production of the New Ford – which was given the designation 'Model A', as it represented a new beginning – began in limited numbers in November 1927, and the press were at last permitted a look at it at the end of that month. On its first public showing, 100,000 people crowded into the showrooms of

Left: the famous Alfa-Romeo 8C-2300 which came second in the 1935 Le Mans 24-hour race and was later used on the road by Mike Hawthorn. The car was designed by Vittorio Jano and was fitted with bodywork by Touring of Milan; its twin-overhead-camshaft, eight-cylinder engine (*below left*) gave the car a top speed of 115mph from its supercharged 2336cc (National Motor Museum, England)

Below: a 1932–3 version of the famous SS One fixed-head coupé, with a six-cylinder, 50bhp, side-valve engine (Coventry Motor Museum, England)

Detroit just to catch a glimpse of the new car, which turned out to be as conventional as the Model T had been quirky, although its design was full of Ford ingenuity, like the petrol tank which formed an integral part of the scuttle, or the short copper strips which connected the distributor to the spark plugs. But what really set the Model A apart from its predecessor was its elegant styling, carried out under the supervision of Edsel Ford, who had created the car as a smaller facsimile of the luxury Lincoln, which had been produced as part of the Ford empire since 1922. For such up-to-date looks, the price was astonishingly moderate: the Model A Tudor sedan, at $495, was no more expensive than the equivalent Model T (and $100 less than the Chevrolet), the Fordor was $570 and the Coupe was $495. Development and new machinery costs totalled $250,000,000 – and Ford met this colossal bill with equanimity and cash from the company's reserves, for when Model T had ceased production, Ford could count $350,000,000 in the bank. . . .

By comparison, Europe could show nothing on so grand a scale: William Morris, who had built up production of his well liked Bullnose models to over 54,000 in 1925, and gained British market dominance, did not even have a

Above and left: a 1934 Rolls-Royce Phantom II, with Thrupp and Maberley coachwork, commissioned by the Maharajah of Rajkot; the Maharajah's motto is displayed on the car and it can be roughly translated as 'an impartial ruler of men of all kinds of faith' (Stratford Motor Museum, England)

Below left: a beautiful Hispano-Suiza 68bis, with Saoutchick coachwork and an 11.3-litre, 250bhp, pushrod V12; this splendid machine was put together in 1934 (Peter Hampton)

Below: a 1935 Buick convertible, driven by a Mr G. G. Wood, waiting for the judges in the RAC Rally and Coachwork competition at Eastbourne, Sussex, in that year

moving production line until the early 1930s. Chassis were just pushed down the factory in rows, getting nearer the exit as they approached completion. The same, on a lesser scale, applied at Clyno, who were still matching Morris prices to the penny with a car that was in many ways superior. Then they made two fatal mistakes – building a huge new factory at Bushbury, a Wolverhampton suburb, and introducing a 9hp model to forestall the rumoured introduction of the Morris Eight. They tried to build a '£100' version of the Nine, but the new model, officially christened 'Century', became known as the 'Cemetery', as its introduction was instrumental in sending Clyno to an early grave, one of the first victims of the depression that was about to force many motor manufacturers out of business. The Rootes Brothers, Kent-born motor traders who were building up a car-building empire by snapping up companies which had run short of cash, like Humber and Hillman, could have bought Clyno for around £86,000, but preferred to see this admirable make go out of business. Henry Meadows, the engine manufacturer, and a former works manager of Clyno, had plans to revive the marque during the late 1930s, but the re-armament programme put an end to his plans.

Right: a 1934 Talbot 105, with a six-cylinder engine of 2970cc, which gave the car a top speed of more than 90mph; this model was fitted with a preselective gearbox, built by Georges Roesch, in which the lever was needed only for down-changes (National Motor Museum, England)

Below and left: a 1935 Auburn 851, with a supercharged 4585cc engine, giving a power output of 150bhp and a top speed, via the two-speed rear axle, of 100mph. Each car was hand-built and carried a plaque to guarantee that it had been tested to over 100mph (National Motor Museum, England)

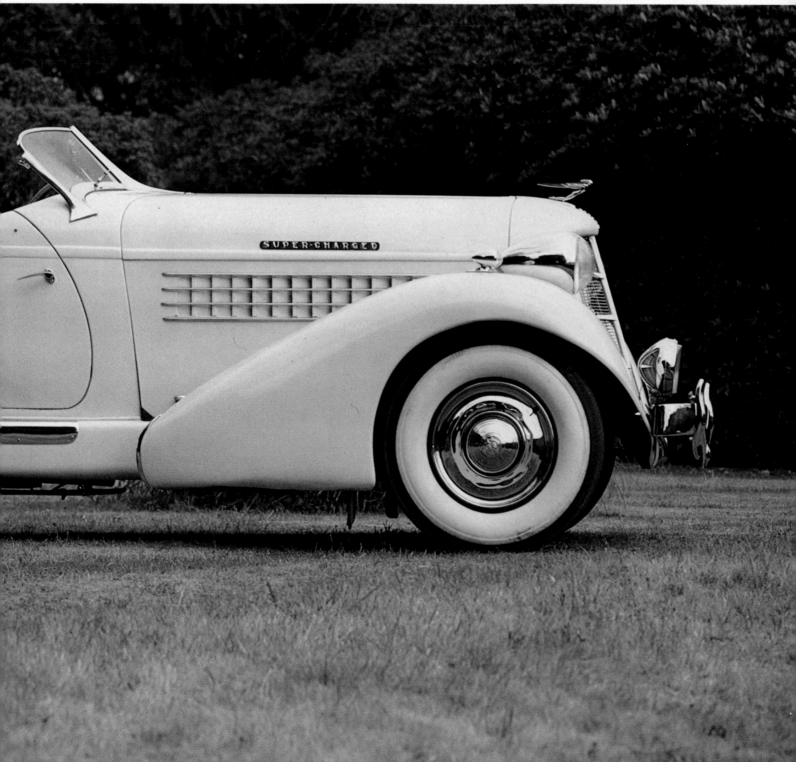

The depression proved that, henceforth, the race would definitely be to the strong, and lack of finance and the inability to compete on equal terms with the mass-producers, who could practise the economies of scale (and who, indeed, had often snapped up their former suppliers, to further minimise costs of components) drove some of the most respected names in the industry – Bean, Swift, Star, Calthorpe – out of business. One make, however, which had collapsed before the onset of the depression, had done so because of incompetent marketing. The shock was that much greater because the firm in question was Wolseley, one of the oldest names in the British motor industry, who had introduced a new model known as the 'Silent Six' for 1925; its radiator mascot was six little Klu-Klux-Klansmen standing in a circle. Customers, expecting the model to live absolutely up to its name, were apt to return their car to the factory for replacement if they heard the slightest sound emanating from the engine. The company ran into so much trouble from this cause that, by 1927, they were bankrupt, owing £2,000,000; William Morris stepped in and bought up Wolseley for £730,000.

By the end of the 1920s, it was evident that the smaller independent motor

manufacturer was a dying breed; in 1919, over eighty different companies produced a total of 25,000 cars (or an average of 300 per firm), while a decade later there were forty motor manufacturers in Britain, who built 239,000 cars between them, an average of 6000 each. The motor vehicle had obviously come to stay, for there were 2,260,500 motor vehicles on the roads of Britain, paying a total of £27,040,384 in licence duties; 1,042,300 of these were private cars, paying an average horsepower tax of £13 18s 6d each, while 339,500 were petrol or steam goods vehicles, average duty £26 5s 6d.

Perhaps even more significant were the statistics from the United States, where production during 1929 reached a record level of 5,337,087, a figure a million greater than the previous year's output, and one that would not be beaten for another twenty years. And of those cars, nine out of ten were closed, an exact reversal of the 1919 figures, when nine open tourers were sold for every sedan.

Cars were more powerful now and people needed a vehicle that could be used reliably in all kinds of weather.

Top: a 1935 Hillman Aero Minx, with a 10hp side-valve engine and fastback, pillarless coachwork by Thrupp and Maberley (Coventry Motor Museum, England)

Above: this is the sports version, 508S, of Italy's most famous family saloon of the 1930s; this particular model was built in 1935 and was renowned for its excellent brakes and high gearing, the latter of which gave it a cruising speed of 70mph from its 1100cc engine (National Motor Museum, England)

CHAPTER 11

Opulence gives way to Economy

One of the earliest British motor-manufacturing companies was the Wolseley concern, whose first cars were designed by Herbert Austin, better known for selling cars under his own name. In 1927, however, the Wolseley organisation was forced into liquidation and was taken over by Lord Nuffield's Morris company; rationalisation of the range was slowly put into effect, thereafter, Morris engines replacing the Wolseley units, in all cases, by 1938. The model pictured here was made before this time, however, being a 1936 21 hp saloon, with a straight-six 3-litre engine. Somewhat inconveniently, the body was not fitted with a boot lid, access to the luggage compartment being gained by removing the rear seat
(Coventry Motor Museum, England)

The 1920s, then, were a decade of sweeping changes, a decade in which the external form of the motor car altered radically, if not beyond all recognition, and in which its mechanics made unprecedented progress, most particularly in the opposed respects of starting and stopping. Electric starting and four-wheel braking became accepted as commonplace where, before the war, they had only been fitted by the most adventurous of manufacturers. Hydraulic brakes had been invented as early as 1918 by the aircraft manufacturer Malcolm Loughead (better known by the phoneticised version of his name – 'Lockheed') and first fitted in production to the Duesenberg of 1920, although as they were then truly hydraulic, using a water-based fluid in compression, such brakes were generally mistrusted. And when they appeared on the cheaper American cars, with their 'sudden-death' wraparound band brakes, vicious in the dry and totally useless in the wet, there was further reason to treat them with suspicion. Henry Ford, indeed, would have nothing to do with hydraulic brakes, and regularly published homilies on the superiority of mechanical brakes (although by that time hydraulics had become eminently trustworthy).

Other notable trends of the latter part of the decade were the adoption of coil ignition in place of the more reliable – but more complex and costly – magneto (and the relegation of the starting handle from its fixed abode on the nose of the crankshaft to the tool kit), the general acceptance of flexible engine mountings

to minimise vibration, the abolition of scuttle-mounted petrol tanks feeding the carburettor by gravity in favour of the rear-mounted tank with some kind of pump or vacuum device for fuel supply. Cars became easier to look after, with the introduction around 1928 of cellulose paint in place of coach varnish and the availability of chromium plating, which reduced the care of brightwork from the daily rubdown with polish necessary in the days of brass, nickel plate or german silver to an occasional wipeover with a damp rag.

Transmissions, too, altered dramatically, with the announcement of syncromesh in 1928 and the relatively short-lived vogue for free-wheels in the final drive. In 1927, Packard introduced the hypoid-geared back axle, which permitted a dramatic lowering of the overall height of the car without the need for a dropped chassis; better roads were another factor permitting the building of low-slung vehicles.

One remarkable invention of the 1920s which failed to catch on was the original 'run-flat' tyre, invented by 16-year-old Fred Rapson, whose father was a noted tyre manufacturer. This tyre had an inner high-pressure tube within a low-pressure outer cover, so that in the event of a puncture, the motorist could

drive to the nearest garage, with the weight of the car taken by the high-pressure tube. And the tread of the low-pressure tyre was detachable, so that it could be replaced when the tyre wore out. . . .

Body design showed many minor improvements, like the adoption of safety glass (although this didn't become compulsory in Britain until 1937) and the advent of the sunshine roof, which had been pioneered by a pre-war Labour-dette limousine body on a Silver Ghost Rolls-Royce. Luggage boots began to be built into the rear of the body, and passenger comfort and roadholding were enhanced by the general adoption of shock absorbers on the suspension. By the end of the decade, cars were appearing on the road with independent suspension; front wheel drive had made a tentative appearance, and the Armstrong-Siddeley and Cotal 'self-changing' epicyclic transmissions brought semi-automatic gear selection into practical use.

Above: this straight-eight limousine was made at the height of Packard's 'classic' period in 1936. The mid 1930s were important times, as far as Packard models were concerned, because 1935 saw the first slanting radiator grille *(right)* and front-hinged front doors, while wire wheels, solid front axles, mechanical brakes and automatic chassis lubrication disappeared in the following year

As the car was maturing, so the companies that built cars were changing. The older, smaller companies were either turning to the production of relatively high-priced specialist cars, or vanishing from the scene, unable to compete with the mass-producers. The great manufacturing corporations were gaining muscle; during the 1920s General Motors took a European stake with the acquisition of Vauxhall in Britain and Opel in Germany, while Morris and Rootes, both former cycle and motor agents, were expanding their manufacturing empires, Morris even attempting to compete in the French market by taking over the Léon Bollée factory at Le Mans to build a 12 cv Morris-Léon Bollée which failed to achieve lasting success, although it was apparently better-built than the company's English products.

In the winter of 1927–28, somewhat implausible reports of an 'understanding' between Ford and General Motors began to appear in the Press; Henry Ford was stated to have agreed to purchase a 'substantial holding' in General Motors, while GM were supposed to have promised 'not to fight Mr Ford's new motor car if Mr Ford did not invade the high-priced motor-car field'. As Chevrolet was edging ahead of Ford in terms of sales, the whole business was obviously journalistic invention.

But the thing which really marked the 1920s was the rise of the small car, notable milestones being the Peugeot Quadrilette and the Austin Seven. In 1928, Morris had announced their Eight, which had an overhead camshaft, and which was thus a descendant – if on the wrong side of the blanket – of the Hispano-Suiza aero-engine, which Morris's new acquisition, Wolseley, had manufactured during the war years, applying the knowledge gained therefrom to the design of their post-war models. So the new Morris was really a Wolseley.

Soon, however, it had a companion which *did* admit its parentage, the Wolseley Hornet, the smallest six-cylinder car on the market, announced in the spring of 1930. But this Snark also turned out to be a Boojum, for the new car was almost indistinguishable from the Morris Eight, except for the two extra cylinders and a few inches of chassis added to accommodate them. The most noticeable difference was the price, which at £195 was £60 more than the comparable Morris, and the braking, which was Lockheed hydraulic rather than the mechanical system of the four-cylinder car. After the initial ecstasies – 'speed . . . effortless, exhilarating, from the staid forties through the smooth fifties to the swift sixties' – had died away, the customers decided that the Hornet wasn't exactly stunning value for money, and the model's sales began to fall away. So, after only eighteen months on the market, the Hornet, having failed in its manufacturer's aim of 'providing first-class express travel in a small car for the first time' was replaced by a design whose meretriciousness was far more studied.

The New Hornet cost only £3 10s more than its predecessor, and on the surface appeared to be an entirely new design, carrying a portly sixlight saloon body 7 ft long on a wheelbase of just 7 ft 6 in, and within an overall length of 11 ft 7½ in. This, of course, didn't leave much room for an item of such minor consideration as the engine, which had a few inches lopped off by replacing the vertical shaft which drove the dynamo and camshaft by a two-stage chain and belt drive. This was engineering by the standards of Procrustes, and, to carry the simile further, the docked power unit was shoehorned into the forward extremities of a chassis with the torsional rigidity of a bedstead. Pushing the engine forward over the front axle meant that the radiator had to lean over backwards to make room for it, while the forepart of the sump had to be amputated to accommodate axle movement. Ostensibly to increase passenger comfort, but probably also to reduce stresses on the flimsy, overloaded chassis, softer springs were fitted, and, to judge by contemporary opinion, all this jiggling about with weight distribution and suspension endowed the New Hornet with excellent road-holding – provided that it was going straight ahead on a perfect road surface. Corners proved the full horrors of letting the stylist and the salesman override the engineer's better judgment.

The cynicism which had overtaken the motor industry as manufacturers strove to maintain sales in the face of the depression was amply exemplified by the introduction seven months later of a sporting version of the Hornet, the

Two views of the Packard 115 coupé, of 1937. This model had a great deal in common with the 120, which had been introduced two years earlier; one major difference, however, was that the 115 was fitted with a 3.6-litre six-cylinder engine as opposed to the straight-eight of the sister car, which by 1937 had grown from 3.7 litres to 4.6

Hornet Special, supplied in chassis form to coachbuilding companies, who cloaked its deficiencies in bodywork of exaggeratedly sporting aspect, so that the end result usually looked like something designed for the adolescent readers of the *Wizard* or *Hotspur*, with an aggressively louvred bonnet held down by leather straps, stoneguards on the headlamps and all the other accoutrements deemed necessary by the Walter Mittys of the Kingston Bypass.

Describing the new model, *The Autocar* hedged enough bets to build a maze: 'It is implied that the chassis is not sold as a racing job, but as a basis which is structurally correct and upon which keen coachbuilders can develop whatever they desire, for the capability of high performance is present in the design, and all the much desired refinements for speed work are already incorporated. The extent of the performance will largely be a matter of selected body style'.

Blame the shortcomings of the chassis on the coachbuilder, then . . . and perhaps the best summing-up of the Hornet Special came, again, from *The Autocar*: 'It is a most seductive motorcar'.

Seduction seems to have been the main aim of quite a few motor manufacturers in the difficult days of the slump as they busied themselves with the

newly discovered art of selling sizzle, not steak, making plenty of employment for men such as C. F. Beauvais, an ex-staffman on *The Motor*, who suddenly blossomed forth as a much vaunted automotive stylist.

It was the activities of such window-dressers which prompted Ernest Appleby to remark, waspishly, in 1931: 'There are cars on the market today, the sales of which would not be increased by the bare chassis . . . there are one or two which as complete cars are most imposing, but when one opens the bonnet it is difficult to find in it the engine, so small is it in comparison with what one expects to find'.

It wasn't, of course, an entirely unexpected situation, for sales of small-engined cars had been on the increase for some time, and the most popular models were now those of 10 hp and under; the trouble was that motorists would insist on demanding all the equipment on a baby car that they had hitherto demanded on larger vehicles; and a crop of ludicrously proportioned saloons and coupés was the inevitable result. Final-drive ratios had to be lowered to cope with the extra weight, with the consequence that economy suffered and high-revving engines needed reboring at laughably short intervals – sometimes after 10,000 miles or less. . . .

Reading the correspondence columns of the contemporary press, one comes to the inescapable conclusion that motorists were then obsessed with running costs. But when an enterprising American firm attempted to abolish running expenses entirely, there were surprisingly few takers.

The company in question was the American Austin Company, of Butler, Pennsylvania, founded in 1930 with the bold idea of introducing the Austin Seven to the American market, which had been gravely affected by the depression to the extent that during the years 1930–32, personal income deteriorated by 42 per cent, car production fell by 75 per cent and expenditure on automobiles was down by 75.4 per cent. It was against such a backdrop that the American Austin firm launched 'the most sensational sales plan ever introduced in the motor world'. Quite simply, the scheme was to give every purchaser of a $435 Austin – or, at least, every purchaser living in Pittsburgh or Butler – free motoring for the first year (or 7500 miles) that the car was in his ownership. Provided that the owner always bought his petrol and oil from a Gulf Refining Company garage, and had his car serviced at the specified intervals, all the costs would be met by the American Austin company.

Russell K. Jones, sales vice-president of American Austin, explained the reasoning behind the scheme: '"Free Motoring" is the natural result of an

Above: up to 1930, Nash concentrated on a range of six-cylinder-engined cars, but that year saw the introduction of a 4.9-litre straight-eight with overhead valves. This engine was steadily developed until 1942 and found homes under a great many different bonnets; the example shown here is a drophead coupé of 1937

analysis of our first year's sales and service experiences. There was a definite indication that Austin prospects and purchasers were always interested in the bantam's economy. Those who owned the cars knew about this economy. The public at large remained unconvinced and somewhat sceptical. We accepted the burden of proof and the result is "Free Motoring".

'The Austin under "Free Motoring" (or otherwise) offers the lowest cost power transportation in the world, including the streetcar and motor cycle. "Free Motoring" will rid us of the old sales bugaboo that "you could pay another hundred and get a larger four". You can; but under the new plan the Austin first cost of $435 does not have to be supplemented by any maintenance costs for 7500 miles, so that at the end of that mileage the cost to the purchaser is still $435. On the other hand, by adding the lowest average maintenance cost for other fours for 7500 miles to their lowest initial price, you get over $720. In other words, we offer a transportation saving of $285 or more for the first 7500 miles, or year, over that of our nearest price competitor. That means over $23 a month saving.

Above right: Oldsmobile built a number of six and eight-cylinder-engined models during the 1930s and this is the company's 'Six' of 1937, with a 4.2-litre engine producing 95 bhp at 3400 rpm
(Skokloster Museum, Sweden)

'Our plan, which will be tried elsewhere than in the places named when opportunity presents itself, is offered to persons with pruned budgets. We know it will work because in the last few days, when only a few persons outside our plant knew anything of it, we have been besieged with telephone calls, wires and letters asking for more details.'

Keen efforts were made to promote the scheme: a fleet of Austins fitted with radio loudspeakers cruised through the business districts of Pittsburgh and Butler broadcasting the details, but it seems that even in times of depression, the average American wasn't prepared to countenance motoring in something as tiny as the Austin, even though it had been restyled to suit indigenous tastes by Count Alexis de Sahknoffsky, better known for his work on Peerless luxury cars. The car was regarded as a joke, and appeared as such in a Laurel and Hardy film of the day, where its inability to accommodate Oliver Hardy's huge bulk was emphasised hilariously.

So the original manufacturers of 'the bantam car' went into liquidation in 1934; their successors fared a little better and, when the War came, designed the original Jeep. However, their factory wasn't capable of building the Blitz buggy in sufficient quantities, Willys and Ford came along with similar designs, and the company ceased production.

227

Left: in 1932, Ford's British subsidiary moved from Manchester to Dagenham, where, initially, American cars were assembled. However, 1933 saw the introduction of the first all-British Ford, the 8 hp model Y, which was made available in two and four-door form, and was powered by a 940 cc side-valve four. This example was made in 1936
(National Motor Museum, England)

Right: the Humber Vogue of 1936; this model was introduced by Humber in 1932 and was aimed at women drivers. Although not as slow as some of its predecessors, the Vogue was underpowered, having a heavy body and a 12 hp engine of 1700 cc
(Coventry Motor Museum, England)

Below: Ford of Britain introduced a smaller version of the V8 in 1937, this one having a 22 hp engine of 2227 cc, as opposed to the 30 hp and 3622 cc of the bigger car. This particular example is seen on the Torquay Rally of 1937, followed by a Delahaye type 135

It's odd, because cars based more or less on the Austin Seven were successfully built in France (Rosengart), Germany (Dixi and BMW) and even Japan, where the Nissan Jidosha Kaisha built it as the Datsun (though they improved the styling and chassis design), which had the advantage that it was so small that its drivers didn't need to take a driving test.

If British-designed baby cars couldn't make the grade in America, an American-designed baby car could – and did – change the face of light car motoring in Europe. The story started in 1929, when Ford of Britain began work on an immense new factory on reclaimed marshland at Dagenham in Essex. While the factory was under construction, the depression hit Europe, and sales of the Model A Ford, even in its smallbore 14.9 hp 'beat-the-taxman' guise, began to sink. It was apparent that although the Model A was a light car in its homeland, it was regarded as over-expensive to run by European motorists. And when the vastly expensive Dagenham factory opened in 1931, having cost £5 million – one would probably have to add two noughts to the figure to realise its present-day value – the company was desperate.

Not that it showed it to the outside world, however. To the motoring press, Ford of Britain seemed supremely optimistic and serene: 'In a period of difficulty and world-wide depression, the gigantic Ford undertaking at Dagenham was conceived and brought to fruition. It is an example of heroic

228

Streamlining found its way on to several cars of the 1930s, and some of those models were very sleek indeed. The Peugeot 402, which was introduced in 1935 with a 2.1-litre engine, was certainly streamlined, but its body was so wide that the chassis had to be fitted with special outriggers in order to support the weight. Even the headlights were concealed behind the radiator grille so as not to cause any obstruction to the airflow, as can be seen on the 1937 model pictured here
(Peugeot collection, France)

Ford to let him have a light car that could be produced to save Dagenham from financial collapse. Ford agreed, and work on the design started in October. Engineering staff worked unceasingly on the task, even the 67-year-old Henry Ford wielding a spanner in the construction of the prototypes. Development time of this new 8 hp model must have been an all time record, for the designers first put pencil to paper in October 1931, and by February 1932 sixteen prototypes were running on the road.

Henry Ford wanted to produce this new model under a new marque name – 'Mercury' – and the prototypes were built with this name on their radiator badge, but Perry insisted that the car, soon christened Model Y, should be marketed as a Ford. It was unveiled to the public at the Ford Exhibition at the White City in February 1932 when the oldest Ford dealer, A. E. Rumsey of Bristol, dapper in gold-rimmed glasses and goatee beard, stepped forward to pull a dustsheet from one of the prototypes.

When they heard that the proposed price of this stylish little saloon was £120, which undercut both Austin and Morris, Ford dealers could scarcely contain their joy.

231

'Nothing like it has ever occurred in the motor industry in this country,'
Perry wrote to Edsel Ford. 'Have never seen Ford dealers so enthusiastic . . .
Public opinion and press everywhere proclaim 8 hp car just what is wanted
here . . . Anticipate that many months will elapse before we can overtake the
demand.'

And within a year of Perry's original request, the Model Y was in production
and selling well. Out of 55,339 cars built at Dagenham in 1933, no fewer than
32,958 were Model Ys, and Ford of Britain was at last established as one of the
Big Three in terms of sales.

The Model Y had dragged the company back from the edge of disaster, from
a dreadful situation where Dagenham was living from hand to mouth; there
was no exaggeration in the statement by a Ford director that: 'The Model Y
was our only salvation'. By 1934 the Y held 54 per cent of the British market for
cars under 9 hp.

Now Morris fought back, installing moving production lines at his Cowley
factory and introducing a new 8 hp model whose styling was a blatant crib of
that of the Model Y, but offering a number of refinements like hydraulic

Above: a typical American street scene of the early 1930s

Left: this Wolseley 25 hp sporting convertible was made in 1937 by the Wolseley workers, as a Christmas present for Lord Nuffield; the Series II version of the car went into limited production in 1938
(National Motor Museum, England)

braking and a chassis strong enough to bear open tourer bodywork in unmodi-fied form – the Dagenham directorate was always rather concerned about the rigidity of the Y's chassis when endowed with open bodywork, and only catalogued saloons, leaving outside specialists to cater to the fresh-air fiends.

The Morris Eight sold well – 100,000 by July 1936, less than two years after its introduction – but Perry had a dramatic ace up his sleeve. By cutting out unnecessary frills, the price of the Model Y was reduced from £120 to £115, then to £110. Finally, at the Ford Exhibition in the Albert Hall in 1935 came the dramatic announcement: 'A saloon car at £100, not only roomy and comfortable, but exceptionally economical'. Production costs and, more importantly, profit margins, had been cut to the very minimum to achieve this figure . . . but it achieved the desired result.

It was the first time a fully-equipped four-seater saloon car had been offered at £100; previous attempts to market a car at this figure had produced only austere open cars, like the Morris Minor £100 side-valve model announced as the chimes of midnight heralded the new year of 1931, and available only as a two-seater painted 'naval grey'. This didn't sell at all well, and Rover's con-tribution to the economy car stakes, the rear-engined £85 Scarab, didn't sell at all, for it was withdrawn from the market as soon as it was announced in 1931.

But the Ford Popular struck exactly the right note, and once again saved the day for Dagenham: Ford's share of the '8hp and under' market, which had dropped to 22 per cent in 1935, soared to 41 per cent, giving the company over 22 per cent of the total market. Dagenham was firmly established as the biggest Ford operation outside the USA; although the Model Y was also built in Ford factories in France, Germany, Spain, Australia, New Zealand and Japan, it never achieved significant sales in those countries.

Its successor, the 7Y Ford Eight of 1937, was designed in Dagenham, and was to set the style for British Ford economy models for more than two decades to come.

Right: the Standard Big 9 saloon of 1932, with a 1287 cc, side-valve, four-cylinder engine, which gave the car a top speed of about 55 mph

Below: the Lagonda company produced its first V12-engined cars in 1937, in the shape of the V12 and Rapide; these were followed in 1938 by a more sporting version of the Rapide called the Le Mans, an example of which is pictured here. The 4480 cc engine, common to both models, produced 225 bhp in the Le Mans, 50 bhp more than the Rapide; the increased power output was due to a raised compression ratio and four, instead of two, carburettors (Stratford Motor Museum, England)

CHAPTER 12

Classic Cars of the Thirties

While the mass-producers were coming to rely more and more on the smaller sorts of car as the Depression reshaped buying habits, luxury car makers went in entirely the opposite direction, building bigger and more flamboyant cars than ever. The 1920s had seen Ettore Bugatti's magnificent aberration, the Royale, with a straight-eight single ohc engine of 12.8 litres (the prototype's power unit displaced 14.7 litres!) based on one of Bugatti's aero-engine designs. But this car, originally intended for kings and heads of state, never reached its intended clientèle and, at half-a-million francs for the chassis alone, only found six purchasers among super-rich commoners between 1927 and 1933, so Ettore Bugatti, never one to let a good engine go to waste, adapted this power unit to drive high-speed railcars, one of which set a 122 mph record in 1936. All the Royales produced are now jealously guarded collectors' items, and at least one Bugattiste is so anxious to own an example of this model that he is reversing the original design progression by building a replica of the 'Golden Bug' round a railcar engine. . . .

A year or so after the Royale appeared, the American Duesenberg brothers, Fred and August, put *their* concept of the super-luxury car on the market, encouraged by their backer, the flamboyant Erret Lobban Cord. Advertising superlatives (which for once in an American while were justified) greeted the appearance of the Duesenberg Model J in December 1928: 'It is a monumental answer to wealthy America's insistent demand for the best that modern engineering and artistic ability can provide . . . Equally it is a tribute to the widely-recognised engineering genius of FRED S. DUESENBERG, its designer, and to E. L. CORD, its sponsor, for these men in one imaginative stroke have snatched from the far future an automobile which is years ahead, and therefore incomparably superior to, any other car which may be bought today'.

The new Duesenberg had a straight-eight twin-ohc engine with four valves per cylinder displacing 6.9 litres, with a claimed output of 265 bhp at 4250 rpm: the chassis, which was exceptionally rigid in construction, came in two wheelbase lengths, short (11 ft 10 in) and long (129.5 in), although one specially commissioned limousine had a wheelbase of 14 ft 10 in. The standard of engineering was exceptionally high, and much use was made of aluminium in the car's construction; according to *The Motor*, the Model J was the world's most expensive car, with a chassis price of £2380, while typical American convertible bodywork brought the cost up to £3450. The Duesenberg looked better when it was fitted with open, sporty bodywork; somehow more formal carriagework didn't seem to sit the chassis so well. Not so long ago the author saw a Model J *sedanca de ville* which, although undoubtedly a very fine car, looked a little too high and narrow for its length. But the Duesenberg was a successful model considering the times that it was born in, with sales averaging one a week during its production life of 1928 to 1937, and is still one of the most sought-after of all antique cars. Current price, if you can find one, of a well preserved Model J Duesenberg is approaching £60,000 . . .

Doubtless you would have to pay even more for the highly exotic Model SJ Duesenberg, fitted, as its title suggests, with a supercharger, a centrifugal blower in the American idiom, running at five times crankshaft speed and boosting power output to a claimed 320 bhp, giving the car a top speed of 129 mph (the unsupercharged J was capable of 116 mph), and the ability to reach 100 mph from rest in 17 seconds. It was not a typical American car of its day. . . .

Nor, indeed, was the V12 Twin-Six Packard, whose 7298 cc power unit was silken-smooth, yet gave sizzling road performance. Introduced in 1930, this was Packard's second venture into dodecuplicity of cylinders, for they had built the original Twin-Six in 1916, and sold over 35,000 of them before production ceased in 1922. Designer of both Packard V12s was Colonel Jesse G. Vincent, who had gained his original inspiration from a V12 Sunbeam aero-engine imported into the United States just after the outbreak of World War I. This second V12 Packard lasted in production until 1939, and was bodied by the great American coachbuilders of the day; with a price tag of $4000–$6000, the Packard V12 represented excellent value for money, and a total of 5744 was

Daimler have long been renowned for building large, luxurious limousines and this Straight 8, of 1937 is no exception, with its 4½-litre engine. The example shown here was originally owned by a Lady-in-Waiting to Her Majesty the Queen (Coventry Motor Museum, England)

built. A front-wheel-drive variant, built in 1932, didn't reach production.

Not that this was the only American V12, for Franklin, Lincoln and Pierce-Arrow announced luxury models with this engine configuration, while Cadillac, having persevered with the manufacture of V8s since 1915, brought out both V12 and V16 models during the 1930s. The other great American V16 of the 1930s was the Marmon, which had an 8-litre engine and made its appearance in 1931; to rival Cadillac and Marmon, another famous American quality car maker, Peerless, made plans for a V16, and built a prototype with an elegant Murphy body before falling sales caused them to abandon car production in 1931. Soon afterwards, however, prohibition was repealed, and Peerless resurfaced . . . as the Peerless Corporation, brewers of Carlings Ale, having decided that quenching America's thirst was a less risky business than pandering to its taste for luxury.

Nor were big V engines restricted to American manufacturers, for the Daimler company had been building their Double-Six since 1926, and continued to build it in capacities varying from 3743 cc to 7137 cc for the next decade, encouraged by Royal patronage; King George V had several Double-Sixes in his stables. Like its French contemporary, the Voisin V12, the Daimler Double-Six compounded complexity by not only having twelve cylinders but having twelve *sleeve-valve* cylinders . . .

Voisin, never noted for the conventionality of his engineering, also built a straight-twelve, again with the sleeve-valve engine that was his hallmark, while the Bucciali brothers, who used V12 Voisin engines in front-wheel-drive chassis, made a sixteen-cylinder 'Double-Huit'.

In 1931, Hispano-Suiza introduced their most spectacular model, the 9425 cc Type 68. As a publicity stunt, that great French motoring journalist Charles Faroux drove one of the first Type 68s at high speed from Paris to Nice and back, the car going straight from the run into Hispano's showrooms for the duration of the Paris Salon de l'Automobile. During that time, not one drop of oil is reported to have fallen from the hard-worked car. A couple of years later, the decision was taken to market the Type 68*bis*, which had a 20 mm increase in stroke, bringing the swept volume to a respectable 11,310 cc, making this almost certainly the biggest production car of the 1930s.

By contrast the V12 Rolls-Royce Phantom III, announced in 1936, was almost a baby car, with an engine of 'only' 7.3 litres, but a performance that was decidedly un-Rolls-like. A couple of years ago, the author rode in a magnificently preserved Rolls P III belonging to the lady rally driver, the Hon Mrs Victor Bruce, who, despite her petite build and 79 years, was still capable of handling this massive car with perfect safety at speeds considerably over 80 mph . . .

Perhaps the most curious engine configuration of the 1930s was that announced right at the beginning of the decade by the National Factory of Automobiles of Barcelona. Although it never made production, the 3993 cc Nacional was a most interesting design, which had an engine constructed largely of elektron alloy with steel cylinder liners, and whose duralumin connecting rods ran directly on the crankshaft without bearings. Only two forward gears were provided, with maximum speeds in these ratios of around 40 and 80 mph respectively. And what was noteworthy about the cylinder layout of the Nacional? It had ten cylinders in line.

A multiplicity of cylinders was not to remain the prerogative of the plutocrats for long: that arch-leveller, Henry Ford, worried by the fact that Chevrolet sales had overtaken Ford, due not only to the hiatus in production when the Model T gave way to the Model A, but also to the fact that the Chevrolet had six cylinders against the A's four, decided to bring the V8 engine, hitherto only used in expensive luxury cars, into the mass-production market.

The luxury V8 Lincoln was already being manufactured under the Ford banner but, like all the other V8s currently in production, it was costly to build, with its cylinders and crankcase cast separately. Ford was convinced that the way to mass-produce a V8 was to cast crankcase and cylinders in a single unit, a task then regarded as impossible by everyone except himself.

In May, 1930, the first experimental unit was completed; then followed

months of trials as the design engineers attempted to build a prototype that could be translated into production terms. Some thirty different cars were made, and they even gave the octogenarian inventor Thomas Alva Edison a spin in one of them; but nothing seemed to satisfy Ford: 'He seemed to be getting madder and madder . . . he felt we weren't yet on the right track', recalled one of the engineers.

Then, in December 1931, the 68-year-old Ford personally took charge of the work, labouring like a human dynamo. The energy of the man must have been amazing . . . and this must have been the most fascinating era in the Ford Company, for two immortal designs were being simultaneously developed under Ford's personal supervision, the V8 and the 8 hp Model Y; both were ready for production in a staggeringly short space of time.

The V8 was announced to the public on 31 March, 1932; known in Ford terminology as the Model 18, it shared the streamlined radiator shell and more modern styling of the recently introduced Model B (Edsel Ford had insisted that the latter should be referred to as the 'Improved Model A', but his edict was generally ignored). Performance of the new model was electrifying, for it had a power-to-weight ratio unknown among its contemporaries: unfortunately, its cable brakes and overall chassis design were not really up to 80 mph motoring, and it was not long before the Model 18 gave way to the vastly better Model 40. When that happened, the Model B was phased out, and soon all American Fords were V8s. But in Europe, where taxation authorities disliked powerful cars, the V8 attracted a high rate of duty, and several Continental countries were offered the B40, which retained the less heavily taxed Model B power unit which, incidentally, soldiered on throughout the decade in a variety of guises, surviving into the 1940s as the motive power for Spanish-built Ford trucks.

For those who could afford it, however, V8 motoring was a revelation, as *The Autocar* witnessed in 1936: 'To drive a V8 for the first time is to sample virtually a unique motoring experience. Everything that this machine does is achieved remarkably easily. It suits the laziest driving mood with its almost exclusively top-gear running abilities, as well as providing in the fullest measure a swift car for point-to-point travel when such is wanted. This car may be got moving by using first and second gears for just a few yards, and then the engine will pick up at once and pull away smoothly on the quite high top gear ratio. It runs thereafter even in slow-moving traffic and conditions that involve taking right-angle corners without the slightest need for a change-down to be made. Hills are the easiest prey to the car, all normal main-road gradients being treated as acceleration bursts if the driver wishes . . .'.

Forty years on, it's a view that can be endorsed wholeheartedly, for the author's first experience of 'the greatest thrill in motoring', as Ford advertising called the V8, was in Northern France with a 1936 Model 68 V8 which, despite the vast change in road and traffic conditions since it was built, could hold its own with most 1970s popular cars, cruised at 50–55 mph and had perfectly acceptable ride and roadholding. And in 1936 one could buy a fully-equipped Ford V8 saloon for just £250, a similar price to cars of only 10 or 12 hp from other British manufacturers (for by this time the V8 was built at Dagenham instead of being shipped over from Canada).

Indeed, the equipment and performance of these American cars put them in a class by themselves, even though their styling might not have wholly coincided with European taste. Some years ago, the author was talking to a motorist who had interspersed a succession of Rolls-Royces with a 5-litre Hupmobile Eight around the year 1936, and he remarked, 'the American car didn't suffer too badly in the comparison!'.

Features which we nowadays take for granted, such as radios, synchromesh gearboxes and independent front suspension, first appeared in mass-production terms on American cars.

Cheaper motoring really entered the realms previously reserved for the exotica when the straight-eight Graham appeared in 1934 with a supercharger as a standard offering. A six-cylinder version was announced in 1936, capable of 90 mph, and boasting overdrive on the upper two of its three gears; a button

Above: a rare example, assembled in Britain, of Citroën's famous 7 cv model, with independent suspension, front-wheel drive and unitary construction. The saloon version was long used in France by the police and was probably hardier than the convertible
(National Motor Museum, England)

Left: the 1934 Graham-Paige Straight 8, which was fitted with a centrifugal supercharger rotating at 5¼ times engine speed to give the car a top speed of 95 mph

on the dashboard controlled the operation of this overdrive, which, when the button was pulled out, engaged automatically at speeds over 40mph, and disengaged when the speed fell below 30mph, when a freewheel came into operation.

Overdrive had first appeared in 1934 (although some earlier cars had a geared-up top speed, which wasn't quite the same thing) on that remarkable (and ugly) car, the Chrysler Airflow, whose 'back-to-front' design was the result of wind-tunnel testing, and proved to be too extreme for the average purchaser, who liked a car to have a recognisable bonnet (so later Airflows had a curious 'widow's peak' grafted on to their front contours). Although it wasn't a great success, the Airflow did condition the public for the streamlines that were to come from other makers, and, in this context, it's worth noting that the wind-tunnel had become part of the car stylist's stock-in-trade relatively early on, although its use was by no means universal. Ford had developed an experimental streamlined car in their wind tunnel as early as 1930, and in 1932 used wind-tunnel techniques to improve the airflow around their new Lincoln models. In view of this, recent claims that the wind-tunnel wasn't used in the

Cal Breer designed a range of aerodynamic cars in the 1930s, which were sold as Chryslers and De Sotos. They were known as Airflows and all of them had engines mounted ahead of the front wheels, although the rear ones were driven. This is the cheapest Chrysler version, sold in England as the Heston and powered by a 4.9-litre, eight-cylinder engine; it was made in 1937, the year in which the model was dropped (National Motor Museum, England)

development of the Lincoln-Zephyr, the first Ford product to have a monocoque body/chassis unit, seem surprising for its shape was every bit as slippery as that of the Airflow. Developed by Dutch-born John Tjaarda under the patronage of Edsel Ford, the Lincoln-Zephyr kept the Lincoln name afloat at a time when falling sales of its more conventional models seemed likely to cause the marque to vanish from the scene altogether. Its sleek, unconventional lines even drew qualified praise from the English press: 'A certain amount of adjustment is needed as regards the unusual appearance, but from all points of view a remarkable car has been produced'.

Ford advertised that driving a Ford was the
greatest thrill in motoring and, arguable though
that statement may be, the smart V8, *above*, was
an exciting and fine car

It wasn't long before streamlining was all the rage in Europe, too; Panhard gave birth to the curious 'Dynamique', with spatted front wings and 'China-closet' curved windows at the sides of its narrow windscreen (which boasted *three* wiper blades) and grilles over the headlamps which were miniature replicas of the sloping radiator grille. The Art Deco interiors of these Panhards were every bit as eccentric as their outward appearance.

Paul Jaray's work for Maybach attracted attention, too . . . but mostly was regarded as a Showtime eccentricity: 'Reminiscent of submarine practice, the Maybach', commented *The Motor*'s man at the 1935 Paris Salon, 'with barrelled body and wings . . . the headlamps are recessed into the wings'.

With his Aerosport, which appeared at the same Salon, Gabriel Voisin returned to a theme he had successfully used on racing cars a decade before: the body as full-width aerofoil, with wheels set in the pontoon wings which formed an integral part of the design. To the eyes of 1935, the Voisin looked thoroughly odd, but then the design was a quarter-century ahead of its time; it is, indeed, vaguely reminiscent of the Mark II Jaguar range of the 1960s . . . It was far more futuristic than the 'car of tomorrow' shown at the 1936 Salon by Peugeot, which would have passed almost without remark had it not been for the aircraft-type stabilising fin fitted at the rear of the bodywork. Because of this useless appendage, the Peugeot attracted more attention than another truly prophetic vehicle at the same show, the Czechoslovakian Tatra 77a, designed by Hans Ledwinka, which, like the Voisin, had full-width aerofoil bodywork, although it went further by mounting its air-cooled V8 engine and transmission at the rear of the backbone chassis. 'Everything', claimed the car's catalogue, 'which science has allowed to be conceived or established has been put to practical use in the design of the Tatra car, without regard for traditional attitudes. Everything is new about this car, whose bold concept attains perfection . . . The economy resulting from the latest developments applied to the Tatra is unbelievable. The car is so perfect that its engine works without effort with unequalled results. Its longevity is increased because it is mechanically more perfect . . . For twelve years, Tatra has been using independent suspension, and has been followed in this respect by manufacturers the world over, proving the correctness of the views of the pioneer.'

Unfortunately, the Tatra achieved little success outside its homeland, unlike the contemporary light car, also streamlined and also fitted with an air-cooled rear engine, which was also shown for the first time in 1936 by its designer, Ferdinand Porsche. But then Porsche had a more powerful backer than Ledwinka, for his 'KdF-Wagen' ('Strength through Joy Car') had been developed under the patronage of that most enthusiastic of motorists, Adolf Hitler, who proposed that the car should be available to Germans at a price of around £55. The more who bought, the lower the price would be, Hitler claimed; but the true *raison d'être* of this 'People's car', or 'Volkswagen' was that it would keep the car-buying public's money inside Germany, thus

Above: Maybach, renowned for their massive V12-engined cars, built a range of six-cylinder vehicles in the mid 1930s; this is a 1936 SW38, which featured an engine of 3.8 litres

Above right: the amazing Panhard Dynamic of 1937. It featured, apart from unique styling, a backbone chassis, torsion-bar suspension, worm drive and a central driving position (later discarded for the more-normal left-hand drive)

Below right: the most successful motor car, in terms of numbers produced, was the Volkswagen Beetle; this is the first example made by the Wolfsburg company

strengthening the Fatherland's currency . . . moreover, when War inevitably came, it would be very easy to adapt the Volkswagen for military use.

At the 1938 Berlin Motor Show, Dr Goebbels, the Nazi Propaganda Minister, said 'The Twentieth Century is the period of the motor car. Since the National Socialist revolution, politics no longer lag behind the development of applied science. Politics show the direction applied science is to take . . . The export of motor vehicles in 1937 exceeded the 1932 production total'.

To emphasise the direction in which politics would now push applied science, the Führer opened the Show with a speech giving the official Party line on the Volkswagen. 'The people's car will soon be produced', Hitler claimed. 'It will make life pleasanter and satisfy the longing of thousands for the motor car. In time, it will become the general means of transport for the German people'.

Excusing the delays in getting the Volkswagen project under way, Hitler continued: 'If we have not progressed so rapidly in the production of this car as was done in other spheres, it is because there were two main difficulties to be overcome. First of all the requisite purchasing power had to be created and, secondly, lengthy research had to be made to produce this low-priced

machine with a maximum performance for the minimum horse power. The proposed car will not only be the best, but the cheapest car in the world, and will give 100 per cent service'.

Few Volkswagens were, in fact, built before the war, and even Adolf Hitler, one suspects, might have been surprised that the car to which he had been sponsor would survive until the 1970s and become the best-selling car of all time in the process. It had been, apparently, originally inspired by one of Ledwinka's earlier designs . . .

At the same period that he was backing the Volkswagen, Hitler was also pouring money into the Mercedes and Auto-Union Grand Prix cars, to ensure Nazi dominance on the racing circuits of the world, and had ordered the construction of a system of high-speed motorways – *Autobahnen* – of which some 800 miles had been completed by 1937, at a cost of £56,000 a mile.

The construction of specially-designed motor roads had been mooted as far back as the 1890s, when schemes for a motorway from London to Brighton were published: but it took a dictatorship to introduce the concept to Europe.

Even outside the totalitarian states, the face of motoring was altering

radically, with production concentrated more and more in the hands of the big batallions, who were thus able to educate the public into buying cars which were, in many ways, inferior to those they supplanted, though the new models were bedizened with all kinds of tempting gadgets. Many motorists of the 1930s were, anyway, first-time buyers, who didn't have a standard of comparison. And there was now a vast number of motorists – they were no longer an eccentric minority, for a survey taken in 1935 proved that there were some 35 million motor vehicles in use throughout the world.

Inevitably, this growth of motoring led to an increase in restrictions on the motorist. In 1936, for the first time, British motorists had to undergo a driving test, and a 30 mph speed limit was imposed in towns. American motorists, it seems, fared even worse: 'Detroit motorists who get into trouble with the police are liable to be sent to the city's new psychopathic clinic, where experts decide whether or not the erring ones should be allowed to drive. Seventeen

Top, left and right: one of the great luxury cars, this Packard of 1939 spent its working life in Sweden with the Swedish Tobacco company. Its power unit is of the straight-eight variety (Skokloster Museum, Sweden)

Above: this 1939 Cadillac 135 bhp V8 was part of the Swedish Royal Family's collection; a similar car was used frequently by King Gustav V (Skokloster Museum, Sweden)

standard traffic offences are staged with the aid of model cars. 'Patients' must spot them all, and also describe what action should be taken when various emergencies arise'.

By 1937, the American economy was on the upturn: sales of cars were second only to those in the record year of 1929, though because of this there were no startling innovations in the new car models. 'It is not the habit of the industry to make daring innovations in the midst of a good buying cycle,' wrote an American journalist. 'Such innovations are considered to be better saved for the day when car owners must be prodded to buy new vehicles.'

Nevertheless, there were improvements: wheelbases were generally longer and bodies larger to give more interior space, while headroom was increased by lowering the floor level, which also helped to give passengers more leg room. Seats were wider, by as much as six inches, and luggage boots were more capacious. Engine sizes were on the increase, always a good economic pointer, though some of the extra power was obviously needed to cope with the increased weight of those bigger bodies – and with all those accessories now deemed necessary by American motorists. Most of them now had heaters fitted to their cars, often in conjunction with windscreen defroster, while some 30 to 35 per cent of new car buyers were reported to be ordering radios to be fitted to their cars, though the general trend towards all-steel bodies had caused car radio manufacturers some reception problems. The all steel 'turret top' roof had appeared in 1935, and since then, bodies had become almost entirely made of steel, with wood retained only as a medium to nail the upholstery to; this development was due because steel mills were now capable of rolling wider steel sheets, and because the art of pressing and welding steel had made notable advances. But whether Chevrolet were justified in describing the all-steel body on their 1937 models as 'crashproof' is a debatable point.

America was now unquestionably the world's most car-conscious country; the world-wide average number of people to each car was 66, in America the average was only 5.6. Second most car-conscious country, surprisingly, was New Zealand, with 10.5 per car, followed by Canada, with 10.9 per car and then Australia, with 13.8 per car. There were 24.5 Frenchmen to each French-registered car, while in the United Kingdom the average number of people to every car was 30.6.

At the far end of the scale came China, with 13,123 Chinamen to each car. . . .

Since many of the world's countries had no indigenous motor industry, there were obvious export outlets; America sold between 9 and 13 per cent of its total output to overseas customers during the 1930s, while Britain, admittedly with a smaller annual production, had increased its export sales to more than 17 per cent by 1937. The total export figure of 1936 was almost double the over-seas sales made in 1933. The turning point in British car exports was apparently 1931, when Britain went off the gold standard, making English cars financially more attractive to overseas buyers. A typical example was that of Vauxhall, who in 1929 exported only 150 cars; in 1931 the figure had risen to 800, by 1932 it was up to 1750, more than doubled the following year to 3650 and in 1934 reached 6800. Of course, Vauxhall was helped by being part of the General Motors organisation, which meant that the company could take advantage of its adoptive parent's assembly plants across the world for sales and service facilities, as well as for the conversion as necessary to left-hand-drive.

Ford, of course, had assembly plants all round the world, and Rootes were also establishing footholds overseas, encouraged, no doubt, by reports like the one which stated: 'In particular, the Hillman Minx has proved a "best seller", not least because of its roominess in its own horsepower class – a point appreciated in most overseas countries, where men are men'.

They usually are, of course, and one can hardly imagine the overbodied Minx having much appeal as a virility symbol, though one Mr Bhattarchargee of Calcutta was recorded as owning a fleet of three of them. . . .

There were, too, the prestige sales of British cars to foreign royalty: Rolls-Royce cars, of course, led this field, followed by Daimler and their alter ego Lanchester, for these two oldest of British firms had combined during the

Below: a 1935 Hillman Aero Minx with bodywork by Thrupp & Maberley; this 10 hp side-valve car was to form the basis for the Talbot and Sunbeam Talbot Tens
(Coventry Motor Museum, England)

Below right: a 1939 Dodge Custom 3.6-litre sedan
(Skokloster Museum, Sweden)

Depression. But humbler makes appealed to the humbler monarchs: Prince Mahomet Ali of Egypt had a Humber Pullman limousine, while an Armstrong-Siddeley saloon was the chosen mount of the Attah of Igbitta Lokojo, from Nigeria.

On the other hand, during 1937, Britain imported £1,515,836-worth of motor vehicles and accessories; oddly enough, considering that there were already rumours of war in the air, the only country to have increased car sales to Britain was Germany, which in 1937 sold British motorists £86,202-worth of motorcars, against £5875-worth in 1936. All other countries showed a more or less marked drop in sales to Britain.

But just imagine . . . in the Spring of 1938 the British motorist with £700 in his pocket could choose from over 400 different cars of around 70 different makes, ranging from the 7.8 hp Austin Seven at £112 to the 23.8 hp Talbot at £695, and there were still the expensive models like the Alfa-Romeo, Bugatti, Bentley, Autovia, Rolls, Hispano at prices in excess of £700. . . .

This was, however, the high point of the recovery from depression: by the summer exports and imports were both in decline. In the first seven months of

1937, American cars worth £415,322 were imported into Britain, compared with £841,585 for the same period in 1937. German imports, £54,720 in July 1937, plummeted to £8708 in July 1938.

And then came Munich. Already the car manufacturing companies were involved in the setting up of 'shadow factories' for the production of war material: now the threat of war with Germany once again proved how vital the motor vehicle was to the nation. Cars were used to evacuate children, invalids and hospital patients from areas vulnerable to aerial attack; they were used to mobilise the ARP and the emergency services; they were used to transport the Prime Minister, Neville Chamberlain, to and from the aerodromes in Britain and Germany in his high-speed dash to the Four-Power Conference at Munich with Hitler, which averted the war for a year.

'And what of the private individual?' asked *The Autocar*. 'Supposing it had been necessary for London to be evacuated, then London alone had 140,000 private cars, capable of carrying, at need, some 500,000 persons, which might well have proved a vital factor in relieving other forms of transport.'

In their inimitable fashion, the British authorities rose to the occasion by discouraging people from owning cars by announcing an increase in the annual road tax from £0.75 to £1.25 per horsepower, and increasing the tax on petrol from 8d to 9d a gallon. This brought the amount contributed to the national purse by the motorist to £104 million, more than one-tenth of the total. Justifying the increase, which was to come into effect from the beginning of 1940, the Chancellor, Sir John Simon, showed once again that the motorist was regarded as having a bottomless pocket: 'Side by side with the reduction of income tax in 1934, my predecessor reduced the private car tax to 15s per horse-power. The users of private cars, who very largely correspond with the income

247

tax paying classes, have, for five years, enjoyed the benefit of this reduced scale of taxation. Therefore, I feel bound to ask them, in these stern times, to submit to a substantially increased scale.'

With bland ignorance of the possible consequences of his proposals, Sir John commented: 'We ought, I am sure, to avoid any measures which would have a generally depressing effect upon industry . . .'.

Shortsighted MPs welcomed the tax on 'luxury motoring' as a means of curtailing the manufacturer of motor cars and lessening the traffic on the roads, together with the burden of their upkeep. It was as though the 19th century mechanophobe, Colonel deLaet Waldo Sibthorpe, who regarded engineers as lower than vermin, was once again stalking the corridors of Westminster to heed the development and progress of the car.

Before the tax came into effect, however, a more effective curtailment of private motoring was declared, as Britain went to war against Germany. Once again the motor vehicle, reviled in peacetime as a rich man's plaything, would prove the vital hinge on which battles were won or lost. More than ever before, this was to be a petrol war. . . .

Below: a 1938 BMW 328 and a Bucker Jungmeister aircraft of the Luftwaffe

CHAPTER 13

Adapting to Survive

Above: during the war, Ford built many four-wheel-drive vehicles; this is one seen leaving the Dagenham, Essex, factory

The French called it the 'Drôle de Guerre', the British called it the 'Phoney War'; under any name it meant that for a while after war had been declared, little seemed to happen. There were a few air raid warnings, some women and children were evacuated from London. Industry, far from increasing output, actually had less work in hand than before. Although the Earls Court Motor Show was cancelled, some manufacturers actually introduced 1940 models. The original Ford Anglia, for instance, was a 'war baby', announced after the outbreak of hostilities.

Ford was in a particularly difficult situation, for the Government was reluctant to place orders with the company, maintaining that the situation of its factory at Dagenham, on the River Thames near London, was too vulnerable.

So Ford camouflaged the factory site under the guidance of experts from the Royal Air Force: 'an elaborate picture was painted on the roof to make the buildings appear from the air as though they were a piece of marshland with tracks running through it.' Even so, most Government departments still hung fire, although the Ford company was still fulfilling a pre-war Air Ministry order for six-wheeler trucks and winches for Balloon Command, while there were small orders for five-ton trucks from other Ministries. And there was a special agreement with the Ministry of Agriculture and Fisheries, dating from the early part of 1939, that Ford should produce tractors against the eventuality of war being declared, to be stored in depots all over England until they should be needed. The Ministry had agreed to order 3000, with the proviso that if war didn't break out, the company would take them back at cost price. In fact, the tractors proved vital, for when war broke out, 3,000,000 additional acres of land were put under cultivation for food crops.

Apart from this, life went on pretty much as usual. Dagenham was still working a forty-hour week, there was plenty of food (although already rationed) in the canteens, cigarettes were still plentiful. However, heads of departments were given secret instructions for immobilising the factory in the event of enemy invasion.

Some V8 engines were supplied for use in a dangerous device called a 'degausser' used to explode magnetic mines from a distance: some of these units were installed in Wellington bombers so that they could detonate these mines by flying over them at a low level.

Then, early in April, Hitler struck. Denmark and Norway were invaded and suddenly the 'phoney war' had ceased to be a joke.

When the war broke out, the War Department owned just over 50,000 vehicles of all types, from motor cycles to three-ton trucks, and had commandeered another 26,000 from civilian users: but when the Low Countries and

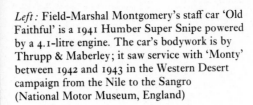

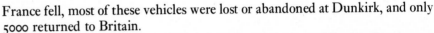

Left: Field-Marshal Montgomery's staff car 'Old Faithful' is a 1941 Humber Super Snipe powered by a 4.1-litre engine. The car's bodywork is by Thrupp & Maberley; it saw service with 'Monty' between 1942 and 1943 in the Western Desert campaign from the Nile to the Sangro (National Motor Museum, England)

Below left: war work on four wheels did not just mean active service at the front; here, a Ford van is busy delivering food at home

France fell, most of these vehicles were lost or abandoned at Dunkirk, and only 5000 returned to Britain.

So motor manufacturers had to work flat out on providing replacements; they also had to adapt their manufacturing skills to the production of a wide variety of military equipment of all kinds under the 'shadow factory' scheme. Leyland Motors, for instance, had opened a vast new engine and transmission plant, which was now turned over to making tanks, bombs and other munitions. Daimler built two 'shadow factories' near its works in Coventry; these were initially wholly engaged in the production of Bristol Mercury, Pegasus and Hercules radial aero-engines.

As the centre of so much of the motor industry, Coventry was particularly important to the British war effort. The Germans, whose anticipations even ran to having aerial photographs of important car factories available in 1939, were obviously aware of this, and their attempts to bring the motor industry to a standstill added a new word to the English language – 'Coventrated', meaning complete and utter destruction by bombing. On the night of 14 November 1940, German bombers destroyed the centre of Coventry, and the raids continued until the following April. The city had preserved much of its medieval heritage, despite its industrialisation, and many historic buildings were destroyed (although the crazy buildings in Much Park Street occupied by Lea-Francis Cars, surely the oldest structure ever used as part of a motor factory, survived).

Around 170 high explosive bombs and mines were dropped on Daimler's Radford factory, which was seventy per cent destroyed – yet production was increased, as the company had expanded into 44 dispersal factories reaching from Newcastle to North Wales.

Among the other casualties of the blitz on Coventry was the famous Motor Mills, birthplace in 1896 of the British motor industry. Daimler had moved out in the 1930s, however, and at the time of its demise the building was being used as an Air Ministry store.

Daimler's contribution to the war effort was extremely varied – gun turrets, parts for Bren and Browning guns, rocket projectors, four-wheel-drive scout cars and armoured cars, buses, and, during the final year of the war, a large Government order was received for a fleet of cars for the use of high-ranking officers once Germany had been occupied.

Other companies, apart from using their normal production expertise, also contributed to the war effort with their byproducts: Dagenham byproducts were used in the manufacture of Toluole and Xylole for explosives and varnish for aircraft fabrics, while the slag from its blast furnace was converted into Tarmac, which was used to build runways for the Battle of Britain airfields. Before the war was over, the runways and dispersal points of fifty-six airfields scattered over ten counties had been constructed of Tarmac reclaimed from the slag from the Ford furnace.

251

Of course, the factories were always on the alert for enemy attack, although it was rare that an air raid was as leisurely as the occasion in 1940 when Ford workers were playing a local team at football on the Ford Sports Ground: the match had to be halted seven times due to enemy action, but was eventually played to a finish, the referee taking note of time lost in the air raid shelters so that full time was played. 'Fords won by four to two,' ran a contemporary report, 'and by the time the last whistle sounded, the field and the factory were ringed with smoke and fire, the largest conflagration being the oil tanks at Purfleet, which were belching flame and smoke many feet into the air.'

Often the raids had more tragic consequences, like the attack on Vauxhall's Luton factory in August of the same year, in which 39 people were killed and 40 injured: despite the heavy damage, the plant was back in production six days later. Vauxhall were another company with a widely varied war production, turning out 5,000,000 jerricans, 250,000 Bedford trucks, armour-piercing

Above left: the fire engine at the Ford works had plenty of fires to put out during the blitz, even though the Ford complex was disguised by being painted to appear from the air to be marsh land

Above: in the desert, four-wheel drive was a necessity and, as often happens, four-wheel drive development took great leaps in sophistication to meet military needs

Below: Ford lorries line up, waiting to be shipped into action. Their durability and ruggedness was remarkable, and some were still working, well into the 1970s, as tow trucks in France and Italy

shells, 4,000,000 venturi tubes for rocket launchers, 95 per cent of the components for the first twelve British jet aircraft engines and Churchill tanks, which were developed from drawing board to production within a year. Over 5,600 of these 38-ton tanks were produced, and a successor was under development when the war ended.

During the early part of the war, there were few restrictions on the movement of labour, and some workers even moved from Dagenham to Coventry in search of higher pay. Others joined up, but before long there was more need for skilled men in the factories than at the front. But by 1941 there was a shortage of suitable employees, and women were being trained for jobs which were formerly thought of as suitable only for men: when the war ended there were 3500 women employed by Ford alone.

Despite the difficult conditions that the motor factories were working under, the vehicles they produced were beyond reproach: they were even sought after by the enemy, as battle orders signed by Rommel, captured early in 1942, proved: 'For desert reconnaisance only captured English trucks are to be employed, since German trucks stick in the sand too often . . . all captured motor transport is to be distributed to the fighting companies for the transport of personnel . . . all German trucks are to be echelon transport (second line transport)'.

Praise came from the Allied commanders, too: Montgomery's famous caravan, and the truck which pulled it, were built by Ford. Three weeks after the invasion of Normandy, 'Monty' found time to write a testimonial to Dagenham: 'The caravan which your works produced for me has come ashore safely in France, and since I came over here I have been using it to the full as my operations room. There is no doubt you have produced a most excellent vehicle'.

A Ford V8 utility car, equipped with desert tyres, was acquired by the Royal Air Force in Cairo in 1942: first it carried Air Chief Marshal Sir Arthur Tedder (who became Lord Tedder, Marshal of the Royal Air Force); then from El Alamein to Tripoli it was the transport of Air Marshal Sir Arthur Coningham. From Tripoli it was shipped to Malta and then to Sicily and Italy, carrying many notable Air Force Commanders, including Air Vice-Marshals Broadhurst, Dixon and Foster, ending its war in Linz, in Austria. In August 1945, Air Vice-Marshal Foster commented that the Ford, although somewhat battered externally . . . is still mechanically absolutely sound and in regular use.'

Officialdom was surprised by the scale on which the motor industry had become accustomed to operate. Although the Carden-Loyd Bren Gun Carrier had been designed round the engine and rear axle of the Ford V8, it wasn't until September 1941 that the Ministry of Supply asked Dagenham to build the complete vehicles. Their initial order called for twenty-five a week.

'That is too few,' the Ford management told them. 'With our capacity, at least a hundred a week can be built, and we do not believe in running our factory except at the highest possible pitch.'

Amazingly, it took several weeks to convince the Ministry that such a rate of output was possible, but in January 1944, two years after the Bren Gun Carrier had gone into production at Dagenham, the factory was turning out two hundred of these complex tracked vehicles a week. Nearly 14,000 were built before the end of the war in Europe.

Perhaps the most amazing achievement of the Ford production methods was the building of Rolls-Royce Merlin aeroengines in unprecedented numbers in a shadow factory at Urmston, Manchester, not far from the old Ford factory at Trafford Park. The aeroengine works, in production within a year from the start of work on the foundations, covered nearly 45 acres, and eventually employed 17,316 workers, of whom 7200 were women. Less than one hundred of this total had ever had anything to do with aeroengines before joining Ford, and only three hundred or so knew anything about car engines. Nevertheless, before its closure in 1946, the Urmston factory had produced over 34,000 Merlin engines, not one of which failed the exacting requirements of the Royal Air Force. One intriguing aspect of this project is that the jig boring machines which were vital to its success were supplied by a firm from Switzerland in

1943, which meant that they were shipped to Britain via German-occupied France and Spain. The Germans had to agree to this unusual move because the Swiss insisted on their right, as neutrals, to trade with all belligerents. The Germans, who needed Swiss light machine tools, were forced to speed their own downfall. . . .

Sadly enough, when Ford of America were asked in their turn to produce Merlins (this was in 1940, before the USA entered the war), Edsel Ford and Charles Sorensen approved the venture, but were over-ruled by the 77-year-old Henry Ford, whose curious ideals of neutrality and pacifism dictated that no engines should be built for Britain . . . so Packard eventually took on the task. Later that year, however, Ford and General Motors cooperated in the production of Pratt & Whitney radial aeroengines.

Although America didn't come into the war until 1942, its motor industry had been supplying the Allies since 1939: in 1939-40 the French government had ordered large quantities of trucks, which were being shipped when France fell to the Germans, so were hurriedly diverted to England. Here, improvised assembly plants were set up in all kinds of unlikely places, from the airship shed at Cardington built for the ill-fated R101 to a tram shed in Wigan. Here, in June 1942, the first Jeep ever assembled in Britain was completed. The Jeep – officially known to the US Army as 'Truck, ¼-ton, 4×4, Command Reconnaisance' – was the result of a US Army specification of 1940, for which prototypes were built by the American Bantam Company (who had tried unsuccessfully to introduce the Austin Seven to the American market), Willys-Overland and, later, by Ford. The final design of Jeep was an amalgam of all three designs and, as such, was produced by all three companies, although Bantam switched to other war work before Pearl Harbor. Willys, on the other hand, persisted with the Jeep after the war, and a developed version is still in production, although it is now far more refined than the original 'Blitz Buggy', of which hundreds of thousands were built: at the peak of production, a Jeep was leaving the Willys assembly lines every 1 minute 20 seconds.

In March 1941, the American Government had passed the Lend-Lease Act, under which materials and know-how were made available to the Allies on the premise that by pooling knowledge and resources, they could win the war more quickly. Under this scheme, the US supplied some $42,000,000,000-worth of material and services to 44 countries, especially Britain and the USSR.

Until Pearl Harbor, however, private car production continued almost unabated, with sales of well over four million cars in both 1940 and 1941. But once America entered the war, the skills of the industry were wholly employed in the manufacture of military equipment. There was little problem in the mass-production of trucks and Jeeps, and tanks and other fighting vehicles posed few difficulties. But at the request of President Roosevelt, Ford built a vast new factory at Willow Run, near Ypsilanti, Michigan, where four-engined Liberator bombers were to be built on production line methods. Needless to say, there were vast problems involved, and at one stage the venture

The quarter-ton Jeep, built by Ford and Willys, was *the* famous vehicle of World War II and did much to keep the allies mobile in the worst of conditions. In the photograph above, the infantry is advancing in its Jeeps, along a road near Coutances, in Normandy, in July 1944; in the other photographs, *below and right*, a model from that year is seen in retirement near the National Motor Museum
(National Motor Museum, England)

gained the nickname 'Will It Run?'; but by late 1943 all the problems were solved, and in 1944 the plant was turning out three to four hundred Liberators a month.

The production figures achieved by the American automobile industry during the war were staggeringly huge: 4,131,000 engines, 5,947,000 guns, 2,812,000 tanks and trucks, 27,000 aircraft, and millions of smaller items from saucepans to atomic bomb equipment. . . .

Although the military vehicle in the front line had been afforded great – and well deserved – attention (after all it was the trucks of the 'Red Ball Express' which had kept the Allied armies in France supplied after D-Day), the poor motorist who needed a private car for his war work on the home front was hedged about with bureaucratic restrictions of the most annoying sort. New tyres were in short supply, yet motorists could be fined for using bald tyres while waiting for the new ones to arrive.

Petrol was rationed, yet the rationing seemed sometimes to be carried out on an arbitrary basis, as one British munitions worker complained in 1943: 'Drastic cuts long ago eliminated those who had any hope of getting to work by

alternative means of transport. The remainder are so carefully controlled that the exact number of working days for the quarter is declared in advance and petrol is doled out to the nearest half-gallon. Even a single day lost through illness is reported to the Divisional Petroleum Office, and coupons for petrol to cover it have to be surrendered at the end of the period. Now, apparently on instructions from London, the DPO has slashed allowances so that people are only able to go to work for 50 days out of the 75. They are invited to "stay with friends" or sleep at the office for the remaining nights. My only friend with a spare bed near my work happens to be of the opposite sex, and I don't think she would at all appreciate that suggestion. . . .

'It comes particularly hard when one sees American troops running round to the local dance hall with British girls in their Service vehicles at night and to read of MPs and Government officials using chauffeur-driven limousines to go to the theatre'.

There were, of course, ways round the regulations for the ingenious: cars could be persuaded to drag themselves along powered by cumbersome producer-gas outfits generating a fairly combustible gas from charcoal or manure, while those who could not obtain new pneumatic tyres were offered a curious device called a 'Getuhome', which consisted of wood segments linked together by a turnbuckle mechanism which tightened it on to the bare rim. 'Looks like an ordinary tyre, strong and durable and *will* get you home,' claimed the optimistic manufacturer.

Despite all the restrictions, however, the private motorist could look forward with anticipation to peacetime, when vehicles making full use of all the technological lessons learned during the war. 'Wherever extreme conditions of service have to be met, or intricate machinery devised or constructed,' commented *The Motor*, 'technical knowledge of enduring value has been gained. Supplementing the laboratory and test track, many theatres of war have provided ready-made proving grounds where natural forces and conditions have caused nearly as much destruction as the direct attack of the enemy.'

But for many motorists the anticipation was to be prolonged well after VE-Day, for the bureaucrats had also learned a great deal from war conditions. It was to be a long time before those war-developed cars were readily available to those who were placing orders for early delivery. . . .

The German equivalent workhorse to the Jeep was the Volkswagen Kübelwagen, based on the Volkswagen car chassis. The amphibious version, the Schwimmwagen, had a shorter chassis and four-wheel drive. It used an 1131 cc engine and could reach 50 mph on land and 7 mph in the water

CHAPTER 14

Weathering the Utility Years

Victory in Europe didn't bring the expected millennium for the British motorist, for motoring was very low on the list of priorities of the post-war Socialist government – although restricting and taxing the car owner seemed to be higher up the list. New cars *were* available in 1945, but you needed a Ministry of War Transport Licence to order one, and then had to wait an indeterminate period before it was delivered (unless you had the money and the contacts to buy on the Black Market).

Purchase tax, introduced during the war to discourage the market in so-called luxury goods, remained on cars, although it was removed from household appliances, such as electric fires and refrigerators. Said the Chancellor of the Exchequer, Hugh Dalton: 'There is too much congestion on the roads at home . . . the industry should concentrate on exports . . . I have been asked to take the purchase tax off cars sold in this country, but regret that I cannot do this now. I have been told that the trade want a definite statement, and I shall give it. I cannot hold out any hope of removing the tax for some time to come . . . The motor industry and would-be purchasers of private cars in this country should, therefore, proceed on the assumption that the purchase tax is here to stay.

'I hope that the motor industry is going to export a lot more than it sells at home. There is a great block on the roads at home and great opportunities for trade abroad. There is today a sellers' market for cars, as for other British exports, in many different parts of the world, and I hope that the motor industry will fully exploit it. This is a time for exporters not only to renew contacts with old markets but to find their way into new ones – and there is, of course, no purchase tax on cars which manufacturers export. To this extent, therefore, the export trade is stimulated, as it should be'.

This was pure doctrinaire claptrap, and only Dalton's parliamentary colleagues applauded it: the unfortunate manufacturers, beset by material shortages of all kinds, coped magnificently with the order to export half their production, despite the fact that most of their products were only pre-war models with minimal updating, and had originally been designed for the peculiar requirements of the British market with no view to sales overseas. Both Government and industry were unrealistic in their view of the situation, for the manufacturers had forecast a production of 600,000 cars in the year 1947, but only managed to build 147,767: the Government set an export target of 100,000 cars for 1946, which turned out to be 80 per cent of total output for that year!

The motor industry had one particular bugbear among the ranks of the Government, and his name has become part of the mythology of austerity: ask anyone to recall the evocative images of the late 1940s, and it's inevitable that among a list that's bound to include things like snoek, whalemeat, Civic Restaurants, ration books, Dick Barton and the Berlin Airlift will be Sir Stafford Cripps.

Cripps, whose thin, bespectacled, ascetic face seemed to personify austerity, was president of the Board of Trade and later became Chancellor of the Exchequer; although he made many statements which were received with scorn by those to whom they were addressed, few of his remarks attracted more attention than his speech to the Society of Motor Manufacturers and Traders in November 1945 in which he attempted to dictate the future marketing policy of the car industry.

'We must provide a cheap, tough, good-looking car of decent size,' said Cripps, 'not the sort of car we have hitherto produced for the smooth roads and short journeys of this country. And we must produce them in sufficient quantities to get the benefits of mass-production. That was what we had to do with aircraft engines, and so we concentrated on two or three types only and mass-produced them – not a dozen different ones in penny numbers. My own belief is that we cannot succeed in getting the volume of export we must have if we disperse our efforts over numberless types and makes'.

Commented a Manchester motor trader: 'Sir Stafford Cripps has told the motor industry how to build cars; no doubt another wise guy in the Govern-

ment will now show us how to sell them . . . The retention of the purchase tax will reduce the sale of new cars in Britain to negligible proportions. That means relatively few cars will have to bear the overheads of selling and distributing costs, and prices must therefore be high'.

Certainly there was no comparison with pre-war prices: the cheapest car on the British market in November 1945 was the 8hp Ford Anglia, at a basic price of £229, boosted by purchase tax to £293 7s 3d, against its 1940 price of £140. Some post-war prices were totally unrealistic: while a Hillman Minx cost £396 17s 3d (inc PT), a Sunbeam-Talbot Ten, which was virtually identical apart from a better-finished body, was priced at a total of £620 9s 6d, which fact attracted some irony from enthusiasts.

With tyres almost unavailable and 'Pool' petrol rationed to enough for around 270 miles a month, motoring was a fairly gloomy business, and those who can

Top: despite having styling similar to many pre-war American motor cars, the Jowett Javelin was rather different underneath, with its flat-four engine – unfortunately, the car-buying public thought it was too radical, so it was not a great success; neverthelsss, 30,000 examples were manufactured

Above: at the sporting end of the British post-war market was the Healey. This is a 2.4-litre model, designed by Donald Healey and A.C. Sampietro, which was the fastest series-production saloon of its day; this actual car was raced into thirteenth place in the 1948 Mille Miglia by Count Lurani

remember the empty streets may well wonder where Hugh Dalton got his vision of unacceptable congestion, for car ownership was far from universal. At the end of the war there were only just over a million private cars on the road; the author can recall only two motor owners in his own fairly long street at that period, a builder who ran a three-wheeled James Handyvan and a family with an aged Morris Minor saloon which spent more time, it seemed, being pushed than running under its own power. Some mornings the only traffic was the leisurely milk cart, although he discovered the relentless onward march of progress when the milkman's horse was supplanted by an electric milk float (which broke down more frequently than the horse, and didn't know the round so well . . .).

Fortunately, one threat of State intervention in motoring proved empty – although it was a forecast of things to come . . . Late in 1945 *The Star* carried a disturbing feature: 'A people's car? State may enter motor industry. The Government contemplates entering into the motor trade in competition with the manufacturers'.

Although Americans had torn up their petrol coupons on VJ-Day, they too

Above right: Sir Alec Issigonis's first design for the Nuffield Organisation was the Morris Minor of 1948. It had a unitary-construction body and torsion-bar front suspension

had discovered that the State was not finished with its interference, although in this case it was the manufacturers who were to be incommoded. Once the war in Europe was over, the American industry was granted permission to build 200,000 cars during the remainder of 1945, provided it could obtain enough of the necessary materials to do so. But raw materials were rare, and a series of wildcat strikes made them even rarer – and far more expensive. Into this situation was flung one Chester Bowles, the Price Administrator, who blandly announced that maximum prices for new American cars should be 2 per cent less than 1942 prices in the case of General Motors models (Chevrolet, Oldsmobile, DeSoto, Cadillac) while Ford, Chrysler and Studebaker were restricted to increases of 1 to 9 per cent. This meant, for instance, that a 30 hp Ford now cost the equivalent of £210, while a Studebaker was less than £225.

Complained Henry Ford II, who had taken over the running of the Ford

Motor Company from his octogenarian grandfather: 'It costs us $1041 to make a car . . . but we are restricted to selling it at a maximum of $780'.

Retorted the altruistic Mr Bowles: 'Mr Ford is selfishly conspiring to undermine the American people's bulwark against economic disaster', (but weren't the motor manufacturers American people, too?).

As in Britain, restrictions of this kind served mainly to bolster the sales of aged derelicts, pre-war cars often changing hands at well over their price new . . . often over the post-war price for the same model. American buyers did have the advantage that their war had started in 1942, and that therefore pre-war models were that much newer, but it was a mixed blessing, for the exaggerated styling of the early 1940s had not been to everyone's taste. A survey of American motorists in 1945 showed that most of them wanted four-door saloons, painted black, light grey or dark blue, with ample headroom, larger windscreens and side windows and – the view of 75 per cent – cars with a plain exterior finish rather than chromium-plated ornamentation on grilles, louvres and wings. Needless to say, the stylists ignored this latter remark, for this was the era of the full-width 'dollar grin' radiator grille.

One New York motoring correspondent was in no doubt about his feelings on seeing the new 1946 Oldsmobile: 'The grille has been further widened and lessened in height. The bumper is more massive and wraps further round the front wheels. Alas, the effect is more and more like some nightmare creature coming up for air from a thousand fathoms!'.

However, the fickle public bought the cars anyway . . . they liked the novelty of their cars to be restricted to mere external show, and there was no future for the unconventional, like Powel Crosley's sub-compact Hotshot, Preston Tucker's rear-engined Torpedo or a bold design proposed in 1945 by the Alsatian motor manufacturer, E. E. C. Mathis, who had destroyed his factory in Strasbourg and escaped to New York when the Germans overran France. Mathis and Ford had had an uneasy alliance in the 1930s to produce the Matford car, but now the Frenchman had no intention of competing on the mass-production market. Instead he planned to make an 'ultra-light car, utilising plastics and weighing less than its five passengers'. He had, in fact, built some prototypes in France before the war, and such a venture would probably have succeeded in his homeland, but there was no future for it in America.

Americans didn't even trust new marques of car, for when Henry J. Kaiser, who had a formidable reputation as a wartime producer of military material, attempted to break into the monopoly of the Big Three – Ford, Chrysler, General Motors – he couldn't build up a sufficiently strong marketing network for his Kaiser-Frazer and Henry J lines, took only five per cent of the market in 1948 and faded away completely thereafter.

Although the world was car-hungry, it could still be quite finicky about its diet. . . .

260

Below: this 1952 Lea-Francis London Motor Show car is a 2½-litre sports, which uses a 2496 cc, four-cylinder engine. It could reach a top speed of 102 mph, by courtesy of its 125 bhp power unit

Bottom: three famous MGs. They are Y-type 1½-litre saloons of 1953

This was odd, because the public was clamouring for new cars: in fact, if you believed a somewhat equivocal comment by *The Times*, they would buy anything on wheels that was offered to them.

'In most countries today,' reported the paper, 'the shortage of motorcars is so acute that motorists exercise very little discrimination in buying a car. They consider themselves fortunate if they can acquire any new car, of any make, nationality and engine power. This partly accounts for the present demand for British small cars in the United States, where motorists normally prefer cars of high power and large body size.'

In fact, it didn't account for it at all, for the 'small British cars' which were making such an impact on the American market were cars which didn't compete with existing US models at all, and attracted an entirely different kind of customer. One British model which particularly enshrined itself in American automotive mythology was the MG TC Midget, a sports car of pre-war character which offered lively handling and quick acceleration, and could consequently run away from any large American gin-palace on a twisting road, although the larger car was very likely faster in a straight line.

Left: American influence on English styling is seen in this Austin A90 Atlantic of 1950

Below: the Alec Issigonis-designed Morris Minor introduced in 1948 was to have been a front-wheel-drive car. However, when it reached production, it was conventionally driven and proved to be one of the most reliable cars ever designed.

Right: the beetle-back Standard Vanguard was a milestone in motor-car styling when it was announced
(National Motor Museum, England)

Austin exported many small cars styled on transatlantic lines, although again it was almost certainly their 'nippiness' which sold them rather than Americans buying in desperation: the Austin A90 Atlantic even set up a number of American speed records, and so the old bomber factory which housed Austin's export division was kept fully occupied.

There were some curious features about the British export drive, but none more odd than the case of the Citroën factory at Slough, where components were shipped in from France, assembled into complete cars for the British market – and fifty per cent of them were then solemnly exported overseas again!

By 1950, British factories were exporting some 350,000 cars out of a total output of 522,515, although the impetus of the export drive was now beginning to fall away, partly because the countries to which Britain was exporting were now building cars to meet their own requirements, partly because the British products were said to lack reliability and to deteriorate at an unacceptable rate.

Fortunately, the old taxation system based on cylinder bore had vanished in 1947, replaced for a year by a tax of £1 for every 100 cc of engine capacity, thereafter by a flat-rate tax of £10; this did at least give British designers the

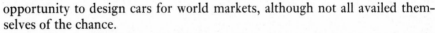

opportunity to design cars for world markets, although not all availed themselves of the chance.

Austerity and shortages, indeed, meant that some new designs had to remain on paper: Morris designer Alex Issigonis designed a bulbously streamlined light car with torsion-bar independent front suspension, front-wheel drive and a flat-four engine. It emerged in production form with the chassis and styling intact, but with the side-valve Series E engine of pre-war vintage driving the rear wheels through a conventional transmission. It didn't matter, however: the Morris Minor would prove to be a car with inbuilt longevity, and even after production had ended some two decades later, Morris Minors of all ages would still be a common sight on British roads.

Oddly enough, the Morris Minor had rather similar styling to the German Volkswagen, which had been put into limited production in 1945 in a factory gutted by Allied bombing, after British experts and Henry Ford II had rejected the design as having no commercial future. Commented the British: 'This car does not fulfil the technical requirements which must be expected from a motor car. Its performance and qualities have no attraction to the average buyer. It is too ugly and too noisy. Such a type of car can, if at all, only be popular for two to three years at the most'.

This was the car that would become the most popular model of all time, with sales considerably exceeding the all-time record of fifteen million plus set up in 1927 by the immortal Model T Ford (although it must be admitted that the Model T achieved its record in far less time in a much smaller overall market).

France's concept of the utility car was the 2 cv Citroën – 'four wheels under an umbrella' – with an 8 bhp 375 cc flat-twin engine driving the front wheels, a project developed in secret during the German occupation, as indeed had Renault's postwar offering, the 4 cv, which had its four-cylinder engine at the rear. This was the first model to be produced by Renault after its nationalisation in 1944 – the company's founder, Louis Renault, had been accused of collaboration with the Germans and died in prison – and was nicknamed 'Cockchafer' or 'Little pat of butter' because it was painted with yellow ochre confiscated from the Afrika Korps. This was to become the first French car whose sales exceeded a million, and it was to be built for fifteen years, up to July 1961.

Italy's biggest manufacturer, Fiat, was concentrating on economy, too, with the post-war version of their 500 cc Topolino ('Mickey Mouse') and its larger 1100 cc and 1500 cc sisters.

So the 1940s came to an end, with Europe concentrating on economy and America exuberantly extravagant. Automotive engineering was certainly moving forward: unfortunately good taste was heading in the opposite direction.

Below: the French equivalent of the Morris Minor was the 4CV Renault saloon. Cheap and easy to produce, it was, along with the 2CV Citroën, the 'motoring for everyone' car in France

CHAPTER 15

The Flamboyant Fifties

Below: one of the first British cars to be a size away from the economy vehicles of the late 1940s and early 1950s was the Ford Consul; this is a 1955 drophead coupé version (National Motor Museum, England)

Right at the beginning of the 1950s, the British motor industry was staggered by a merger which was more of a shotgun wedding than a marriage of convenience, bringing two great rivals together. William Morris had become Lord Nuffield, but had now lost interest in the empire he had created, and was finding increasing solace in his prolonged cruises to Australia; his former lieutenant, Sir Leonard Lord, now headed Austin, and had once sworn that the only reason he would return to Morris would be to take it apart 'brick by bloody brick'. But Austin and the Nuffield Group did merge to form the British Motor Corporation, although there was little rationalisation of model ranges, and the old Austin-Morris rivalries seemed to persist. And the group's share of the market, originally about fifty per cent, began to slip steadily downward.

Of course, this may have been due as much to the fact that the rest of the British motor industry was catching up technically as to any residual bitterness between Nuffield and Lord: Ford introduced its first truly modern range in 1950 with the Consul, with an ohv four-cylinder engine, hydraulic brakes,

Left: the six-cylinder brother of the four-cylinder Ford Consul was the Zephyr; this is a 1953 example

Below: sports motoring in the early 1950s was available to the less well off in the form of myriad kit cars, manufacturers of which sprung up everywhere. The wealthy, however, could acquire magnificent cars like this 1954 AC Aceca

Below right: a 1950 Daimler Consort DB18 (Coventry Motor Museum, England)

Bottom right: one of the most popular sports saloons of the 1950s was the Sunbeam-Talbot; this is a 1954 example

independent front suspension and integral body/chassis unit, and followed this soon after with the similar, six-cylindered Zephyr.

'Judged both on performance and on value for money, the Zephyr is a very satisfactory car,' commented *The Autocar.* 'It is quiet yet lively, roomy without being cumbersome, and it had a quiet modern line without the vulgarity often produced by the addition of excess ornamentation.' The test concluded with a masterly piece of ambiguity: 'It goes and stops and handles well'.

Soon after this, Ford announced a unit-constructed small car, the 100E Anglia, whose 1935-designed power unit was also used in a remarkable survival from the Mesolithic age of motoring, the Ford Popular, the cheapest real car on the British market, whose styling dated back to 1937. It was produced in the old Briggs Motor Bodies factory at Doncaster, which meant that manufacture of bodywork for the unorthodox Jowett Javelin had to stop: and Jowett ceased car production. Remarkably, the crude little Ford Popular remained in production until 1959.

Unfortunately the new-look Fords seemed to attract the attentions of the gadget-lover, for above all the early 1950s were the era of the bolt-on gimmick: amber plastic bug-deflectors in the shape of birds decorated the bonnet top, chromed masks sat like eyelids above the headlamps, windscreens were given overhanging peaks like the eyeshade of a Hollywood newspaper editor, 'portholes' lined the bonnet. Bad taste was rampant.

Nowhere was bad taste more evident during this period than in the United States. American cars smirked their way into the 1950s behind chromium-plated radiator grilles of surpassing vulgarity: they ended the decade with front-end styling reminiscent of the head of some deep-sea fish and tailfins like rocket-powered guppy. Nor is the piscine analogy far-fetched, for a promotional

film made by Ford of America around 1956 showing a car stylist at work, bathed in a dim, religious light, emphasised that he took inspiration from natural forms – like a tank-full of tropical fish. Then the film showed this Renaissance man take up his pencil, as though he were a medieval monk about to illuminate a psalter – and design a futuristic car that was as impracticable as it was re-pellent. Fortunately this was a flight of fancy that was not about to be launched on an unsuspecting public.

'Cars of the future' were very much in the corporate minds of the American motor moguls in this period, although quite why is something of a mystery, save that their appearance at motor shows did go some way to accustoming the public to the shape of cars to come – a sort of cushioning against bodyshell-shock.

Cadillac started the tailfin vogue in 1950, the modest kick-ups at the tips of the rear wings acting as something of a relieving touch to the ponderous styling of the new models, which were the first Caddys to sell over 100,000 in a year; the fin vogue reached its peak on cars like the 1959 Buick LeSabre, on which these lethal-looking appendages were half-a-car long.

Right: styling gone quite mad. This Cadillac had a body by the French coachbuilder Saoutchick

Below: flowing lines can be used quite subtly as with this Bentley Continental

For America, the 1950s began badly, with the outbreak of the Korean War;
yet this major international disturbance had little effect on the sale of motor
vehicles, which that same year exceeded 8,000,000 for the first time ever
(6,665,863 of these were cars).

Despite their excesses of styling, American cars were all pretty much alike
underneath: most had V8 engines of around 100 hp, with six-cylinder power
units reserved for the lower price ranges; suspension was generally by independent coils at the front and leaf springs at the back; sealed-beam headlights,
radio and heater were regarded as virtually indispensable. On models with
manual gearboxes, a steering-column gearchange made room for three on a
bench front seat, but removed all precision from the operation of changing
speed. The provision of a column change, with all its complex linkage, must
have been extremely costly compared with the simplicity of the 'stick shift',
especially to an industry reputed to count the cost of every washer.

There was an alternative, however, and motorists were prepared to pay extra
for it. Automatic transmission, which had made its first tentative appearances
in the 1930s, was now reliable enough to be put into mass-production. The fact
that many of the early automatic boxes only possessed two forward speeds was
immaterial, for those big V8s made up in torque what they lacked in economy.

One of the first manufacturers to go automatic was Buick, who in 1950
became the fourth manufacturer to achieve sales of over half-a-million cars in
a year – and nearly 430,000 of these were fitted with the new Buick Dynaflow
torque-convertor transmission. Madison Avenue outdid itself in coining names
redolent of speed and power for these early automatic transmission: 'Tip-Toe
Hydraulic Shift with Gyrol Fluid Drive', 'Hydra-Matic', 'Powerglide',
'Ultra-Matic', 'PowerFlite'.

It was definitely marketing, not engineering, which sold cars in the America
of the 1950s: in fact, these Rockets and Firedomes and Silver Streaks were only
in their element on the dead-straight turnpike highways, and under more
demanding conditions their road-holding deficiencies were emphasised to the
full. However, the great marketing dream turned to a nightmare in 1959 when
Ford introduced the Edsel, designed after thorough market research, and
discovered that public taste could be expensively fickle. The motorists for
whom the Edsel had been designed failed to buy it, and production was
curtailed inside two years, with only 35,000 cars sold. The marketing men had
failed to anticipate a move away from large cars, an error of judgment that cost
Ford an estimated $250,000,000.

By the end of the decade, America was definitely warming to the compact,
partly to combat the success of imported European cars, which were introducing American drivers to new standards of economy and roadholding (and if
you can remember just how vague the steering was on some European small
cars of the late 1950s, you'll get some measure of the directional imprecision
that the average American monster of the epoch must have possessed).

273

Mind you, America's idea of 'compact' was a long way from Europe's concept of small cars. Oldsmobile and Buick entered the field late, in 1960, with a 3.5-litre V8 power unit which was to be adapted for the British Rover later in the decade. Oldsmobile's F85 compact was 15 ft 8 in long, two or three feet longer than the average medium-sized European car.

Europe, though, didn't have the advantages of wide-open spaces and cheap petrol which had encouraged Americans to think big (though growing urban congestion was showing the US industry the disadvantages of this policy); imported petrol and, on the Continent, taxation systems which penalised large engines, had conditioned Europeans to regard the optimum size for a power unit as being below 2 litres. Citroën's advanced and sharklike DS19, introduced in 1955, for instance, was a big car in everything but engine size. Despite having hydraulic power for steering, brakes, clutch operation, gear engagement and suspension trimming, the 22 cwt DS had a four-cylinder power unit of only 1.9 litres, relying on its slippery shape for efficient speed.

Only a year after the introduction of the DS, Europe had been given a salutary reminder of the finite nature of petroleum resources in the wake of the

Right: by 1964, fins and chrome had disappeared from most American motor cars, they now being plainer, smarter and tidier, if still as large; this as an Oldsmobile F-85 Deluxe Station Wagon

Below: seen at the 1952 London Motor Show was this Bentley R-type, with bodywork by Freestone & Webb

Suez War when the fuel supply routes were closed and fuel rationing had to be imposed. There followed a brief period of happy hitch-hiking for the majority of the British public, those without transport being given lifts by those who could get petrol. By careful choice of which vehicles you waved your thumb at, it was possible to extend your motoring experience in the most intriguing way. On one day during this adventurous period, the author rode in (or on) vehicles as diverse as a mid 1920s Sunbeam tourer and a window cleaner's ex-WD BSA motor bike!

Even when the rationing was over, there was always the thought that it could happen again, and manufacturers and the motoring public suddenly began to take seriously a new breed of cyclecar which had, indeed, begun to appear before Suez, but was then regarded as something of a joke. One of the first such cars was the Isetta, a strange device like an Easter egg mounted on a roller skate, powered, if that is the appropriate word, by a rear-mounted 245 cc engine with only one cylinder.

It was followed by the Heinkel, a similar vehicle (similar enough for the two makers to go to law about design resemblances) with a 198 cc engine capable of

Above: the famous Mercedes-Benz 300SL 'gullwing' of 1957; this car had what was probably the nearest thing, in a production model, to a true space-frame chassis, made possible by the high sills and the lift-up doors

Left: the mid 1950s had their own share of economy models. This is an Isetta Moto Coupé, commonly referred to as a 'bubble car'

Right: Germany produced the Messerschmitt Tiger as an economy vehicle. The engine had to be started the 'wrong way' if one wanted to travel backwards. Note how the cockpit bears more than a passing resemblance to that of the famous Messerschmitt fighter aircraft (National Motor Museum, England)

Left: a busy scene on an *Autobahn* near Stuttgart in Germany in 1960

Below: Alec Issigonis's front-wheel-drive idea finally achieved fruition with the Mini, introduced in 1959. The Mini came with incredible roadholding as standard equipment and many firms rushed to do tuning work on the little cars. BMC later marketed their own sports version, as seen here, albeit with non-standard alloy wheels, and this bore the famous Cooper name

returning 86 mpg and propelling the vehicle at over 50 mph on the level.

Their shape naturally earned these little creatures the nickname 'bubble cars', although their makers liked to think of them as 'cabin cruisers'. One of the strangest was the little Messerschmitt Kabinenroller, built by the erstwhile German aircraft manufacturer; this had tandem seating for two moderate-sized adults and a child under a plastic cockpit cover. It had handlebar steering and a 191 cc Sachs two-stroke engine which had to have its direction of rotation reversed to achieve a 'reverse gear'. There was also a supersports version of this car, the KR500 Tiger, which had a 500 cc engine and four wheels instead of three, as obstructions like manhole covers were liable to upset the roadholding of the original model.

The bubble-car vogue was a short-lived one, for these little cars were noisy, cramped and not over-reliable, although at one stage in 1960 the British-built Scootacar was, at £275, the cheapest enclosed car on the market (it looked rather like a perambulating phone box and was built by the Hunslet Engine Company, who in 1903 had produced a car with the ominous name of Attila).

The car which was to prove the downfall of the bubbles arrived in the autumn of 1959, and stemmed directly from the swing to small cars caused by Suez. This was no cramped two-and-a-bit seater with a minuscule scooter engine, however, but a proper four-seater, four-cylinder car in which maximum use had been made of a minimum of space by clever design ideas like a transverse engine, with the gearbox in the sump, driving the front wheels and variable-rate rubber suspension. It was called the Morris Mini-Minor, and its designer was Alec Issigonis, who had previously been responsible for the Morris Minor. There was an attempt to market an Austin version of this car under the annoying title 'Austin Se7en', but it was the 'Mini' title which stuck (and coincidentally gave a new word to the English language). The Mini proved to have outstanding handling, and was soon being used for racing and rallying; its major fault was one which was not apparent to the public, but to the manufacturer, for this advanced design was expensive to produce in relation to the price which could be asked for the finished product. Ford engineers took one of the early examples apart for analysis, concluded that on the sort of production volumes then being achieved it would be hopelessly uneconomical for them to try and build a similar car, and instead designed the thoroughly conventional, roomier Cortina, which appeared in 1962 after the space in the Ford range between the Anglia and the Consul had temporarily been plugged by two short-run 'stop-gap' designs, the Classic and the Capri, and which, selling in similar price ranges to the little car, proved its most serious competitor.

'You've never had it so good' was the political slogan which ruled the Mini's natal year, and indeed 1959 had seen an unparalleled crop of new designs; apart from the Issigonis baby, there had been the Triumph Herald, designed by Harry Webster, the Aston Martin DB4GT, 6¼-litre V8 light-alloy engines for Rolls-Royce and Bentley, the Ford 105E Anglia, the Daimler SP250 (a rather

ugly glassfibre-bodied sports model), the MGA 1600, the Sunbeam Alpine, Hillman Minx with Easidrive automatic and new models from AC and Armstrong-Siddeley.

There was another slogan which was soon to affect motoring in America, however. Chevrolet had broken away from tradition to produce the Corvair compact, which had a flat-six air-cooled engine mounted at the rear and swing-axle independent rear suspension. Its unfamiliar handling characteristics led to a crop of accidents and a book written by a crusading lawyer, Ralph Nader. The book's title? *Unsafe at Any Speed* . . .

Top: a 1959 Aston Martin DB4, which used the straight-six twin-cam engine. Producing 240 bhp, the engine gave the car a great performance

Above: a 1956 Armstrong-Siddeley Sapphire is typical of the British luxury motor car of the 1950s with very conservative styling

Right: a Jensen Interceptor of 1969, with Vignale bodywork

Left: the Amphicar found only a very limited market and was one of the strange vehicles that appeared on the roads and in the water of the early 1960s

Below: the Gordon-Keeble represented a brave attempt to market a specialist high-performance sports car in Great Britain. However, the car failed, probably because it was priced too low and the resultant profit not great enough to keep the company going

CHAPTER 16

Styling brings Sales

It was clever packaging rather than engineering which sold cars in the early 1960s: two-tone paint jobs and vestigial fins were common on middle-range British cars, although interior appointments were distinctly spartan. Dashboard design was generally of a low standard, with much pressed metal in evidence, and instruments of poor design, although models as diverse as the De Luxe Mini and the MkII Jaguar range featured 'instrument-shaped instruments' of admirable clarity. The Jaguar, indeed, also offered a high standard of interior luxury – leather seating and polished wood – at reasonable prices. On the whole, however, the average car of the first part of the decade was a pretty dismal prospect, although it obviously pleased the customers, for sales continued to rise until 1964, when they dropped back slightly. Annual sales had first passed the million mark in Britain in 1958: in 1964 they were up to a record 1,867,640 of which some 600,000 went for export.

All, however, was not well with the industry: Standard-Triumph, having just announced the new Herald model, found themselves unable to finance the necessary expansion, so combined in 1960 with the Leyland Group, hitherto more closely connected with commercial vehicles. Not long after the merger the Standard marque was allowed to celebrate sixty years of production and then quietly phased out, as it was felt that the word 'standard' had become so debased since the make's debut in 1903 that it was no longer relevant. Once it had signified a criterion; now it just meant 'basic'.

Then Ford of America made a massive cash bid, which brought Ford of Britain entirely under their control. However, fuelled by successful models like the Anglia and the Cortina, Ford was in expansive mood, marked by the construction of a modern headquarters building costing several million pounds at Warley in Essex in 1963, and the opening of a new factory at Halewood on Merseyside the same year. Halewood, representing an investment of some £70 million, was a major step in a policy of decentralisation which created, in effect, production lines several hundred miles long, engines from Dagenham being shipped to Halewood and the truck factories at Langley and Southampton by special trains, and gearboxes from Halewood and back axles from Swansea being moved cross-country by the same method. This was theoretically the best interpretation of Henry Ford I's dictum that a factory must have the best possible transportation links. Stoppages at one factory can disrupt national production however.

There were complaints from some political quarters that, with Vauxhall owned by General Motors, the new set-up at Ford brought half the British industry under direct American rule; there was little justification for such anxieties, however, for, quite apart from the fact that both Ford and Vauxhall were left to operate as virtually autonomous units, producing cars specifically designed for their own markets, the massive cash resources of their respective parent companies were used to finance the building of new factories, and thus the creation of many new jobs. It was during the early 1960s that Vauxhall

built a new factory at Ellesmere Port, also in the Merseyside development area, to produce a new version of its 1-litre Viva model.

It was American cash which was to prove the salvation of the Rootes Group which, having just opened a Scottish factory to build its new rear-engined Imp light car, found itself in financial trouble, and needed bailing out. With Government approval, the Chrysler corporation took a £27 million stake in the company in 1964, and three years later put in another £20 million; the final takeover came in 1973.

As for the other two big companies in the British market, these began the Sixties as rivals and ended the decade as a unity. For seventy years, the groups which were now known as the Leyland Motor Corporation and the British Motor Corporation had been rolling along like corporate snowballs, gathering company after company, although by the mid 60s both seemed to have run out of inertia. The last act of rivalry was the acquisition of Jaguar in 1966 by the BMC, which gave the corporation an entrée into the prestige-car market; shortly afterwards, Leyland bought Rover to prevent BMC from having it. Even during the 1950s, the economic signs pointed towards a merger between the motoring giants, and a succession of Managing Directors, including Leonard Lord, Joe Edwards, Sir William Black, Sir George Harriman and Lord Stokes, had paved the way for the eventuality. In association with the Labour Government's Industrial Reorganisation Corporation, Leyland and BMC considered a rescue operation for the ailing Rootes Group. This was not a commercially sound proposition and Rootes was acquired by Chrysler. The Government-supported concept of a British corporation large enough to compete with the increasingly sophisticated continental manufacturers was sufficient to create the basis for the merger, which took place, not without considerable difficulty and bitterness, in the February of 1967. The company is still evolving through rationalisation of model ranges and streamlining of internal administration procedures, and is now the second largest automotive company in Europe.

Against the understandable complexity of the BLMC range, the other big European companies relied on simple model ranges of perhaps three or four distinct types: small, medium and large. Sporty cars gained sufficient variety to appeal to the mass of car-buyers by offering a wide range of trim and equipment, so that two identical bodyshells could leave the factory, one as a basic spartan model designed for fleet use, the other as a comfortable limousine with, for instance, wooden door-cappings and a high level of interior appointment. From such companies it is therefore possible for a customer to choose, within the options offered, the size of car, performance, degree of sophistication and accessories to suit his own requirements.

The only real exception to the rule that a big company should keep its range simple seemed to be Fiat, which in the mid 1960s had a basic lineup of eleven different models, but as the company had a virtual monopoly of the Italian

Above: Opel was one of the many companies in Germany who rose from relative obscurity in the 1950s to great heights of success in the 1960s and 1970s; this is the Commodore GS of 1969

Above right: the Ogle-designed Reliant Scimitar 3-litre V6 of 1966 was the car which evolved into the Scimitar GTE, a whole new concept of motor car

Right: TVR of Blackpool have concentrated on sports cars and, in their teenage history, on one basic design of car. However, during its time of production, that basic design has evolved steadily to keep up with the times. This is a 1969 Vixen with a specially tuned 1650 cc Ford Cortina engine

Left: the AC Cobra was the last 'hairy chested' sports car built in England. This car, a seven-litre Shelby Cobra, was constructed in America. Boasting a genuine 550 bhp+, this actual car could reach 60 mph from rest in a shade under four seconds

Below: the Swiss luxury motor industry in the 1960s was catered for solely by Monteverdi; this is one of Peter Monteverdi's 375 High Speed coupés built in Basle

market, with something like 75 per cent of total sales, perhaps they could afford to be a little profligate in their marketing.

On the other hand, Volkswagen, who during the decade joined the Mercedes-Auto-Union group, found that stark simplicity had its drawbacks, too. At the start of the 1960s, the old VW Beetle was still selling strongly, backed up by enthusiastic press reports of its durability, but technical progress during the decade began to leave the Beetle behind – it was, after all, a child of the '30s – and Volkswagen began tentatively to diversify, offering models with the same basic layout but modern styling, although with hindsight these 'modernised' VWs seem to have dated far more quickly than the Beetle.

The unfortunate Beetle was one of the victims of Ralph Nader's *Unsafe at any speed* campaign, although it seems that the crusading American lawyer was over-emphasising his arguments to gain the maximum of publicity. Especially in America, the motor industry and the legislature over-reacted, and the environmentalist lobby, boldened by the success of its onslaught, moved in for the kill. Figures were issued claiming – although exactly how such things could be measured was unclear – that, annually, motor cars emitted 60 million tons of carbon monoxide, 12 million tons of hydrocarbons, 6 million tons of nitrous oxide, a million tons of sulphur oxide . . . and a million tons of 'smoke'.

These arguments were given some credence by the freak atmospheric conditions prevailing around Los Angeles, where atmospheric pollution can form a dense smog layer over the city, although the inhabitants' predilection for using a car to go even the shortest distances, and to regard anyone actually seen walking as some kind of freak, did not aid the situation.

Politically, there were easy pickings to be made out of the situation, and Senator Ed Muskie put a bill before Congress proposing that exhaust emissions from a motor vehicle should be 95 per cent clean before they were released to the atmosphere. This virtually meant that the exhaust gas had to be purer than the air sucked into the carburettor, but it sounded impressive, and soon manufacturers were attempting to meet this impossible standard by fitting all kinds of 'de-toxing' devices to ensure that engines ingested all their own harmful waste-products. Needless to say, power units did not benefit from their coprophagous diet, and performance and efficiency deteriorated. So much underbonnet equipment was needed to meet these requirements that Ford's engineering laboratories jokingly announced that the standard test to see whether a European Capri converted to meet California emission laws had all the appropriate plumbing was to empty a bucket of water over the engine. If any ran out underneath, there was sure to be something missing.

Having now forced the makers of all cars sold in America to conform to a standard intended to beat freak weather conditions, the environmentalists launched a campaign aimed at the additives included in fuel to promote more efficient combustion. Tetra-ethyl-lead, which had permitted increased engine compression – and hence efficiency – when it was first put on the market at the end of the 1920s and regarded as a miracle additive and personified by a Betty Boop-like character called Miss Ethyl, was now reviled as a causer of brain damage, and plans made to phase it out.

Engines thus became less competent at burning their fuel, petrol consumption went up and in a world increasingly aware of the finite nature of its oil reserves, could one argue that the environmentalists were proposing the right solutions?

Many of these environmental lobbyists seemed to be non-motorists, misunderstanding completely the role of the car in society, and instead of encouraging manufacturers to produce cars with impeccable steering, braking, roadholding and acceleration – cars which were safe to *drive*, a criterion which the majority of manufacturers were already aiming at – they forced through legislation to ensure that a car was safe to *crash*!

In order to be able to sell in many markets, therefore, manufacturers nowadays have to spend vast sums of money in deliberately writing-off brand-new cars in carefully controlled crashes to prove the integrity of the passenger compartment. One particularly regrettable aspect of the situation was that the environmentalists succeeded in killing off the mass-produced convertible

in America at the beginning of the 1970s, as open tops were dangerous in the unlikely situation of a car being inverted. It apparently did not occur to these people to insist on the standardisation of roll bars.

One expensive blind alley followed by manufacturers in response to such hostile lobbying was the 'Safety Car', various concepts of which were built in America and Europe in the early 1970s, and most of which succeeded in looking like highspeed bulldozers. Heavy, clumsy and inelegant, it seemed that the only thing that they could do successfully was to run into solid obstacles!

Although road-building programmes were being instituted with zeal during the 1960s, the constraints on the use of cars were multiplying with equal rapidity. For instance, in 1965, Britain's new non-motoring lady Minister of Transport announced that as a temporary experiment, a nationwide maximum speed limit of 70 mph would be instituted. It gives some idea of the credence that can be given to a politician's concept of 'temporary' when one considers that at the time of writing, eleven years later, that 70 mph maximum is still in force.

Since then, the cancer of overall speed limitation has spread to most countries, either as a result of fuel economy measures or because of the attitude of the safety lobbyists. The facile argument that 'speed kills' is not really defensible, because the majority of drivers keep to self-imposed limits, and the faster driver is normally more aware of what is going on. It's the slow, half-asleep motorist who often causes accidents by his total oblivion of what other road users are doing. But of course when an image of 'responsibility' for such

exponents of creeping paralysis has been created for political ends, one can hardly accuse those slow drivers of being a menace to the more rapid drivers on the road!

Faced with such unreasonable legislation, and fearing that the situation could only deteriorate in the future, the keener motorists began to seek solace in the ownership of cars built in happier days, whose driving required some little skill and which, in short, made driving within the limits still bearable. During the 1960s, therefore, demand for veteran and vintage cars grew apace, and Prices began to rise. Unfortunately, the increase in value of such vehicles also attracted the 'investor', who just saw an interesting car in terms of its potential increase in capital value, and was prepared to salt it away and rarely, if ever, use it. The activities of such gentlemen priced many of the true enthusiasts out of the market, and forced them to look to more recent cars of interest for their recreation.

But in that context, when one looked back on the 1960s, one realised how very few truly classic designs had appeared in that decade. Maybe the future held something better?

Below: Triumph used a straight-six engine in their successful 2000 series cars, introduced in 1963. This is the Mk II 2.5 Pi, introduced in 1971 which used a 2½-litre Lucas fuel-injected version of the power unit. Producing 132 bhp, the engine gave the car a top speed of 112 mph

CHAPTER 17

The Seventies and Onward

Even though the decade is scarcely half over, the 1970s has been one of the most dramatic episodes in the history of motoring, with the motor industry lurching between optimism and despondency as the victim of international politics which at one stage seemed to threaten its entire future.

The 70s opened well enough for the British industry, although Ford, Vauxhall and Chrysler all had their share of industrial unrest. By 1973, optimism was the keynote.

Reported *The Times*: 'The fruits of a bumper 1972 are already being reflected in plans for 1973. The Society of Motor Manufacturers and Traders says that the British industry is geared to produce 2,500,000 cars and car sets (for assembly overseas) this year. This compares with 1,900,000 last year. Mr Gilbert Hunt, the society's president and also chief executive of Chrysler UK, talks of a four to five per cent rise in home demand and a twenty per cent rise in exports . . . Much is at stake for the country's biggest earner of foreign currency this year'.

Mr Hunt's optimism was, however, misplaced; at the end of 1973 the Arab–Israeli War erupted, bringing the Arab oil embargo in its wake. For maybe half a century, there had been forecasts that one day there would be problems in obtaining Middle East oil: faced with the reality, European governments instituted all kinds of restrictions, from limits on the amount of petrol that could be bought at one time to car-less Sundays. Most of these measures were mere windowdressing, introduced to bring home the seriousness of the crisis to the general public, for cars used only a tiny proportion of oil imports, the bulk being used by industry and public services.

Far from rising, British sales fell by almost 200,000. Soaring raw materials, prices and wages caused new car prices to rise at an alarming rate – nearly 40 per cent in a year in some cases – and savage taxes were placed on petrol to curb demand.

The worst of the oil crisis was soon over, but it left a vastly changed motor industry in its wake. The salvation of British Leyland, faced as it was with massive losses, lay in the hands of the government, and the company was 'taken into public ownership'. Whilst it is arguable that such a drastic step might not necessarily be certain to increase the company's commercial efficiency, there is little doubt that without Government intervention at the time, Leyland would look quite different today. Chrysler, too, was in trouble, although as it was an American-owned company, the British Government could hardly take it over as it had British Leyland: but again millions of pounds were handed over to keep Chrysler in Britain.

To an outside observer, it might have seemed like unfair preference; after all, the other British motor companies were trading in the same market. But both Ford and Vauxhall, using shrewd marketing and attractive model ranges, actually increased their share of overall sales, Ford, indeed, nudging the British Leyland makes (lumped together for statistical purposes, although still marketed under their old marque names) out of first place during the early part of 1976, although Leyland made efforts to retaliate.

There were, indeed, doubts about the government's understanding of business management: the civil servants didn't always seem to be pulling in the same direction as the Leyland management. As witness the announcement by Whitehall in September 1976 that British Leyland was planning to invest some £100 million on the development of a successor to the Mini. As this car wasn't due to be put on the market for another three to four years, the announcement was premature to say the least, and broke all the industry's normal rules of confidentiality over forthcoming models. The press reported that the Leyland directors were 'furious', and that the leak had caused a drop in the sales of the current Mini. There were also doubts about the economic viability of such a model, as all the leading European companies were already active in this area of the market, known to the manufacturers as the 'B' car class.

The main problem with building small cars – and the fuel crisis had really only advanced a swing to such economical vehicles – is that a great deal of them needed to be built before they become financially attractive. After all, the

Left: a classic sports car, the Pininfarina-designed Ferrari Dino 246GT

Above: the GTE started the trend of sports/estate cars and other manufacturers quickly jumped on the bandwagon; this is BMW's 2000 Touring or 2002 Touring, depending whether you live in England or Germany!

Right: the Hillman Imp was the basis for this small sports car built first in Essex and then in Lincolnshire. It is the Ginetta G15

plant and labour costs are virtually those of a larger car, the only saving being on metal and other raw materials.

Ford solved the problem neatly by building their Fiesta in three strategically-placed factories; at Dagenham, at Saarlouis in Germany and in a new, purpose-built plant at Almusafes, near Valencia in Spain, where Fiestas would be built not only for the booming Spanish market but also for other southern European countries. The necessary raw materials could therefore be bought in quantities sufficient to keep these three factories supplied, the 'economies of scale' meaning that components could be purchased or produced at the minimum unit cost. Typical of the new generation of small cars, the Fiesta was a two-door model with hatchback tailgate, and offered a wide range of options and trim – even a luxury Ghia model. Small no longer meant 'austere'.

The launching of the Fiesta in 1976 also proved a new truism: in order to think small, a company had to be very big. And, in general, the climate of the 1970s was inimical to the limited-production, specialised manufacturer. Aston Martin almost vanished and Jensen *did* vanish; only those specialists like Rolls-Royce or Morgan who catered for a readily identifiable minority of well heeled motorists could face the future with some assurance.

In fact, the period was marked by huge groupings, both national and international, either as straight commercial mergers, or as looser comings-together where companies retained their independence but pooled resources for the development of some technical resource, such as a new design of power unit. Typical of the latter type of arrangement was the Comotor company, formed jointly by Citroën (who were owned by Pardevi, a Swiss company owned 51 per cent by Michelin, 49 per cent by Fiat) and by Audi-NSU (who were a subsidiary of Volkswagen); Comotor, whose factory was in the Saarland, produced Wankel Rotary engines, a type of power unit which seemed to hold

Left: Citroën produced a 'car of the 1950s' with their DS of 1955 and, in the 1970s, produced the CX series which were as futuristic as their predecessors. Here is a CX2200 Pallas which, like all other Citroëns, has a very low drag coefficient

Below: Lotus marketed their famous 7 from the late 1950s right into the 1970s. This is a Mk IV car which sports a 126 bhp big-valve twin-cam engine. When Lotus decided to drop the model, production was taken over by Caterham Car Sales who built the earlier, and more popular, Mk III

Below: the NSU Ro80 was the second car to feature Felix Wankel's rotary-engine design, the first being the rare NSU Spider. The front-wheel-drive Ro80 also featured a three-speed manual gearbox with a torque converter and a clutch operated by a hypersensitive switch in the gear lever

out possibilities of being more easily adapted to meet American exhaust pollution levels. Just to complicate the merger picture still further, by 1976 Citroën had come under the control of the privately-owned Peugeot company (which for a decade had been operating a joint research, development and investment programme with the state-owned Renault company!). First fruit of the Peugeot-Citroën alliance was the Citroën LN minicar, referred to in the French press as 'a little lion with Javel sauce', which used a two-door Peugeot 104 bodyshell and a 602 cc, flat-twin, air-cooled power unit and transmission from the 3 cv Citroën.

So the new generation of cars for the late 1970s were really quite conventional restatements of established themes. Comfort, of course, was greatly improved on the majority of them, and features like heated rear windows, servo-assisted disc brakes became common standard fitments; but most of the refinements were relatively minor ones. Faced with the reality that motorists were changing their cars less frequently, manufacturers began using phrases like 'the long-lasting car', and Porsche came up with a car that would 'last for twenty years' (although as there were still fifty-year-old cars in daily use, one felt that they

could have been a little more ambitious). Such trends caused the prophets of the automotive future to trade in their crystal balls for utility models.

In 1966 the *Wall Street Journal* looked ahead to transportation in the year 2000, and forecast a 'dazzling, Buck Rogers-like world of plush, electronically controlled ground vehicles and 6000-mile-an-hour airliners'.

Ten years later, their view of the future was more cautious: 'Today's airline passenger or motorist should be able to step into a vehicle of the early 21st century and feel right at home'.

Coupled with this attitude was that of the protagonists of public transport, who wanted to drive people away from the privately-owned motor car and force them to use what Americans called 'mass-transit vehicles' – buses and trains. But these were no longer economically viable alternatives to the car: however expensive owning a motor vehicle had become, public transport had become more expensive still, and with services pared to a minimum, especially in rural areas, the use of public transport became only a desperation measure for many people.

Politically-biased 'consultation groups' talked grandly in their big brotherly way about increasing the cost of petrol still further so that the motorist would be frightened out of his car and on to the public transport by the 'perceived cost of his journey'; but what they seemed unable to comprehend was that for the family motorist the car would always win. On a train and bus four travelled at four times the cost of one, but in a car, four travelled at a quarter the cost of one. Nevertheless, the pressure groups continued to press for cars to be abolished, despite opposition from many people.

When, in 1975, Henry Ford II was called to testify before the US Joint Economic Committee, he was questioned persistently about his attitude towards Federal aid to the car industry to enable it make the 'inevitable' conversion from building motor cars to building mass-transit vehicles.

Commented Mr Ford: 'That's one problem we at Ford are not worried about. The real mass-transit system in the United States is the Highway system and the automobile, which are responsible for more than 80 per cent of all trips to work and all trips between cities, and for more than 90 per cent of all trips within cities. The automobile business is now about 75 years old. Most of the United States has been built within that period, and the building pattern has been made possible by the unprecedented convenience, flexibility, comfort and low cost of motor vehicle transportation.

'Even if it were possible, the United States has better things to do with its resources than build a 19th century transportation system – and then build a

Below: the kit-car and specialist-car industry, which got off the ground in the early 1950s, continued to flourish in the '60s and '70s in various forms. This is the Dri-Sleeve Moonraker Bugatti replica, which was one of the best. The car used an ordinary Ford Cortina engine; only seven were built, however

Right: the Porsche 911 series matured from very quick sports cars in the 1960s to among the fastest 'supercars' of the '70s with the Carrera and Turbo; this is a Targa-roof 911S

19th century country so that we can somehow make do with primitive transportation.

'There is room and need for better public transportation in many places. But better public transportation will take few people out of cars and probably will not even halt the long, steady decline in public transportation usage. The few new rapid transit systems built in recent years all have drawn their riders from buses, not cars. They can be built only with enormous outlays of public funds, and generally can be operated only with additional large subsidies to cover the growing gap between revenues and operating costs.'

What, however, of the car's alleged over-use of non-replaceable fuel and raw materials? The latest statistics available in 1976 showed that the known recoverable reserves of petroleum totalled 660,000,000,000 barrels, enough for some 34 years. And much of the world's surface remained undrilled – ninety per cent of all the oil and gas wells ever drilled in the world had been drilled in the United States. Other potential fuel sources included oil shale, tar sands, coal and organic waste matter: it seemed as though the internal combustion engine would be around for a long time yet. And 80 per cent of the

Below left: a 1973 Cadillac Eldorado 8.3-litre car, which has everything either automatic or power operated. This front-wheel-drive car even has lights that come on automatically when the daylight fades

Right: the first example of Lotus's 'up-market' cars, the Elite. This is a luxury four-seater car with a highly efficient four-valve twin-cam engine and the best roadholding and handling of any front-engined road car ever built

Below: the only American sports car in production in the 1970s was the Chevrolet Corvette Stingray, this being a 1973 7.5-litre automatic

materials used to build a car could be recycled to build new cars.

Manufacturers were, nevertheless, investigating alternative forms of power. Steam and electricity had been tried and found wanting at a very early stage in the development of the motor vehicle, although there were persistent attempts to revive the electric car, at least for urban use. All one could say of the electric vehicles of the 70s was that until they could surpass the performance of their Edwardian forebears, and until some revolutionary lightweight battery could be perfected at a moderate cost, they would never be a viable rival to the petrol engine. And the pollution from an oil-burning electric generating station could amount to more per electric car than anything emitted by a petrol vehicle's exhaust.

More promising, perhaps, was the Stirling engine, a modern development of a 'hot-air' power unit originally – and appropriately – devised by a Scottish clergyman in the early 19th century; the 1970s Stirling operated on a closed-cycle 'hot-gas' system of some complexity, but was remarkably unfastidious in its dietary requirements. The Stirling, claimed its protagonists, could run on any fuel from peanut butter to nuclear energy with equal efficiency, and by the mid-1970s Ford were running Stirling-engined cars on their proving grounds, while a Stirling engined bus had been built in Holland.

Meanwhile, governments were understandably taking a parsimonious look at their oil imports. In America, Congress decreed late in 1975 that the average fuel economy of all cars produced in a year by each manufacturer should rise in stages to 27.5 miles per (US) gallon by the 1985 model year, representing a 100 per cent improvement over the fuel consumption of 1974 models.

'To achieve so big a change in so huge an industry in so short a period,' claimed Henry Ford II, 'we must start right now and we have little time to hesitate or change direction along the way.'

The motor industry world-wide, it seemed, was entering a period of unusual uncertainty, although there was evidence that the public was becoming tired of excessive government interference in their freedom to buy and use motor vehicles. Henry Ford II summed up the problems ahead in a speech to the Automotive World Congress at Dearborn, Michigan, in July 1976: 'Outside the United States, will the trend towards government control and ownership of auto companies continue, and how far will the march towards social democracy go? How will world trade in motor vehicles be affected if manufacturing and marketing are increasingly aimed at protecting jobs and generating export income rather than profits? Can private, profit-orientated enterprise survive in anything like its present form in the face of growing support for such measures as worker participation in management, compulsory profit sharing and compulsory distribution of stock to workers and unions?'.

The motor industry is now ninety years old, and in its lifetime it has transformed the face of the world more than any other. The problem now is: can the industry survive the social changes it has itself instigated? The answer is most probably yes.

The Jaguar XJS, seen here in automatic form, used the 5.3-litre V12 two-cam engine first seen in the last E-types. Not only did the XJS have magnificent acceleration and top speed (155 mph), but it was one of the quietest tourers ever available. The XJS, despite its conservative instead of *avant garde* styling, represented motoring of the 1970s: sophisticated, silent, quick and expensive, a far cry from the chugging and puffing vehicles that graced our roads (or tracks) of the motor-car age in its infancy

Chronology 1690-1976

This brief chronology lists, year by year, the milestones in the motoring story, together with photographs of the important cars, so that the speed and scale of development of the motor car can be seen at a glance.

1690 Denis Papin, inventor of the pressure cooker, makes the first proposal for a piston-driven road vehicle.

1769 In Paris, Nicolas Joseph Cugnot makes the first recorded run in a self-propelled steam vehicle, and becomes history's first motor accident, knocking down a wall.

1770 Cugnot builds a larger carriage, still preserved in Paris.

1770 Cugnot steam carriage

1801 The first successful motor vehicle, built by Richard Trevithick, runs through Camborne, Cornwall, but goes up in flames four days later.

1803 Trevithick's second steamer shipped to London, where it makes several successful trips, but frightens the horses and arouses public hostility.

1805 The first-ever internal-combustion engined vehicle built in Switzerland by Isaac de Rivaz. With a foot-operated exhaust valve, it can only run for a few yards.
Oliver Evans puts wheels on his massive steam dredger and drives it through Philadelphia and into the River Schuykill.

1805 Evans *Orukter Amphibolos*

1816 Reverend Robert Stirling files patents on Stirling engine. Nobody understands why it works.

1829 The first long-distance automobile tour, from London to Bath, made by Goldsworthy Gurney's eighteen-seater, six-wheel steam coach, not without incident.

1830 Walter Hancock's steamer *Infant* begins regular service between Stratford, East London, and Fulham, West London.

1831 British Commission says that steam carriages are practical. Sir Charles Dance operates three Gurney steam carriages between Gloucester and Cheltenham, the world's first scheduled passenger service by automobiles. It lasts only a few months.

1834 Walter Hancock establishes a chain of garages and service stations in London for his passenger-carrying steam omnibuses.

1845 Pneumatic tyres patented by R. W. Thomson of Edinburgh.

1860 J. J. Etienne Lenoir's gas carriage described in *Le Monde Illustré*.

1860 Lenoir gas carriage

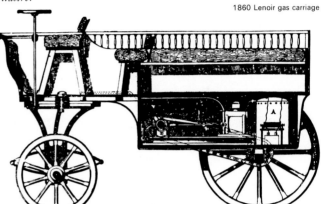

1863 Lenoir's second carriage, with a 1.5hp engine, used for several journeys from Paris to Vincennes – six miles in three hours – running on 'liquid hydrocarbon'.

1864 Lenoir makes history's first export sale of a car, to Alexander II, Tsar of Russia.

1865 'Red Flag Act' passed in Britain; restricts 'Road Locomotives' to 4mph on the open road, 2mph in towns, preceded by a man carrying a red flag (which was not required by law after 1878).

1868 Tangye steamer *Cornubia* exported to India.

1879 George B. Selden files 'master patent' for the automobile in the United States.

1885 Gottlieb Daimler and Wilhelm Maybach convert a horse-carriage to petrol power with a four-stroke engine.

1886 First successful runs of the Benz three-wheeler, the first petrol car to be designed as an entity, not converted from a horse carriage.

1886 Benz

1888 John Boyd Dunlop re-invents the pneumatic tyre.
Magnus Volk begins limited production of electric carriages; one is sold to the Sultan of Morocco.
Karl Benz begins limited production of his three-wheeled cars; but has few orders.

1889 Panhard & Levassor acquire French rights for Daimler's new V-twin engine.

1890 Not being interested in producing cars themselves, Panhard & Levassor grant automotive licence for the Daimler engine to the Peugeot ironmongery business.
Daimler-Motoren-Gesellschaft set up in Cannstatt, Germany.

1890 Panhard & Levassor

1894 Benz Viktoria

1894 Benz Velo

1891 M. Levassor changes his mind, and designs and builds a rear-engined car.
Daimler UK rights acquired by Frederick R. Simms, who at first applies the engine solely to motor launches.
French inventor Ferdinand Forest, who in 1885 built an opposed-piston engine with low-tension magneto ignition and a spray carburettor, produces the world's first four-cylinder petrol engine with mechanical valve operation. He will later build the world's first six-cylinder engine, but as both these epoch-making power units were used in boats, not cars, history will tend to ignore him.

1892 Levassor devises the archetypal form of the motor car, with front engine, sliding-gear transmission and rear-wheel drive. It will be known as the *Système Panhard*. In 1893, one of these cars is sold to the Abbé Gavois, a parish priest, who will use it for the next forty years.

1893 The brothers James and Frank Duryea build their motor buggy in Springfield, Massachussetts. Although Lambert, Nadig and Schloemer have all built cars earlier than this, the Duryea is accepted as America's first practicable motor car. However, it is crude compared with the Benz and Daimler vehicles shown at that year's Chicago World Exposition.

1895 Sir David Salomans holds Britain's first motor exhibition at Tunbridge Wells, Kent.
The first indoor exhibition of cars in Britain is held a month later, in November, at the Stanley Cycle Show. One of the five exhibits is the Hon Evelyn Ellis's Panhard, in which the future Edward VII has just had his first petrol-car ride.
After years of revision, Selden's master patent is at last granted in the USA.
De Dion and Bouton produce their first petrol engine.
J. J. Henry Sturmey founds *The Autocar* magazine.
The Lanchester brothers build their first car.
The first car to run on Michelin pneumatic tyres is a Peugeot *L'Eclair*.

1896 Harry J. Lawson launches the Daimler Motor Company in Coventry: the British Motor Industry is born.
Parliament raises the speed limit to 12mph; Lawson organises the Emancipation Day Run from London to Brighton.
American pioneers Henry Ford, Charles Brady King, Ransome Eli Olds and Alexander Winton all complete and test their first cars.
Duryea brings two cars over to Europe for the Emancipation Day event.
Léon Bollée's voiturette is the first car to be sold with pneumatic tyres as standard.
Lawson forms the Great Horseless Carriage Company (later the Motor Manufacturing Company), and seeks to gain control of the British motor industry by acquiring rights to all the vital Continental patents.

1893 Duryea

1894 Benz begins 'mass-production' of the Velo and Viktoria; in 1895, his company will build 135 motor vehicles.
America's first car factory opened by Henry G. Morris and Pedro Salom of Philadelphia to build Electrobat electric cars.
Elwood Haynes and the Apperson brothers collaborate to build an automobile in Kokomo, Indiana.

1896 Ford

1897 Francis E. and Freelan O. Stanley are the first Americans to produce steam cars commercially.

First large-scale attempt to build cars in America is made by the Pope Manufacturing Company (the country's principal cycle makers) of Hartford, Connecticut.

Sturmey drives a Daimler from John O'Groats to Lands End.

F. R. Simms forms the Automobile Club of Great Britain and Ireland.

First four-cylinder Cannstatt-Daimler ordered by Emil Jellinek.

Death of Emile Levassor.

1898 Stanley

1898 Panhard-Levassor abandon the tiller for wheel steering.

The first De Dion Bouton voiturette appears.

Louis Renault builds his first car, using a De Dion engine and live-axle drive.

Coventry-Daimler's first four-cylinder model appears.

Napier build their first power unit.

1898 Panhard

1898 Daimler four-cylinder

1899 Ransom Eli Olds begins production of the Oldsmobile. Other companies to begin production this year are: FIAT, Sunbeam, Wolseley, Albion and Isotta-Fraschini.

The first Gardner-Serpollet steam cars appear (Léon Serpollet built his first car in 1887).

1900 The Thousand Miles' Trial, organised by the ACGBI, demonstrates the reliability and efficiency of the motor vehicle to the British public, many of whom had never before seen a car.

Gottlieb Daimler dies; a week later the decision is taken to produce the Mercédès, named after Jellinek's teenaged daughter, and designed by Wilhelm Maybach.

American car production totals 4192, sold at an average price of $1000 each.

1901 Mercédès

1901 Lanchester cars go into production.

Cannstatt-Daimler introduces the Mercédès, 'the car of the day after tomorrow' (although none of its technical features is new in itself).

1902 First attempt to drive round the world; but Dr Lehwess's Panhard caravan *Passe Partout* fails to get further than Nijni Novgorod.

Frederick R. Simms founds the Society of Motor Manufacturers and Traders.

The Mercédès-Simplex appears, a vast improvement over the 1901 model.

1902 Mercédès Simplex

1903 Motor Car Act passed in Britain raises speed limit to 20mph, introduces numbering of cars and driving licences (but no test).

First SMMT motor show at the Crystal Palace (London already has two other motor shows, the Cordingley and the Stanley).

Marius Barbarou designs a new front-engined Benz, the Parsifal, to replace the old rear-engined, belt-drive model developed from the 1885–6 prototype.

Henry Ford founds the Ford Motor Company after two earlier attempts to go into car production have failed.

Association of Licenced Automobile Manufacturers formed in America to administer the Selden patent, and sues Ford, among others, for alleged infringement.

Spyker of Holland build a six-cylinder, four-wheel-drive racer.
Napier announce the first series-production six-cylinder car.
H. M. Leland founds the Cadillac Motor Car Company in Detroit.
The Vauxhall Iron Works of London build their first car.

1903 Benz Parsifal

1904 Danny Weigel drives a 20hp Talbot 2000 miles non-stop.
Motor Car Act becomes law on New Year's Day.
Ford exports to Britain for the first time.
Mr Rolls meets Mr Royce, and decides to market the Royce car.
Delaunay-Belleville begin production.
Rover, builders of bicycles since the 1880s, begin car manufacture.

1904 Rolls-Royce

1905 Herbert Austin, general manager of Wolseley, resigns to
found his own company at Longbridge, Birmingham.
Automobile Association founded to combat the police 'trapping' of
motorists alleged to have broken the speed limit. Sergeant Jarrett of
Chertsey catches so many motorists that he is promoted to inspector
within the year.

1906 Rolls-Royce Limited floated; the motor trade regards the
capitalisation as a catch-penny scheme.
Ford introduces the $500 Model N; America produces 33,500 cars
in the year.
Racing driver Vincenzo Lancia founds his own company (his father
was a wealthy soup manufacturer).
Adams of Bedford make 60hp Antoinette V8 aero-engine.
Exports of British cars to France total two per month; exports of
French cars to Britain total 400 plus per month.
Charles Glidden of America starts his second round-the-world trip
on his Napier.

1907 A 32hp Pilgrim car wins the vapour emission trials organised
by the Automobile Club, which has just been awarded the Royal
accolade by King Edward VII.
Over 60,000 cars are registered in Britain.
Rolls-Royce introduce the 40/50hp six – 'the best car in the world';
under RAC scrutiny, the 40/50 *Silver Ghost* covers 15,000 miles
with only one involuntary stop, at a total cost of £281 8s 4½d, £187
of which was replacement tyres. Forty hours' labour costs comes to
£16 13s 7½d!
A 45hp Hotchkiss also completes a 15,000-mile test, in which it wore
out 46 tyres (value £550).

1907 Pilgrim

1906 Hotchkiss

1908 General Motors Company founded by William Crapo Durant.
Cadillac awarded the Dewar Trophy for standardisation of
production parts.
First Model T Ford built; first year's production totals 8000.

1909 De Dion Bouton introduce their V8, first significant
production model with this engine configuration.
Daimler (GB) adopt the Knight sleeve-valve engine.
Cadillac becomes part of General Motors.

1908 Model T Ford

1917 Cadillac V8

1910 British Parliament rejects proposal to tax petrol.
Death of the Right Honorable C. S. Rolls in a flying accident at
Bournemouth.
Cars are taxed on horsepower ratings devised by the RAC in
Britain.
'The New Motoring' craze at its peak, spearheaded by Morgan, GN
and Bédélia.
Ettore Bugatti begins production at Molsheim, Alsace (German
territory until 1919).
Four-wheel braking offered by Crossley, Arrol-Johnston, Argyll,
Isotta-Fraschini.
Experiments made with wireless installation in a car, although the
equipment is very bulky.
Sankey pressed-steel detachable wheel introduced.

1911 First overseas Ford Factory established at Trafford Park,
Manchester; soon becomes Britain's biggest motor manufacturer,
with an annual output of 3000 Model Ts.
After protestations that they are not going to abandon the
production of steam cars for petrol, the White Company does just
this.
Cadillac are the first company to offer electric lighting and starting as
standard on their 20/30hp model.
The Selden Patent Case ends with victory for Ford – Selden Patent
'valid but not infringed'.

1912 S. F. Edge resigns from Napier company after a dispute,
taking £160,000 'golden handshake' to keep out of the motor
industry for seven years. So he turns to pig farming and cattle
breeding with great success, and also backs motion-picture
production.

1916 Packard Twin-Six

1913 Henry Ford applies the moving conveyor belt to magneto
assembly; full assembly-line production comes early the next year,
cutting time taken to build a chassis from $12\frac{1}{2}$ to $1\frac{1}{2}$ hours. Sales rise
to 182,809.
Cycle and motor agent William Morris, of Oxford, introduces his
10hp Morris-Oxford light car.
Mechanical direction indicators make a tentative appearance.
Lincoln Highway Association formed to lobby for a proper
transcontinental road across America.
Fiat build 3251 cars in the year, Renault 9338.

1913 Morris Oxford 'Bullnose'

1914 Ford workers have their daily pay raised to $5, an industry
record.
Over 200 makes of car on the British market.
Renault taxis used to carry French troops to repulse German
advance on Paris.

1915 Cadillac announce their V8.
Packard introduce the V12 Twin-Six, inspired by Sunbeam aero-
engine designs.
The banker Nicola Romeo takes over the Anonima Lombardo
Fabbrica Automobili of Milan, which therefore becomes
Alfa Romeo.
Dodge adopt the Budd pressed-steel body.
Everyone who buys a Ford Model T this year gets a $50 rebate
because sales have passed their target figure.
Fergus owner-driver car announced.
William Foster & Co of Lincoln build the first successful tank.

1917 Herbert Austin knighted.
Henry Leland resigns from Cadillac, founds Lincoln Company to
build Liberty aero engines.
Chevrolet and General Motors combine.

1918 Car registrations in America exceed five million for the
first time.

1919 André Citroën takes over the Mors factory and begins mass-
production of his Model A.
Henry Ford buys out all the other stockholders in the Ford Motor
Company for $100 million.
Post-war models introduced by Hispano-Suiza, Guy, Enfield-Allday
and Bentley all show aero-engine influence in their design.
S. F. Edge takes over AC cars.
Isotta-Fraschini introduce the first production straight-eight.

1922 Isotta-Fraschini 8

1920 This year fifty per cent of all motor vehicles in the world are
Model T Fords.
Sudden slump closes many American factories as the post-war
market for new cars collapses. Britain's McKenna Duties have put
33.3 per cent tax on imported cars.
Sunbeam, Talbot and Darracq combine to form the STD group,
with resultant confusion of badge-engineering, especially among
their racing cars.
The Motor-Car Act taxes cars in Britain at £1 per RAC horsepower,
crippling sales of the 22hp Model T Ford (but pre-1914 cars pay
only half the horsepower rate, and cars used solely for taking

305

servants to church or voters to the polling station pay no tax at all).
DuPont/Morgan banking interests acquire control of General Motors from Billy Durant; Alfred P. Sloan takes over the running of the group's affairs.
America's first production straight-eight announced by Duesenberg.
Work starts on the Great West Road and Purley Way – Britain's first motor bypasses.
France has 350 car manufacturers.

1920 Model A Duesenberg

1921 Lincoln V8 appears: Henry Ford will take over the company in 1922.
Production of the 3-litre Bentley begins.
Morris cuts prices by up to £100 to boost flagging sales – and doubles his turnover, building 3077 cars in 1921 against 1932 the year before.
Billy Durant borrows $7 million to found Durant Motors.

1922 Lincoln V8

1922 3-litre Bentley

1922 Introduction of the Austin Seven.
Clyno begin car production.
Marconi begin experiments with wireless receivers in Daimler cars.
Over a million Model Ts produced by Ford.
Lancia markets the Lambda, which combines unit body/chassis construction, independent front suspension and V4 engine.
Trico (USA) introduce the electric windscreen wiper – although the vacuum wiper has been around since 1916.
Leyland Motors acquire manufacturing rights to the Trojan.
C. F. Kettering and T. H. Midgley introduce tetraethyl leaded petrol in the USA.

306

1923 Austin Seven

1923 Cecil Kimber builds the first MG, based on his Morris-Cowley sports conversions.
Triumph, famous Coventry cycle manufacturers, build their first car, the 10/20hp.
Ford Model T production peaks at over 2 million.

1923 Triumph 10/20

1924 Walter P. Chrysler begins production of the car bearing his name.
DuPont develops quick-drying enamel in the USA, enabling car production to be speeded up.
Napier abandon car production for aero engines.

1924 Chrysler 70

1925 Morris produces 54,151 Bullnose Oxfords and Cowleys.
General Motors acquires Vauxhall Motors of Luton as a European bridgehead.
Ford's British factory produces its 250,000th Model T, which makes a triumphal tour of Britain.
First popular British car with all-round hydraulic braking – the Triumph 13/30.
The Phantom I Rolls-Royce replaces the Silver Ghost, in production since 1906.

1926 In Germany, Benz and Daimler combine to form the Daimler-Benz AG.
The Coventry Daimler Company announces the Double-Six, with a 7136cc V12 sleeve-valve engine.
The General Strike produces London's first commuter traffic jams.
Clyno become the third biggest British motor manufacturer, turning out 300 cars a week in Wolverhampton.
London's first traffic lights.

1927 Model T Ford production ceases after nineteen years and over fifteen million cars. Lowest price during that period – $290 (£65), a record for a conventional motor car.
Wolseley company fails, and is acquired by William Morris.
Chevrolet takes over the top-selling position in the American motor industry as Ford changes over to production of the Model A.
Studebaker and Oldsmobile pioneer the use of chromium plating.
Stanley Steam cars cease production.

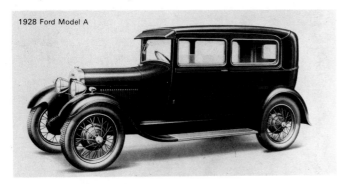
1928 Ford Model A

1928 Motor distributors Rootes Limited acquire the Humber and Hillman companies.
Chrysler buys Dodge for $175,000,000.
Clyno attempt to market a £100 version of their new 8hp model – and fail.
Cadillac pioneer synchromesh gearchange.
Alvis produce Britain's first catalogued front-wheel-drive car.

1929 US car production reaches 5,337,087, a peak that will not be exceeded until the 1950s. A total of 26.5 million cars is registered in the USA this year.
Karl Benz dies, aged 85.
Clyno goes into liquidation.
Armstrong-Siddeley fit a Wilson preselector gearbox as an option (standard from 1933) – preselector gears were fitted to the marque's ancestor, the Wilson-Pilcher from 1901–1907.

1930 Sir Dennistoun Burney, highest-paid inventor of World War I, builds the Burney Streamline, with rear engine and all-round independent suspension. Twelve are sold, one to the Prince of Wales.
Daimler fit fluid flywheels in conjunction with preselector gearboxes to produce semi-automatic transmission.
Car sales fall as the Depression deepens.
Henry Royce knighted.
The Veteran Car Club formed to preserve early motor cars – the first organisation of its kind in the world.
British Parliament abolishes the 20mph speed limit (largely ignored by motorists and law enforcers for many years) and introduce compulsory third party insurance.
Cadillac bring out a 7.4-litre V16.
Morris fits hydraulic brakes on his larger production models.

1930 Burney Streamline

1931 Vauxhall introduce syncromesh gears to the British market on the Cadet.
Bentley Motors goes into liquidation. Napier are interested in buying, but are outbid by Rolls-Royce, who form Bentley Motors (1931) Limited.
Daimler acquire Lanchester, Britain's oldest motor manufacturer.
Morris produce a £100 utility two-seat version of the Minor 8hp model.
Ninety per cent of all production cars are now saloons.

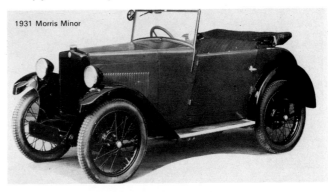
1931 Morris Minor

1932 Ford of Britain moves into its new factory at Dagenham on the north bank of the Thames. All plant and machinery moved from Trafford Park over a weekend so no production is lost.
Rootes Group formed.
The first Ford designed specifically for Europe (in Dearborn), the 8hp Model Y, is announced at the Ford Motor Show at London's Albert Hall.
In the USA, Ford introduces the V8, which sells over 300,000 in the first year.

1933 Ford Model Y

1932 Ford V8

1933 William Lyons founds the SS Car Company in Coventry, building luxury coachwork on modified Standard chassis at remarkably low prices.
Semi-automatic transmission offered on Reo cars.
Ford drops into third place in the American automobile industry behind General Motors and the Chrysler Corporation.

1934 Chrysler introduce the revolutionary Airflow line – and overdrive.
British Transport Minister Leslie Hore-Belisha announces a 30mph limit in built-up areas, pedestrian crossings and a driving test.

Morris Motors instal their first moving assembly line at Cowley.
Sir William Morris becomes Baron Nuffield.
Nazis begin building Germany's autobahn system.
Metallic paintwork available on British cars.
Citroën *traction avant* appears; its development is so costly that the company is virtually bankrupted, and André Citroën is forced to sell out to Michelin.

1935 Ford of Britain introduces the first £100 saloon car, a version of the 8hp Model Y.
A world census shows that there are now 35 million motor vehicles in use.
Screenwash system offered by Triumph.
Rootes Group acquires the Sunbeam-Talbot-Darracq combine.

1936 The first Morgan four-wheeler (but still with the 1909-designed independent front suspension).
Fiat introduce the 570cc '500' – nicknamed Topolino (Mickey Mouse) – which, at a UK cost of £120 combines 55mph performance with 55mpg economy.
Porsche builds the first Volkswagens. Hitler, whose Nazi party is financing the development of the VW, will propose that it will be available at a cost of under £50 on an instalment plan.
Britain still has 45 indigenous car manufacturers.
Sir Herbert Austin becomes Baron Austin of Longbridge.
SS Cars introduce their Jaguar model.

1936 Morgan 4/4

1937 SS Jaguar

1937 The SMMT Motor Exhibition is held at Earls Court for the first time, after being at Olympia since 1905.
Germany now has 800 miles of autobahn – at £56,000 a mile.

1938 Britain raises the horsepower tax to £1.25 per hp – and petrol tax from 8d to 9d a gallon.
Standard Flying Eight is the first small British saloon with independent front suspension.
The Nuffield Group takes over Riley.
British manufacturers begin building 'shadow factories' for war production.

1939 Lincoln division of Ford introduces the customised Continental and the lower-priced Mercury.

1940 Car factories in Britain go over to munitions production.
Germans blitz the centre of Coventry.

1941 Death of Lord Austin, aged 74, and of Louis Chevrolet (62).

1943 Due to war production, American passenger car output is cut to just 139 vehicles.

1945 Standard acquire Triumph, in liquidation since 1939.
SS cars change their name to Jaguar.
Petrol still rationed in Britain; price now 2s, of which 9d is tax.
Henry Ford II takes over control of the Ford Motor Company from his grandfather, Henry Ford I.
British manufacturers are compelled by the new Socialist government to export half their output. Motorists will have to sign a covenant promising not to sell their new cars for a year, to curb the black market in new vehicles caused by this edict.

1946 British Motor Industry celebrates its fiftieth birthday, and the first post-war British designs, from Armstrong-Siddeley, Triumph, Bentley and Jowett appear.
Petrol ration for British motorists increased 50 per cent.
Ford of Britain produce their millionth car, an 8hp Anglia.

1946 Bentley Mk VI

1946 Ford Anglia 8hp

1947 Golden Jubilee of the American car industry.
Henry Ford dies, aged 84.
Bristol and Frazer-Nash acquire the BMW engine as 'war reparations'.
Ettore Bugatti dies in Paris, aged 66.
Louis Renault, accused of having collaborated with the Germans, is imprisoned and his company nationalised.
David Brown acquires Aston Martin and Lagonda.
Standard Vanguard announced.

1947 Standard Vanguard

1948 First post-war Earls Court Motor Show.
Radical change in British car taxation, which has been based on cubic capacity since the war – henceforward all cars will be taxed at a flat rate, initially £10.
Most notable new cars are the Jaguar XK120, the Issigonis-designed Morris Minor and the Citroën 2CV, originally built before the war, and hidden during the occupation.
American motor industry builds its 100,000,000th car.
Rover launch the four-wheel-drive Land-Rover.

308

1948 Morris Minor

1952 Mercedes 300SL

1949 British petrol restrictions eased; more cars available on the home market.

1950 Ford regains second place in the US industry from Chrysler. Petrol rationing ends in Britain – but the fuel tax is doubled. Double purchase tax on luxury cars is halved, although the new-car covenant is extended to two years. Rover demonstrate the world's first gas-turbine car. Ford's new Consul and Zephyr models announced.

1951 Lady Docker's first Golden Daimler shown at Earls Court. Death of Doctor Porsche. The Triumph TR and the Healey 100 are the first popular-priced sports cars to offer 100mph performance. Disc braking and power steering are standard items of US Chrysler specification.

1953 Branded petrols become available again in Britain; the result is a rise in compression ratios to suit the increased octane ratings. Singer announce the first plastics-bodied British production car, the SMX Roadster. New-car covenant purchase scheme abolished.

1953 Singer SMX Roadster

1956 Triumph TR

1954 General Motors produce its 50 millionth car. Nash and Hudson combine to form the American Motors Corporation. Lanchester Sprite is offered with automatic transmission, still a rarity in Europe, although common on American cars. Volkswagen, having rebuilt their factory after it was gutted in the war, are now well enough established to start a vigorous export drive. All new American cars are now offered with tubeless tyres. Ford of America introduce the Thunderbird.

1954 Ford Thunderbird

1951 Austin-Healey 100

1955 Citroën introduce the DS19, with hydropneumatic self-levelling suspension, automatic jacks, power steering and braking. The American motor industry's best year yet, with a total production of 9,204,049 vehicles, of which some eight million are passenger cars.

1959 Citroën DS19

1956 Suez crisis cuts supplies of oil to Europe: rationing re-introduced in Britain and other European countries, resulting in a crop of super-economy bubble cars.
American cars begin to sprout tail fins.
Ford Motor Company stock becomes available to the public for the first time when the Ford Foundation offers over ten million shares.
Pininfarina styles BMC cars.
Daimler discontinues production of the Lanchester.

1957 Ford (US) launches the Edsel.
American Motors discontinues the Nash and Hudson marques.
Fiat introduce a new 500, with vertical-twin air-cooled engine and four-speed crash gearbox.
Lotus launch the plastic monocoque-bodied Elite.
Ford build their three millionth Mercury.
Chrysler's ten millionth Plymouth comes off the production line.

1957 Fiat 500 engine

1961 Lotus Elite

1958 Work starts on the M1 Motorway from London to Birmingham, first proposed in 1924.
New 40mph speed limit on roads round London.
Ford celebrates the fiftieth birthday of the Model T by assembling their fifty millionth car (and reassembling a 1909 T).
Chrysler builds its twenty-five millionth vehicle.
Packard builds its last vehicle.
Enter the 'frogeye' Austin-Healey Sprite.
Sir Leonard Lord becomes chairman of BMC.
British manufacturers produce a record one million cars.

1958 Austin-Healey Sprite

1959 Purchase tax on new cars reduced from 60 to 50 per cent.
Lea-Francis go out on a wave of bad taste with the Lynx.
American manufacturers launch their new compact models to combat the growing imports of European small cars.
Alec Issigonis designs the Mini-Minor.
NSU announce that they will build Wankel rotary-engined cars.
Triumph Herald appears, with all-round independent suspension and Michelotti styling.
DAF begin car production, using the Variomatic transmission.

1960 Lea-Francis Lynx

1961 Triumph Herald

1960 Jaguar Cars take over the Daimler Company.
Japanese industry produces 200,000 cars.
Hillman Minx available with Easidrive automatic transmission.
Ford of Britain introduce the 105E Anglia, their first-ever four-speed model, with its raked-back rear window. This car supplanted the ultra-cheap Popular, which still had the 1935 designed 10hp engine and 1938 styling; the 1954 unit-construction Anglia now became the Popular.

1963 Ford Anglia

1961 Transport Minister Ernest Marples introduces testing of all cars over ten years old in Britain.
British car tax raised to £15 from £12 10s a year.
Sir Leonard Lord becomes Lord Lambury.
Morris produce their millionth Minor.
Commercial-vehicle producers Leyland Motors acquire Standard-Triumph and AEC.
Morris 1100 with Hydrolastic suspension introduced.
BMC production reaches 600,000 vehicles a year.
Ford of Britain introduces the Mk I Cortina.

1964 Ford Cortina

1963 The Leyland Motor Corporation formed. Its first chairman, Sir Henry Spurrier, retires through ill-health four months later and dies in 1964.
Death of Lord Nuffield, aged 86.
Hillman's project Ajax is unveiled in the shape of the 875cc Imp, first passenger car to be built in Scotland since the Arrol-Johnston in 1931.
NSU announce the first Wankel car, the Spyder.
Rover announce the 2000 saloon, with a bodyshell inspired by their T4 jet car. It is voted Car of the Year.
Mercedes 600 appears. With a 6.3-litre eight-cylinder engine and an overall length of 20ft 6in, it carries on the tradition of the pre-war *Grosser* Mercedes.

1963 Hillman Imp

1964 Triumph 2000 launched.
Ford of America bring out the Mustang, which sells 500,000 in under 18 months.
Chrysler acquire controlling interest in Rootes.

1964 Triumph 2000

1965 BMC merge with the Pressed Steel Company.
George Harriman, Chairman and Managing Director of BMC is awarded the KBE.
Motor tax increased to £17 10s.
Labour Government brings in blanket speed restriction of 70mph as a 'four-month experiment'.
AP automatic transmission available on the Mini.
Rolls-Royce's first unit-constructed car, the Silver Shadow, is launched.

1966 Jensen launch the four-wheel-drive, 6.3-litre FF.
The Jaguar Group (Jaguar, Daimler, Guy, Coventry, Coventry Climax, Henry Meadows) merges with BMC to form British Motor Holdings.

1966 Jensen FF

1967 Citroën sign an agreement with NSU for joint production of the Wankel engine.
And kill off Panhard, born 1889, which they acquired in 1965 after holding a share in the capital for ten years.
NSU produce the Ro80, first volume-sale Wankel car.
Leyland Motor Corporation acquires Rover and Alvis.
Ford of Europe set up to co-ordinate the production programmes of British and Continental Ford companies.

1973 NSU Ro80

1968 British Motor Holdings merge with Leyland Motors to form the British Leyland Motor Corporation.
Strikes cripple French manufacturers – Renault lose 100,000 units of production.
Volkswagen produce a new model, the 411, alongside the 1936-designed Beetle.

1969 Volkswagen take over Audi.
Jaguar launch the XJ6.

1969 Jaguar XJ6

1970 Range Rover introduced.
GS and SM Citroëns launched.
Ford acquires Ghia of Turin from Alessandro de Tomaso.
Mercedes build the experimental triple-rotor-Wankel C III.
The first water-cooled Volkswagen, the K70, unveiled.
British Leyland launch the five-speed Maxi and drop the Minor.
Chrysler 160/180 range built in France by Simca for European and British markets.
Japan, with a monthly output of 200,000 cars, is now the world's second biggest motor manufacturer.

1970 Citroen GS

1971 Jensen drops the FF and is taken over by Norwegian-born, American-based Kjell Qvale.
Ralph Nader, having crucified the Chevrolet Corvair in his 1965 book *Unsafe at any Speed*, turns his attention to the VW Beetle.
Aston Martin, in financial difficulties, is sold by the David Brown Group to financiers who continue production of the DBS.
Jaguar V12 revealed.
Aero-engine division of Rolls-Royce goes into liquidation.

1972 British motor industry produces 1,900,000 cars in this year.
Datsun of Japan becomes the second biggest importer of cars into Britain.

1973 The Arab–Israeli War causes oil supply restrictions and threats of petrol rationing.
50mph speed limit imposed in Britain until fuel supplies are stabilised.

Ford opens automatic transmission plant in Bordeaux.
Volkswagen beat the Model T Ford's production record with the Beetle.
British motorists queue for petrol.

1974 Peugeot take over Citroën.
E. L. Cord and Gabriel Voisin die.
Fiat run into grave financial problems.
General Motors cancel plans to build 100,000 Wankel-engined Vegas.
American manufacturers veer away from large-engined cars in search of fuel economy. Their dealers have 80 days' stock of unsold cars on hand – an all-time record.
Ford begin research into highly efficient Stirling 'hot-air' engine.
Mercedes 600 Limousine is the first production car to be sold in Britain at a price exceeding £20,000.
Fiat build a million 127s.
Volkswagen introduce contemporary styled Golf models.

1974 Alfasud

1975 Rolls-Royce unveil the Camargue, priced at £31,000.
Porsche Carrera Turbo, is announced.
Chrysler-UK in financial difficulties, but saved by public finance.
Chrysler's French-produced Alpine brings much needed business.
Volvo gains a majority shareholding in the DAF company.
Volvo, Peugeot and Renault use a communal V6 motor in their luxury models.
Citroën's CX replaces the twenty-year-old DS range and wins the Car of the Year Award.
£200 million injected into British Leyland; it does not prevent the company being dragged down even further by industrial disputes. The British Government's National Enterprise Board now has a 95% stake in the company.
The end comes for Jaguar sports cars as the E-type is superseded by the XJS sports coupé. Similarly, Triumph replace the TR6 with the pedestrian TR7.
Lotus' supercar image consolidated with the launch of the new Esprit and Eclat models.

1976 Chrysler Alpine voted Car of the Year.
Rover's stylish 3500 introduced.
The new Aston Martin-Lagonda is the first car with computerised digital instrumentation.
Audi-NSU experiment with a Wankel engine in the Audi 100.
Ford's first front-drive car, the Fiesta, announced.

1976 Porsche Turbo

Index

Page numbers in roman type indicate that an entry is mentioned in the text on those pages, whereas italic page numbers indicate that an entry appears in a photograph or drawing caption